SECRETS OF SCREEN ACTING

When it was first published in 1993, *Secrets of Screen Acting* broke new ground in explaining how acting for the camera is different from acting on stage. Reaction time is altered, physical timing and placement are reconceived, and the proportions of the digital frame itself become the measure of all things, so the director must conceptualize each image in terms of this new rectangle and actors must "fit" into the frame. Based on a revolutionary non-Method approach to acting, this book shows what actually works: how an actor, an announcer – anyone working in front of the cameras – gives excellent performances on screen.

Patrick Tucker explains how instead of starting with what is real and trying to wrestle that onto the screen, actors can work with the realities of a shoot and move from there towards the real. His step-by-step guide to the elements of effective screen acting is an extension and explanation of a lifetime of work in the field, containing over fifty acting exercises and the tried-and-tested Screen Acting Checklist.

As well as being completely updated to cover new techniques, film references, and insights, this third edition now includes a set of film-clip time codes for each film. These not only itemize the films discussed in each chapter, but also pinpoint the precise moments where each example can be found, so that students, teachers, and professional actors can refer to them quickly and easily.

Patrick Tucker is an accomplished director of the screen and stage. Since his first professional production in 1968, he has directed more than 200 plays in all forms of theater, from weekly repertory to the Royal Shakespeare Company. He was accepted by the BBC Television Directing program in 1976 and has subsequently directed more than 150 television dramas, his most recent (2014) being a Russian situation comedy in Riga (and he has been invited back there to direct a feature film, also in Russian with a Latvian crew). He has developed his unique approach to television and film acting as a separate discipline, and he has lectured and taught all over the world.

SECRETS OF SCREEN ACTING

Third Edition

Patrick Tucker

Illustrations by John Stamp

Routledge
Taylor & Francis Group

NEW YORK AND LONDON

First published 2015
by Routledge
2 Park Square, Milton Park, Abingdon, Oxon OX14 4RN

and by Routledge
711 Third Avenue, New York, NY 10017

Routledge is an imprint of the Taylor & Francis Group, an informa business

© 2015 Patrick Tucker

British Library Cataloguing-in-Publication Data
A catalogue record for this book is available from the British Library

Library of Congress Cataloging-in-Publication Data
Tucker, Patrick, 1941–
Secrets of screen acting/by Patrick Tucker.—3rd edition.
Pages cm
Includes bibliographical references and index.
1. Motion picture acting—vocational guidance. 2. Television
acting—vocational guidance. I. Title.
PN1995.9A26T8 2014
791.4302′8—DC23
2014021712

ISBN: 978-1-138-79340-8 (pbk)
ISBN: 978-1-315-74030-0 (ebk)

Typeset in Bembo
by Swales & Willis Ltd, Exeter, Devon, UK

Printed and bound in the United States of America by
Edwards Brothers Malloy on sustainably sourced paper

CONTENTS

CONTENTS

PREFACE TO THE THIRD EDITION

I wrote the first edition in 1993, and the second in 2003. For this edition, I have completely updated the manuscript, with much more up-to-date examples, and modern references.

The main difference to previous editions is that I have included a large number of examples, giving the time codes for these film clips at the end of each chapter, indicating where the relevant extracts can be found. This means that you can see exactly what point is being made, and see how present practitioners have solved these problems, by watching a download or a DVD.

With modern technology comes a lot of new elements for the actor to consider, and this has meant new glossary items, and a complete rewriting of Chapter 2, which was originally "Film versus television," and is now "Different screens – different effects."

The other main addition to the book is a whole section on **whispering** in Chapter 6, "Sound and vocal levels," as this new phenomenon seems to be gaining ground in our ever changing profession.

The one thing I have not changed are the pictures and drawings, which still show the screen in the now old-fashioned 4:3 Academy ratio. My wonderful illustrator is now no longer with us to change them, but this book allows me to introduce a few more of John Stamp's evocative drawings, as well as retaining all his originals (such as me, still with a nice dark beard).

INTRODUCTION

- *Acting on screen is more like real life.* **Not true.**
- *When acting for television, just make everything smaller.* **Not true either.**
- *For film, it is all in the eyes.* **If only it were that simple.**
- *Do less with your face on screen.* **If anything, the opposite is true.**
- *As an actor, I do exactly the same on screen as I do on stage.* **Oh no you don't.**

Inside this book you will find the answers to the problems posed here – and a whole lot more.

This book was written to answer that simple but profound question: What do you actually **do** that's different when acting or presenting on screen, to be watched either on the big screen or on the small screens of a tablet or smartphone? It is mainly for actors (and teachers of acting), but it also has special chapters for announcers and interviewers and for directors.

The differences between film, television, and stage acting are carefully defined, as are all aspects of being part of the screen business. It tells you what you **do** when performing in one medium or the other. It is invaluable for anyone who has anything at all to do with the screen, large or small.

If you are interested in what actually happens to actors when they get on the screen, then this book may well tell you things you have never come across before. I notice that even the most recent books about screen acting still concentrate on the inner truths of acting, which are very valuable when you are preparing a role, but not so useful when you step onto a set (they say such things as "talk to people as if in real life" – Chapter 6, "Sound and vocal levels," will change your mind on that). This book is not a substitute for these preparations, but deals with the realities and truths of what actually happens in front of a camera.

It is impossible to be neutral when I am talking to you, and equally impossible to find a general term to cover both the sexes. I shall address you alternately by chapter as "she" and "he." This choice is random, and there will be no connection between choice of gender for a chapter and the topic covered in it. The term "actor," of course, covers both female and male performers.

If you could not ride a bicycle, and were cast in a screen drama that needed you to do so, then you would not wait for the day of shooting to climb onto a bike for the first time – you would go and learn the techniques in advance. You would not be dealing with where you were going, or the route to take – just the craft of cycling.

It is the same with screen acting – it is advisable to know the techniques before you start shooting. This book is not about the journey you should take – the actual acting. It is to teach you how to ride that bike.

To help you, I have provided at the end of each chapter details of where to find examples that will show you exactly what I am talking about, where you will be able to see good (and bad) practitioners of our craft putting it all into practice.

And to help you decide if this is the book for you or not, here is a 2014 letter I have just received:

FROM DAVID H. LAWRENCE XVII:

As we were turning around to shoot the scene from the reverse angle, the director looked at me. Like the good cop looks at the perp in a procedural.

He said, simply, "So, David H. Lawrence X-V-I-I. Why are you lying to people?"

I was nervous. It was the second day of my first professional on-camera acting booking ever, a crossboard shoot of the fifth and sixth episodes of Season 3 of the series *Heroes*. I'd been cast, with absolutely no network or studio film credits at all, as the creepy, evil Puppetmaster, the villainous Eric Doyle.

And here was the director of the episode, the incredible Dan Attias, gently accusing me of telling tall tales.

"Why are you telling people this is your first booking? Come on," he continued. "I usually have to have an AD coach any newbies on how to simply ask the right questions on set, to wrangle them away from me so I can get my job done, and here you are, doing things that even veterans take years to learn. Opening yourself up to the camera, walking off and hitting your marks with ease, giving me consistent editing points on your ins and outs, asking the camera operators the right questions for each shot, varying your vocal levels to match the shot size . . . the list goes on and on. And all that tells me, this really isn't your first shoot, is it?"

This wasn't the first surprising conversation I'd had on this three-day location shoot.

Just twenty-four hours earlier, I'd been taken aside by the writers of the episode, and told that I now was NOT going to be shot and killed as scripted. We'd been shooting since early in the morning, and after a few delicious scenes with my love interest, played by the amazing Jessalyn Gilsig, they'd left the set. They returned five or six hours later, and Jeph Loeb, the executive producer on the episode, caught up with me at the meal break and said, "We have to talk."

These are not the words you want to hear on the first day of your first job. The impostor syndrome started cranking away, and I was more than a bit concerned that there had been some horrible casting mistake. That I wasn't meant to be there, that I wasn't up to snuff and that there was going to be a change.

There was a change, all right.

Loeb and the writers took me into a side room and gave me the new sides they'd written in those hours away from set, scenes for the third day of shooting, the day I was supposed to die. As I read the new sides, I was shocked to find that instead of being offed with a handy gun lying on the table, I was to be knocked out with a blow from a chair leg, and sent back to *Heroes'* high security prison.

I blurted out, "Wait! I don't get to do my death scene? I rehearsed all weekend!"

(I know. I know. I'm an idiot sometimes.)

Loeb laughed and said, "We don't want you to die just yet. We are getting things from you on-camera with this character we didn't expect, and everyone's absolutely loving it. We want to keep you around for awhile."

"Awhile" turned out to be three seasons on *Heroes*, some of the most satisfying work in my life.

Back to the director's accusations: The absolute truth is that, three months earlier, I'd been booked on a sketch show called *Frank TV*, but I'd been cut out of most of the sketch I'd been cast in, and there wasn't anything useful for my reel. That was my actual first booking, but hardly something to lay claim to.

So, for me, *Heroes* was huge, and it was my first real credit on TV.

The director pressed me. "So, 'fess up. Why the fib?"

I protested. "No, this really is my first job. You can check out IMDb – I've done student films and a few commercials, but this is my first network episodic."

"So how do you know all these things? You certainly didn't learn how to operate this well on set by working with film students!"

"Oh! That!" I said, as I reached into my backpack for the ratty, dog-eared copy of *Secrets of Screen Acting* I'd been working with for the past fourteen months or so. "Here."

"A book?? You learned all this stuff from a book on acting?" the director huffed, as he started to thumb his way through it. He paused on a couple of pages, his countenance changing from incredulity, to interest, to begrudging admiration. "Oh, no . . . he's telling actors EVERYTHING," he chuckled. He handed the book

3

back to me, apparently satisfied, but clearly amazed that a simple book could offer this kind of preparation.

It was more than that for me. That simple book, the one you're holding in your hands, was life changing.

I'd been working with *Secrets of Screen Acting* for just under a month, when I decided to call Patrick up in London, and ask if he'd be willing to do a daily podcast with me, diving deep into the concepts he puts forth in this book. To my surprise and delight, he instantly said "Yes, my dear!" We ended up recording over 290 episodes of those five-minute podcasts (all available at secretsofscreenacting. com). The dirty little secret is that for me, aside from a lovely collaboration with Patrick, recording those podcasts became a private master class in all that is presented in the print and electronic version of the book, and my skill level shot through the roof. I felt like I had a secret weapon in my hands when I stepped on set. And when *Heroes* hit big, it was like everything fell perfectly into place.

I even added the techniques I learned to my auditioning, headshot sessions, casting workshops, commercial work, and already successful voice-over career. And by the time the audition for *Heroes* came around, I'd been immersed in the process laid out here in *Secrets of Screen Acting*, and I was loving both the artistic and technical side of acting.

As time went on, and I got to know the far more seasoned actors on the shows I worked on – *Heroes*, *Lost*, *CSI*, *How I Met Your Mother*, *The Mentalist*, and countless others – I made a point of asking them how they got the skills they needed to effectively work on professional sets, the skills taught in *Secrets of Screen Acting*. Almost to a person, they said that they didn't have any clue about those skills until they worked opposite actors that did, actors that had learned over time how to handle themselves in front of a camera, and had, over time, mimicked those very same work habits and techniques. It seemed to me that most of these actors followed the classic "master–apprentice" acting tradition, where older and more experienced actors would set an example for the newer cast, and by demonstrating the skills needed to get work done on set, help those newer actors do more of what works, and less of what doesn't.

I can't begin to tell you how valuable this book has been for me. You have, in your hands, a golden opportunity to step aboard the upward express career elevator. Pay attention to the ideas presented here, put them to use immediately in class, at auditions, and on set, and you, too, can shave years of trial and error from your journey.

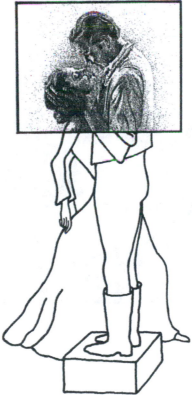

Clint Eastwood and Lee Marvin

Further apart on stage

1

SCREEN VERSUS STAGE

We are all stage actors

Oh yes we are. You may not actually have walked the boards to perform (at least not since school), but every time we want to get our way by putting on an "act," we are "acting," and because it is for someone at a reasonable distance away from us – a "real" distance – it is stage acting.

The child wanting her own way who cries real tears, which are miraculously cleared when she gets it, is giving a particularly convincing "performance."

The stern authoritarian voice you put on when complaining about bad service in a shop is another.

The fawning words and actions we all go through when pulled over for speeding, and the subsequent fake smiles, comprise yet another performance aimed at a particular audience.

These are moments when we are using our words and bodies to convince someone of some emotion or thought that may not, in fact, be the literal truth of what we are feeling, but is the emotion we want the other person to **believe** we are experiencing. This is what stage actors do, too.

Very few of us – especially, funnily enough, screen directors – have experience in acting for the screen or know what the difference would be between this and the acting mentioned above.

When I ask people of no experience, of limited experience, or who are very experienced indeed what the difference is between "screen" performing and "stage" performing, I get surprisingly uniform answers.

From professional actors and students in both the United States and the United Kingdom, here is a selection of the answers I have heard to the following question:

What change would you make, if any, when acting on screen compared with acting on stage?

Do less.

Make it more real.

Make it more intimate.

Tone it all down.

Make it more internal.

Scale down your performance.

Be more still.

Make fewer facial expressions.

Be smaller.

Be more natural.

These are the most common reactions – **and they are all wrong!**

Usually in a list of ten items I am given by a class or group, seven or eight will be variations from this wrong list. One Method drama school in England even graduated its students recently with the declaration that they were probably better prepared for television than the theater, since they had been trained to be minutely realistic – this from a course where over the three years they rarely appeared on a screen or ever analyzed what screen acting might be.

In the old days young stage actors learned from older, experienced professionals, by watching and by acting with them. The young apprentices would play small roles, and stand in the wings watching the master actors at work, hoping one day to be able to copy them and, in turn, to be copied. (See David H. Lawrence XVII's letter in the Introduction.)

How many professional stage productions have **you** seen in your lifetime – that is, productions where you paid to watch and the actors were paid to perform?

Twenty? Fifty? One hundred? Let's be generous, and make it three hundred. (That **was** generous, wasn't it?)

So how many **hours** of professional stage acting have you watched?

Nine hundred? Again, let's be generous, and make it an even thousand – and for most of you, you **know** that you have not experienced that many hours of professional stage acting.

And how many hours of professional **screen** acting have you seen? How many?

Current estimates indicate that by the time you have left your teen years, you have watched between ten thousand and twenty thousand hours of screen stuff.

And yet, most people have no idea what screen performing involves, and always relate their idea of it to **stage** versions of acting.

Strange, isn't it?

To start at the beginning

On screen, you can be seen in anything from a full-length shot of your whole body to a close-up of your face, depending on the size of the shot. I must be able to talk to you about these different sizes, but unfortunately there is no worldwide acceptance of what a size of shot **means**, and there are even variations within countries. My definitions are, I believe, the most widely used, but there is considerable confusion as to what "medium close-up" means, for example, and it is always necessary to describe your shots to establish a common vocabulary. What follows are the descriptions that I shall be using for the rest of the book, with noted variations.

Onto the screen comes a picture of a woman. Her head is at the top of the screen, her toes at the bottom. This is called a long shot (LS).

We now watch a large screen in a cinema, a smaller wide screen in our homes, a smaller image still on a computer or tablet, and a really small screen on a smartphone. Whichever you do, try now watching a blank screen and picture this image on it: the full-length shot of a woman.

Now, how far away would you have to be in a theater to see an actor this size? Yes, it is about sixty-five feet – or the back row of a large theater.

And how do actors convey thought, action, and mood to an audience this far away? Yes, through whole body motions and attitudes as well as loud voices, for it is very difficult to see detailed expressions on their faces.

How my classes *think* screen acting differs from stage acting

- Do less.
- Make it more real.
- Make it more intimate.
- Tone it all down.
- Make it more internal.
- Scale down your performance.
- Be more still.
- Make fewer facial expressions.
- Be smaller.
- Be more natural.

Next shot: the medium shot (MS). Here the woman's head is still at the top of the screen, but now the image is larger, and we can only see down to her waist. This is the usual size of shot when there are two or three people on the screen together.

And in what sort of theater position would you expect to see people **this** size? Yes, at the back of a small theater. Actors here can use some of their facial expressions, but they still have to use their bodies.

Next: the medium close-up (MCU). This is where you see the actor's head and shoulders, with the bottom of the frame cutting across the actors at chest level. Where would you be in the theater now?

9

The odds are you have chosen a very small theater – the front row of a fringe, pub, or off-off Broadway theater – for this size shot is the equivalent to a distance of about ten feet – yes, the medium close-up is the size a person would be **if they were standing about ten feet away – where your television set is usually put**. In other words, there is a relationship with real life for this size, and it is no coincidence that this is the most popular size of shot in television drama.

And how does an actor communicate when the audience is only ten feet away? Well, with subtlety, expressions, small facial tics, and so on, just as they would in a "real" situation.

The story does not end here, for there is another size of shot to talk about: the big close-up (BCU). Here, the face entirely fills the screen, from the eyebrows to the chin. And where would you be in a theater to get **this** view of an actor?

You would probably need to climb into bed with an actor to get your face close enough to "see" her this size, and by the time you were that close, your eyes would be out of focus anyway – so you **never** see a real person in the same way as this gigantic close-up. But it doesn't stop us from using it! It is, if you like, an unreal size of shot, and might correspond to seeing what someone is **thinking** rather than presenting.

Actors on tour with a production that is going to play in different theaters learn to adapt their performances according to whether they are playing in a large, medium, or intimate theater. They alter their performances from venue to venue, from week to week.

Since screen acting involves many different shot sizes, I would state that the screen actor must be prepared to adapt her performance from shot to shot.

In other words, you must change your performance **according to the size of shot.**

• *Long shot (LS):*	**Large, melodramatic style of acting**
• *Medium shot (MS):*	**"Intimate" theater style**
• *Medium close-up (MCU):*	**Reality**
• *Big close-up (BCU):*	**Pillow talk**

Simple now, don't you think?

On page 14 are the shot sizes of an actor: one strip where she keeps doing the same thing with the camera getting tighter and the other where she adapts what she is doing to the size of shot. (Which sequence of shots do you prefer? You can guess which **I** like.) (See *Changing performance with shot size* in *Time codes* at the end of this chapter.)

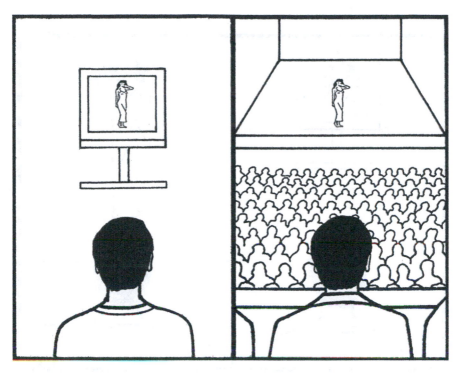

Large theater view

Small theater view

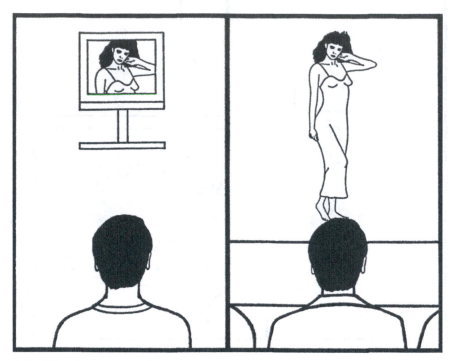

Off-off Broadway or fringe theater view

Intimate view

Watching the stage versus watching the screen

You see, when members of an audience are watching a stage play, they have choices about where to look. They can look at the speaker, or the listener or the servant in the corner. They can study the scenery, the lighting, or even the head of the person sitting in front of them if the play is too boring.

As far as the screen is concerned, there is nothing to look at except the moment presented by the production team. So it **has** to have greater significance, since the audience has to get **everything** from this one picture, rather than having a whole range of images to choose from.

Adjust scale of performance to size of shot

- *Long shot (LS):*   **Large, melodramatic style of acting**
- *Medium shot (MS):*   **"Intimate" theater style**
- *Medium close-up (MCU):*   **Reality**
- *Big close-up (BCU):*   **Pillow talk, putting thoughts on face**

There is another fundamental difference between stage and screen, especially the television screen. In the theater we see the actor by reflected light, while on the screen the image is itself transmitting light. This makes a television image very compelling. We are now so used to watching the screen that when a lecturer I know used a TV screen to show herself to the back of a remote hall, she found that the audience near her preferred to watch her on the screen rather than in the flesh. What was more upsetting was that they still watched the screen when the image went awry, and only "snow" was showing!

From real life to stage to screen

Imagine two people talking to each other in real life. What changes would they make if the moment were to be presented on a stage? Maybe they would talk a little louder, maybe they would turn their shoulders out a little to present more of their faces to the audience, but, on the whole, there would be a very close similarity between the "real life" version and the "stage" version.

And if this moment were to be shown on the screen? Here the changes could be dramatic, with one actor standing **very** close to the other, or standing behind her talking into her hair. If both actors are to be in the same shot, there has to be a radical departure from what they would do in "real" life in order to put them on screen, giving the **impression** of real life. This is called **cheating**. Look again at the pictures at the beginning of this chapter (page 6). The one of Clint Eastwood and Lee Marvin very close together is exactly as

Long shot (LS)

Medium shot (MS)

Medium close-up (MCU)

Big close-up (BCU)

they were in a particular moment of the movie *Paint Your Wagon*. The second picture is how they might be in "real life" or on stage, for two such masculine men would hardly be rubbing up against each other as closely as they had to in the film version.

If this seems a little strange, stop reading this right now and turn on your computer, television, or smartphone to watch a film or television drama **with the sound off** (so you don't get distracted by the storyline). Watch how the actors **really** stand in relationship to each other; see for yourself what the positions are; start noticing (for the first time?) all the **cheating** that goes on to make it all **appear** real. (See *Standing close to each other* in *Time codes* at the end of this chapter.)

There is a lot more on why this cheating is necessary in Chapter 3, "The frame," and Chapter 4, "The camera."

Dramatic structure

The structure of dramas on screen, especially television, is often very different from that of stage dramas, especially when dealing with soap operas or shows with regular characters. Apart from the results of typecasting (where a performance is known before it is seen: see Chapter 7, "Typecasting"), there is also the fact that the normal dramatic form of change and growth cannot be used, for a character has to be more or less the same from episode to episode, from year to year. That is, of course, why people watch serial dramas, to lend some stability to a challenging world. Viewers **like** to know that Agent 007 will, whatever the trauma, survive at the end or that a particular character will always win the court case, and that another character will always lose.

This leads to my Theory of Suffering: Regular television dramas must present characters suffering so that the audience can feel that at least someone they know is having a worse time than themselves. In real life we do not know how events will turn out, whether we will cope well with the unknowns of life, but we **can** tune in and find that our favorite villain is still the same sly dog we remembered all those episodes ago; the detective will always solve the murder case; and our everywoman heroine will always live and fight on to face another emotional crisis on our behalf.

At a conference on soap dramas in Germany some years ago, I presented the idea that American soap operas tend to show rich people suffering while British ones tend to show poor people suffering. I then watched the latest German offering in this form and came to the conclusion that it had middle-class people going through the various traumas on behalf of their audience. The other observation is that the more episodes a soap shows every week, the more events – weddings, murders, abductions, etc. – they have to work through (usually at the expense of character development).

So for the actor – learn how to present the maximum suffering and anguish, and just wait for the jobs to roll in! (I think you can detect some tongue in cheek around here, although John Barrymore, when asked why he chose to perform a smaller part over a larger one in a movie, declared he always went for the character who did the most suffering.)

Screen dramas use far fewer words than stage dramas, for the expressions on the actors' faces often do the work of a script. When they filmed *Amadeus*, a scene that had Salieri speaking twenty-two words in the stage version had just four words for him in the film version – so make sure you are providing all that extra information with your expressions and gestures that would on stage be provided by text. (See *Fewer words for the screen* in *Time codes* at the end of this chapter.)

Actors on stage versus on screen

A lot of actors talk a lot of sense about the differences between the two media (see Richard A. Blum's useful book *Working Actors*), but when asked about acting in the different media they will often tell the questioner what they think people want to hear, rather than what they have experienced.

Because actors chosen to act in the movies come from a pool of thousands, those chosen are usually those who tend to act "naturally" for the screen, whether they know it or not. Some of the reasons they give, then, for their expertise are not always the actual ones. (See *They seemed to know what to do from the start* in *Time codes* at the end of this chapter.)

I worked with a wonderful elderly actor in New York who claimed that there was no difference at all between her work on stage and on screen. She had trained in Stanislavski techniques, and she declared they worked just as well for screen as for the stage. As we continued to work, she would acknowledge that the things I was talking about were, in fact, also what she did. By the end of the workshop I had a long list of things that she now admitted she did differently on screen than on stage. This is not to criticize her (in fact, I come across this very often), but it shows that what she **said** she did with her acting was not what she actually **did**, and she was very skillful and deservedly successful. Many actors will talk about what they think they are expected to say, rather than the reality of working professionally on the screen. (The leading questions asked of them – "You always think the thoughts of the character you are playing, don't you?" – force them into these positions.) I was giving a producer a crash course on directing, when he mentioned that he was considering using a famous actor for his proposed (though never made) film, but was reconsidering since he had recently seen him giving a bad performance. Surprised, I asked to see the offending drama, and was able to tell the producer that the actor was as good as usual, but that the director had made every directing mistake in the book – and he was confusing the bad result with bad acting (you can always use this to explain away less than successful screen outings).

Some experienced actors will make statements along the lines of, "It has taken me all these years to learn to do nothing on screen – I just think it."

16

Young actors, reading this, joyfully rush in to do the same and find to their horror that their performances don't exist, they are invisible. This is because the experienced actor now puts her thoughts onto her face without realizing it, and **thinks** she is doing nothing.

There are two other interesting aspects of this phenomenon. First, as an actor gets more experienced in screen work, she **automatically** does those things I am talking about without realizing it. It's just like when you start to drive a car. It seems impossible to talk and shift gears at the same time, but some while later you can chat along with the best of us. The other reason is even more revealing: A star brings onto the screen not only her face and personality but also our memory of her past successful performances. **This** colors our observations of what she does. When Javier Bardem gives a small glance, we (who know his past performances of violence and action, especially in *No Country for Old Men*) will read menace into it, whereas with an unknown actor giving exactly the same glance, we will have gathered nothing. When Tom Hanks gives an enigmatic look, we (remembering his past performances of honorable characters) read into it a whole lot of subtlety where, if you or I were to be as enigmatic, we would be read as enigmatic. A drinking problem, sexual hang-up or particular neurosis in our stars (all lovingly revealed by the mass media) adds to our appreciation of a performance, and the producers incorporate this background into their casting choices. Now, one has only to see a picture of Robert Downey Jr., for example, and a whole world of assumptions kick in without him having to act a thing – and if any celebrity with recent notorious behavior were to appear in a movie, audiences round the world would project onto her their feelings about her exploits so lovingly detailed in all the newspaper and magazine articles such things attract, and she correspondingly would be required to act less. (See *Noted performances* in *Time codes* at the end of this chapter.)

Differences between screen and stage

Screen	Stage
• Audience told where to look	• Audience chooses where to look
• Very different from "real life"	• Close to "real life"
• Steady state for character	• Character changes and grows
• Change acting style from shot to shot	• Change acting style from theater to theater

---

Kevin Kline directed himself in a wonderful production of *Hamlet* in New York that I was privileged to see, and so I bought the DVD of the film based on the production, also co-directed by Mr. Kline. Interestingly, his performance in the filmed version was very different to that in his stage version, for he was speaking in a voice that no theater audience could hear, and producing real tears that no theater audience would have seen.

King Vidor writes of acting on screen: "I want everything to look real, but not necessarily be real." Elia Kazan, the great Method director, writes that "the art of motion pictures is one of photographing looks, not photographing dialogue."

Screening theater performances

The screening round the world of theater performances is taking off, yet until recently it was quite unsatisfactory. The reason was that for the audience to understand what the actors were thinking, the camera would have to shoot tight shots. The style and approach of the actors were hopelessly compromised: Should they project for the live audience or for the camera? Should they position themselves for the live audience out front, or for the cameras that will inevitably be there on either side of them, trying to "get onto their eyelines"? The end result was usually poor television – and poor theater. The British actor Ian Richardson was in New York and saw that they were going to show a video recording of the famous production of *Marat/Sade* that he had starred in some ten years before. He sat at the back of the auditorium to see it; he was shocked not so much that the audience thought it bad and laughable, but that he found it that way too. He **was** brilliant – at the time it was seen in the theater by the audience, who correctly gave it a standing ovation each night – but the recorded version gave no indication of this.

Today, sending theater shows into movie theaters is much more common, and the reason is that the enhanced quality from digital cameras and projectors means that it is now possible to read the actors' thoughts from wider shots, and so the performances need much less adjustment for the cameras. (Mind you, in those shows I have watched – such as David Tennant in *Richard II* and Kenneth Branagh in *Macbeth* – the star actors still dropped their voices for climactic moments, thus inviting wished for close-ups – see more about this in Chapter 6, "Sound and vocal levels.")

Continuous versus disjointed acting

I have left until last what most people put first: On stage the actor starts at the beginning and goes to the end, building and changing in one long, continuous event, while for the screen the actor is often asked to act scenes wildly out of context and out of time order.

I put it last because, frankly, although it is a major difference, I don't find it changes what the actor has to do all that much. I know perfectly well that it might mean that the screen actor has to perform her last scene before getting to the first one, but actors do that sort of jumping around in stage rehearsals, and although it is a correct **observation** that this is what happens for the screen, I do not see it has any great **effect** on what actors do. After all, they are required to act a scene, so they act it, with as much background and detail as they can.

What the actor **does** then is substantially the same as what she does for any other sort of acting as far as preparation and performing are concerned. No, the differences between stage and screen acting are the more significant ones outlined earlier in this chapter and expanded in the rest of the book.

Chapter 1: Time codes for screen versus stage

(Rounded up to the nearest 5 seconds)

Changing performance with shot size

Awakenings (Robert De Niro knows when the shot changes)	00:49:10
Before the Devil Knows You're Dead (so do Philip Seymour Hoffman and Marisa Tomei)	01:22:40
Bridget Jones's Diary (Gemma Jones is loud in the two-shot, soft in the MCU)	00:01:30
A Few Good Men (Tom Cruise starts very soft, but gets loud when in long shot)	02:00:40
The Fifth Element (Ian Holm and Gary Oldman)	00:51:05
Layer Cake (Kenneth Cranham talks to Daniel Craig louder in the wide shot, softer in the close-ups)	00:11:10
The Lord of the Rings: The Two Towers (very different acting by John Back in his scene with David Wenham between the wide and tight shots)	01:41:10
Master and Commander (Russell Crowe is restrained for the close-up, expansive in the wide shot)	00:31:30
The Third Man (Bernard Lee keeps the letters up high)	00:26:50

Fewer words for the screen

Amadeus (it's all in the expressions for Elizabeth Berridge and F. Murray Abraham)	01:03:00
A Few Good Men (the author made this scene much shorter than in his original Broadway version)	01:15:05
The Magnificent Seven (James Coburn's first line of fourteen in the whole movie)	00:31:45

The Magnificent Seven (and here is his second line)	00:33:00

Noted performances

Catch Me if You Can (in the showdown with Leonardo DiCaprio, the performance would seem boring if it were not played by the known Tom Hanks)	01:48:40
No Country for Old Men (Javier Bardem kills a motorist)	00:04:20
No Country for Old Men (and now he's nasty to a shopkeeper)	00:20:05

Standing close to each other

Before the Devil Knows You're Dead (Philip Seymour Hoffman walks up to be nose to nose with Ethan Hawke)	00:43:30
Carlito's Way (Al Pacino and John Leguizamo smell each other's breath)	01:05:50
Men in Black 3 (Will Smith's neck is urgently talked to by Will Arnett in the elevator)	00:24:45
Notorious (could Cary Grant and Ingrid Bergman get any closer?)	00:22:05
Paint Your Wagon (Clint Eastwood and Lee Marvin getting it together)	00:36:50

They seemed to know what to do from the start

Heartburn (Kevin Spacey's first film, but he looks like a veteran)	01:06:15
Léon (12-year-old Natalie Portman and Gary Oldman)	01:10:30; Extended 01:30:50
The Panic in Needle Park (first film for both Al Pacino and Kitty Winn)	00:34:05

The complete list of films, dates, and directors is in the *Index of films* at the end of the book.

All the time codes are taken from my DVD player in London, with the DVDs bought in the UK, so you can know how many minutes and seconds the clip is from the start of the movie. Where I can, I have noted the different versions of the films.

There may well be variations in the time for different machines and formats, but these should be consistent for your download, DVD player, or computer, and so once you note the differences, you will know where to find each of the above clips.

Arnold Schwarzenegger at the movies

Arnold Schwarzenegger at home

2

DIFFERENT SCREENS –
DIFFERENT EFFECTS

There used to be a big difference between acting for film and acting for television, which is why this chapter was originally called "Film Versus Television." These days, the actor often has no idea of what size screen his work will be shown on, so apart from the difference between single and multi-camera, this chapter is more for background information, with the necessary techniques outlined later in the book.

Film versus television

When I wrote the first edition of this book in 1993, we were still in a situation where dramas were made in multi-camera studios recording on videotape, and shown on Academy ratio screens. Sets were erected overnight for us to shoot on, and taken down overnight to allow a different show to use the studio the next day, and we edited on large cumbersome machines. If we were lucky enough to get into the film world, we were wedded to recording on celluloid and editing physically with scissors, and the results were shown on the big screen or (if inserts to a television program) on the small one.

Nowadays, dramas shot within a multi-camera setup are usually regular series (such as soaps) or situation comedies filmed in front of a live audience; all the rest are mostly shot on a single camera. Everything is recorded digitally, usually on digital chips, with computer-based editing systems. Much more location shooting is involved, and multi-camera shows have permanent sets in custom built studios, and shoot all their exteriors with a single camera. In the film world digital cameras and digital projectors in cinemas mean that the days of using film stock are coming to an end. People now watch dramas on computers and tablets, downloading them more often than buying a DVD, and going to a movie house will also be a digital experience.

All these differences have an effect on the acting required to adjust to the new situations, and this chapter will be addressing these.

What is the difference between the big screen and the small screen? This used to be "What is the difference between film and television?" and as one underemployed film editor asked me, "Which do **you** prefer working with, silver or rust?" He said this because the original chemical used in film stock was silver iodide, which went black when exposed to light, and the first video recordings were made on tape coated with iron oxide, or rust. Nowadays, nearly everything is made digitally, as Keanu Reeves explores in his wonderfully informative documentary *Side by Side*. Major movies are now being made entirely on digital cameras with no film stock at all, and systems are being developed so that the output from the digital camera can be fed directly to the editing computer, with no separate recording medium, and the smaller screens of television are quickly following suit.

The silver and rust comment shows the antagonism often felt toward the small screen and its history of video, with film somehow thought of as the more "pure" medium. Nowadays, the main difference is in the time you are given to make a drama, but even then there is little difference between a major movie and a major drama made for the smaller screen, such as *Game of Thrones*.

Film tends to be shot with only one camera at a time – setups for a big explosion or car crash are the obvious exceptions – so each shot is lined up and filmed, and then the crew and cast move on to the next one.

Shows intended for television are also made with a single camera, just like film only much faster. Contrary to what many people imagine (including many in the profession itself), it is not necessarily better to have many cameras, nor is it slower to shoot with a single camera. On *Brookside*, the soap drama I have done the most work on in the UK, the director had to get an average of ten minutes of broadcastable drama per day out of its single camera system, so in eight shooting days enough is shot for three 25-minute episodes. Excellent work can be done, still using tracks and jib arms, but everyone, actors included, had to be very accurate, talented, and fast, for they were attempting to do things in a filmic way without the budget or time to do so.

Single camera versus multi-camera

For a single camera, the shots themselves are composed and lit as well as possible within the strict timetables we all have to work to, but for a multi-camera setup, the cameras have to be placed where they cannot see each other, and the lighting has to cope with as many as five cameras at the same time, so the shots and lighting are much more compromised.

The **acting** however in the multi-camera setup is done in "real" time. Some actors prefer multi-camera, since it allows them to act for longer chunks, and this longer take has now moved over into the film world, where sometimes in major movies they shoot a complicated sequence with many cameras, not worrying about them seeing each other, as they can digitally edit and change images to give them what they want. (See *Shooting tricks* in *Time codes* at the end of this chapter.)

A normal multi-camera scene would be a long scene lasting perhaps three to four minutes, containing up to forty different shots, with the cameras whizzing about finding new positions to shoot from (in accordance with the director's planning) and the cutter/vision mixer cutting from one camera to another, according to the shooting script.

There are, however, difficulties, as you can spot from the **adjust scale of performance to size of shot** thoughts in Chapter 1, "Screen versus stage." Good multi-camera actors have to be prepared to switch in the middle of a speech from long shot acting to close-up acting. (There are those who don't do any of this; they just act the way they think. This leads to generalized acting and is usually associated with situation comedies.) There are many actors who, once they get into the swing of screen acting, really prefer the single camera, since then they know exactly what the shot is and can pour all their talent and concentration into each one. In *Awakenings*, for instance, there is a shot of Robert De Niro with his arms open wide. In fact, there is a long shot with his arms opened wide, followed by a medium shot with his arms not nearly so wide. Good screen acting technique, Bob! (See *Acting examples* in *Time codes* at the end of this chapter.)

Watching different screens

If we all decided to go and see a film in a movie house today, that is the first point: We have to **decide** to go, and we have to choose where to go.

We travel to **their** place, pay money to get in, and, hopefully, find an auditorium that has some elements of luxury about it. Even if the red plush curtains have disappeared, we still have attendants and people selling us goodies. We sit in a large room with quite a few people and, to help us concentrate on the film, the lights are dimmed while the movie is playing.

When the film starts we gaze up at these **large** creatures who fill our fields of vision. If people near us talk or rustle paper, some of us have been known to hiss "Shhh!" If we do not like the movie, well, we have paid to get in, so often we stay to the bitter end hoping it will get better or at least give us something for our money. When it is over we return to our own homes, and we can recommend (or not) that our friends repeat our experience, for the film will have another showing at the cinema.

When watching on a small screen smartphone, the larger screened tablet or computer, or the wide screen television at home, all is different. For a start, it is easy to watch the small screen without really **deciding** to do so – it just happens to be on so easily.

When we watch the screen, the lights are not dimmed, and the screen is surrounded by elements of **our** lives: our potted plant, our books and papers, our video games ready to be fired up. Look again at the picture of Arnold Schwarzenegger at the beginning of this chapter (page 22). Does it seem familiar?

If anyone moves in the room while we are watching TV, our eyes flick to that person. We often look away from the screen – to talk, to eat, to flirt – why, we even leave the room for a short while in the middle of a program without feeling we are missing much. We talk while the TV set is on, since the **small** creatures have been "invited" into our homes. What's more, if any of them upsets or annoys us at any time – **zap!** We can get rid of them at the touch of a button. And if we are not watching "live," we can stop to go back and look at any bit we like (or dislike) again, pick up any mistakes, freeze frame on the shot of the murderer's feet to see exactly whose shoes they are. In short, the performers work entirely at **our** convenience. (I recently happened to be watching a World War II German propaganda film and was able to freeze frame on a shot of Hitler – with sweaty arm pits! **That** image would have been snipped out if the original filmmakers knew that one day we could push a "pause" button.)

Our relationship to the smaller screens in our homes is just so **different** from our relationship to the big movie screen.

Wide screen television sets, and the universal use of downloads or DVDs means that the theatrical release experience is easier to replicate at home than it was before, and people now set up their own miniature "screening rooms" to enjoy the movie in a way closer to the intended original, although with all the distractions of home. The release of a download or DVD also means that the director can always put back the scenes he wanted that may have been cut from the studio released version, under the title "Director's Cut." (See *Director's cut* in *Time codes* at the end of this chapter.)

Listening to different screens

Watching a film in a movie house you get wonderful surround sound, rich in bass notes. Watching a screen at home can be a very different experience, for the modern thin TV screens have correspondingly thin loudspeakers, and unless you hear it through a sound system, the sound will be very different to that which the program makers prepared. Listening through earpieces is also not as rich a sound as a complete sound system.

The recent BBC *Jamaica Inn* series played well to the critics and program makers at the preview theater (with its nice speakers), but when it was broadcast the BBC switchboard was inundated with complaints that the audience could not understand what the actors were saying. There is more about this in Chapter 6, "Sound and vocal levels," but the difference in speaker quality certainly did not help. (See *Acting examples* in *Time codes* at the end of this chapter.)

Acting for different screens

One of the main differences is that drama produced for television distribution can now be much longer than even the longest movie. With many episodes it is crucial that the actors really build character and relationships over this longer period. As one actor put it to me, a longer series gives you the confidence to relax and be more at ease as you enrich your performance, away from the adrenalin of getting even a small part in a major movie.

The down side of this is that filming will often start before all the episodes have been written, and actors may find that their characters have taken a twist that, had they known at the start, would have changed their acting choices for the first few episodes. I was once having trouble working out what a particular character's sexuality was, and so talked to the actor about it. He told me that, cast as a hairdresser, he had the same question for the producers, but was told that they had not yet made up their minds, so could he play it so that in later episodes they could make his character go in one direction or the other. No wonder he was confused (as was I), and I suspect the audience were too.

William Hurt was cast in the second season of the Glenn Close-led drama *Damages*, but shortly bowed out as he could not work happily the way that a multi-episode drama demands. For others, though, the length of a series allows great development, and even the opportunity of showing many different sides to a character, a high point being Tatiana Maslany in *Orphan Black*, where she gives a detailed and fascinating portrayal of many clones with the same body but very different characterizations. (See *Acting examples* in *Time codes* at the end of this chapter.)

The other main difference in a shoot is the time given for a particular event. For the smaller screens, the crew and producers tend to keep going until the shot is acceptable, and then move on. Only for the larger screen (and with the budget of a movie) is the director given leeway to carry on until the acting is also perfect.

Writing for different screens

In the movies, the filmmakers can often tell a story purely by pictures – a whole series of pictures that by their composition, juxtapositions, and so on give you the atmosphere, mood, and feeling of what is going on. Often in a major action movie, the amount of lines spoken is frighteningly small. One of *The Magnificent Seven*, James Coburn, spoke just thirty-nine words in his fourteen lines in the entire film (apart from chanting "1, 2, 3, 4" in the background of one scene). (See *See not say* and *Tell story with pictures* in *Time codes* at the end of this chapter.)

On a small screen, no program maker would dare leave you alone with pictures for too long, for you look away frequently and, in missing one of the pictures or images, you would no longer be able to follow the story, given all the distractions of home or wherever you are watching your small screen. For programs made just for the television screen, the story will more often than not be **on the sound track**. This means that even if the viewer is looking away (or out of the room) he will be able to follow the story and the action. **That** is why characters talk nonstop in soap operas – they have no choice. They must entertain and inform even when the viewer is in the middle of going to the bathroom, eating a meal, or – and here you can fill in your **own** favorite TV-watching activity. So as actors, be prepared to learn more dialogue for the small screen, and tell more, just with your face, for the large screen.

Shooting for different screens

Finance rules everything, and so being quick is the main attraction for producers in choosing directors, DOPs, first assistants – and actors. Only a major, major film can have the luxury of shooting just a few minutes of finished material a day. For the rest of us, we must act, produce, and light six, eight, even ten minutes a day, rising to fourteen for a fast-shooting episode of a domestic drama.

For a multi-camera drama, of course, you can be expected to deliver a great deal more each shooting day – anything up to fifty minutes of finished drama in one studio day, although the lines would normally be split between quite a number of regular performers.

As you can see, the television actor is expected to digest and perfect a great deal more material than the pure film actor – **and** he gets paid less. No wonder you all want to end up as one of Hollywood's finest!

Modern trends

High definition digital cameras are now being used for mainline movies. The old working professionals plead to use film stock, but the cost of such, the cost of developing the stock – and the cost of sending out cans of films to individual cinemas against the cost of downloading a digitized image – mean that our industry will soon consign film stock to the same quaint box as shooting in black and white.

It is not possible to enjoy the lush productions now being made to be shown on domestic channels if the screen is so small that it is impossible to make out the lavish backgrounds, CGI-created creatures, and wonderful costumes of such works as *Game of Thrones*. Perhaps filmmakers are making sure that their hard work will not be watched on the small screens of smartphones, but at least will be enjoyed on a wide screen at home with proper sound. (See Chapter 3, "The frame.")

On location, and with the ever increasing costs of star performers, major movies are now often filming a scene with more than one camera – and not just for the tricky shots of a car exploding or a huge crowd scene. Two cameras can be used to shoot a conversation between two characters – although this means that the cameras will not quite be able to "get on the eyeline" as well as if one camera is used, but it is a tempting time saver. One camera can also be mounted above another, so that the close-up and medium close-up shots can be filmed simultaneously – not a good idea if the actors are trying to match their performances with the shot size, but good for the quantity of film that can be shot in one day. They are labelled Camera A and Camera B, so now you know what that means in the final credits. (See alternatives to this in Chapter 11, "Directing actors for the screen," and see *Shooting tricks* in *Time codes* at the end of this chapter.)

So there are differences in the way the acting is recorded, differences in the way a program is edited, differences in the way an audience looks at it all, differences in the number of cameras used, and – mainly as it affects actors – differences, vast differences, in the time allotted to shooting any particular moment. And this last difference holds true in today's new world, since even on a digital shoot much more time is given to a drama destined for a movie release than for a release for domestic television sets. You have been warned.

Chapter 2: Time codes for different screens – different effects

(Rounded up to the nearest 5 seconds)

Acting examples

Awakenings (Robert De Niro's arms)	00:49:10
Orphan Black (Tatiana Maslany playing both Rachel and Helena in a diner), season 1, #7	00:14:10
Orphan Black (and here she plays Rachel and Sarah and Alison and Cosima), season 1, #10	00:14:40
True Grit (do your loudspeakers let you understand what Jeff Bridges is saying?)	00:15:45

Director's cut

Apocalypse Now Redux (especially the newly restored scenes of Aurore Clément's only part in the film)	01:58:50; 02:07:55; 02:11:00
Léon (Extended version: charades with Jean Reno and Natalie Portman, cut from the American release)	00:53:35
Léon (Extended: training session with Jean Reno and Natalie Portman)	01:16:20

See not say

Amadeus (four words for F. Murray Abraham)	01:03:00
A Few Good Men (shorter than the Broadway version)	01:15:05
The Magnificent Seven (James Coburn's first line of two words)	00:31:45
The Magnificent Seven (and his second line of just two words)	00:33:00

Shooting tricks

Birth (long, long take ending up on a close-up of Nicole Kidman)	00:25:40
Bridget Jones's Diary (two cameras simultaneously shooting Renée Zellweger singing with different sized shots)	00:05:35
The Graduate (pulling focus from Anne Bancroft to Katharine Ross)	01:06:45
Les Misérables (singing by Anne Hathaway filmed live)	00:26:10
Love Actually (camera goes from outside to inside as Hugh Grant meets lots of people)	00:07:05
The Protector (Warrior King) (Tom Yum Goong) (Steadicam and digi recording; the longest continuous fight)	00:59:15
Russian Ark (camera runs all the time; the entire film is just one Steadicam shot)	all
Side by Side (Disc 2: James Cameron talking about DOPs)	00:06:00
Side by Side (Disc 2: Steven Soderbergh talking about cameras)	00:00:00
Unbreakable (very long foreground shot with Bruce Willis in background)	00:09:25

Tell story with pictures

A.I. Artificial Intelligence (photo reflections show how Haley Joel Osment wants to be part of the family)	00:12:00
A.I. Artificial Intelligence (meal shows what his "parents" think about that)	00:17:45

Close Encounters of the Third Kind (Richard Dreyfus is the last person in the room to see the mountain on the TV, well after the audience)

   Theatrical release 01:09:50; Special edition 01:05:40; Director's cut 01:13:35

Léon (Jean Reno rescues Natalie Portman,   01:16:15; Extended 01:36:45
the gap in their height showing the gulf in
any future for them)

The complete list of films, dates, and directors is in the *Index of films* at the end of the book.

All the time codes are taken from my DVD player in London, with the DVDs bought in the UK, so you can know how many minutes and seconds the clip is from the start of the movie. Where I can, I have noted the different versions of the films.

There may well be variations in the time for different machines and formats, but these should be consistent for your download, DVD player, or computer, and so once you note the differences, you will know where to find each of the above clips.

Clark Gable and Vivien Leigh

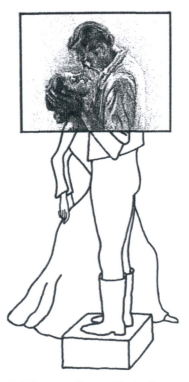

A different reality outside the frame

3

THE FRAME

When we look at a painting, say, a Rembrandt portrait, we do not wonder what is to the left or right of the sitter; we do not wonder what she is looking at; we presume that everything we need to know has been put into the picture – into the frame – by the artist.

Audiences of screen acting apply the same criteria.

We presume that everything we need to know is there, and that **those things not on the screen are unimportant or irrelevant**. This means that if an actor does wonderful things that are not seen, then it is as if she had not done them!

A frame condenses both time and space.

In real life, **or on the stage**, someone holding a cup of tea holds it about level with her navel. This is for both comfort and convenience; it is easy to lift it up to the face or put it down on a table.

Putting this picture inside a frame means that the face is very small and difficult to see. To get a bigger face requires a tighter shot, but then it would look as if she had no cup at all.

So the **screen** actor holds a cup of tea (or a mug of coffee, or a bottle of beer, or a file, or a notebook, etc.) up close to her face, so that when the camera sees it, it looks real, we know what she is doing, and we still see all the expressions on her face.

(Yes, the cup of tea held high looks very silly in real life, but on the screen it looks very natural and "real." Have you watched some screen work yet and found similar examples?)

Don't forget, the audience believes that everything of significance is in that frame; so anything **put** there, even if it is just a teacup, becomes significant. A famous politician in the UK has a familiar motion she makes with her hand when she is making a speech. Although lots of fun is made of it, if you look closely you see that she is keeping her gestures close to her body, and in particular, close to her head. This means that whenever film is taken of her, she ends up with a nice, tight head shot – the camera operator does not have to loosen the shot to accommodate a flailing hand. I think this is skillful screen performing, getting a larger shot of her face, don't you?

This means that **acting** also has to be selective. It is not sufficient just to think or feel an emotion and put it where you think it should be. Just like the cup of tea, if you do not place it correctly, the audience will not see it, and it will be as if it never was.

This is why it is necessary to understand the size of shot and to adjust the business and acting accordingly. Ah, so you should ask the director, "What size shot is this?"

No. You should **not** ask the director, for she will think that all you are after is a close-up and will reply with such a time-honored (and used) phrase as "**You** just do the acting and **I'll** do the directing, O.K.?" It is true that there are artists who care about being seen larger than life to the extent of demanding "another thirty close-ups." (Only stars get away with this.) So there is a danger that directors might assume that you are after such a mythical thing when you ask about the size of shot, rather than trying to learn your craft and using the best technique to get the best result. There are, unhappily, many who are suspicious of your motives and so don't mind keeping you in the dark about what is going on.

Here is a big secret about crews: They all actually **want** the production to be good, good in different ways. The camera crew wants good pictures, the sound department is after good sound, and so on. If members of the crew believe that **you** are out to make **their** contributions look better, then they will naturally fall over backwards to help. No camera operator, for example, wants your fingers flicking in and out of the frame, so if you ask **her** where the cut-off point is, as this is a professional question you will get a professional answer, as the operator will be thrilled that you care about not ruining her shot and will gladly tell you where the frame edge is, and you will be thrilled because you will have found out the size of shot without actually asking for it.

Here is another secret about the frame: Audience members sometimes think that **they** are the only ones who see what's in it.

Let me explain. Let's assume that in your scene another character asks you for money that you do not want to give, and your reply is filmed in close-up. Now, in real life, you would not let your face show how you felt about being asked for a loan, so a mild politeness would come over your face. This might be "real" in that it is what you would do, but it is not how you actually feel.

It is also very boring for the audience, which wants to know the **real** feelings you have. So in the single shot of you, when asked for the loan, your face can show exactly how you feel before the polite look comes over your face. Viewers will feel as if they have been let in on a secret, which they have. They will know how you felt about that moment – and will **not** notice that if you had done such a reaction in "real" life, the other character would have noticed it and asked what was going on.

No, the frame is an aspect of truth, never the real truth. Andrew Wyeth, that wonderful American painter of *Christina's World*, when painting his "realistic" landscapes, would leave out windows of a house or move the position

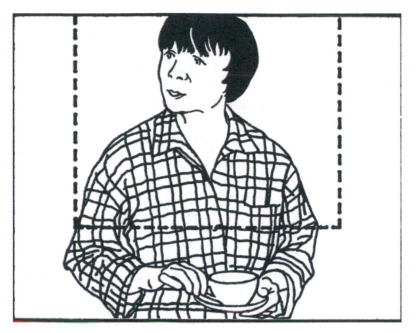

A normal cup of tea

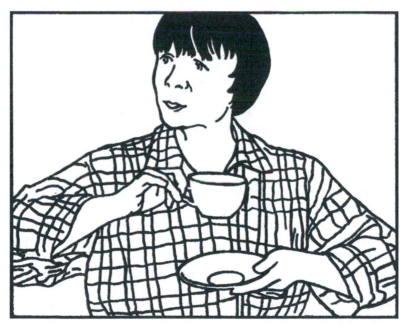

A screen cup of tea

of a tree, because he was interested not in reproducing exactly **what** he was looking at, but in creating a more important and artistically valid painting of how he **felt** about his subject. This transmission of feelings is what art is about; it is why we like paintings and don't just go for a photograph of a place, why we watch and enjoy the work of actors, as opposed to watching real people. There **is** a difference.

Distances

Real people stand a certain distance apart when in a normal social situation (although this does vary from culture to culture), but they never stand as close as Clint Eastwood and Lee Marvin had to. In fact, we have to tear them apart to get them to a "proper" standing distance (see pages 38 and 39).

If we put a frame around the "proper" distance, we would then think they were aloof, and a large part of the screen would not be used. So the distance between them becomes significant on its own account, rather than reflecting a truth. The close version of Eastwood and Marvin looked fine on **screen** when it was framed, but take the frame away and you would think . . . well, you just would not believe that these two men would stand in such an intimate position.

The same happens with Clark Gable and Vivien Leigh in *Gone with the Wind*, pictured at the beginning of this chapter (page 32). I do not know whether he had to stand on a box or whether she had to bend her knees, but I **do** know that it is impossible for them to be in the framed position without such unsuspected activity below the frame. Her forehead below his chin gives a most wonderful **image** of the relationship (which was why it was so planned for, has been so used and is **still** used as an icon after all these years), but in no way does it reflect what the two characters could actually do, or would have chosen to do. It didn't matter that he had bad breath that could be detected at quite a distance: she still had to convincingly kiss him. Incidentally, in the Farsi version of this book they censured this picture – it was obviously too saucy for the religious police! (See *Position cheating* in *Time codes* at the end of this chapter.)

Film star exercise

Go on, try this right now. Pair up with someone conveniently to hand and try to get in to **exactly** the same position as Gable and Leigh. When you are holding yourselves in whatever contortion will be necessary, ask yourself, "How do I feel?" Your answer will be more in the way of pain and embarrassment than wild, unbridled passion!

This a very good exercise – to recompose moments from TV or movies, so that you can **experience** what screen actors have to do, rather than just imagine it. Most such imaginings are of an audience some distance away, drinking in your whole body's story, not of a large and expensive piece of equipment some inches away, with you sitting on blocks, balanced precariously, your nose one inch away from someone who could use a shower. Yes, that glamorous world can be just a touch uncomfortable.

Perception of reality

The addition of a frame alters our perception of reality.

Take a normal situation, where a person comes up to a stranger and asks her a question. In real life, or on stage, there would be a physical gap between the two when the question was asked, for a stranger would never come within the accepted "personal space." If this were to be shot as a screen moment, the director might have the two stand really close to each other because she wants a tight two-shot. This will mean that the actor will **feel** one sort of emotion (**why** am I so **very** close to this stranger?) while she is **acting** another emotion ("Can you tell me the way to the station?").

Have you realized when watching the frame that very often the actors will not address each other directly, but will be positioned where they can only talk to the back of a head? We would of course never do this in real life, but it is a good way of getting both faces to be seen on screen, so we directors often use this cheating within the frame to allow the audience to see both the performance and the reaction to it at the same time. (See *Talking to the back of the head* in *Time codes* at the end of this chapter.)

This is another proof that acting is far from "real" on screen and that, until you are experienced, you **cannot** trust your feelings; to say that it "does not feel right" is not going to make us flock around and sympathize, for we are looking at the framed picture, and if **that** tells the right story, then that is that. As an exercise, I often ask student actors to speak to each other with their noses no more than two inches or three centimeters apart. I film their profiles as they do this, and play it back. Nearly everyone disobeys me – that is, the actors just cannot stand that close to each other, or if they do, they giggle and show extreme embarrassment. They take my instructions, adapt them so it feels good to them by backing off from each other, and then hope to get away with it. Yet from the first time they started watching films, they have seen professional actors do just this. (See *Noses too close* in *Time codes* at the end of this chapter.)

Study dramas on the screen to see what distances actors keep from each other (as always, I advise you to do this with the sound off so you can see what is going on without getting distracted by the story). You will be amazed at how close some have to be, and at how the distance can change wildly from shot to shot, even when the actors are supposedly in the same positions. And also beware of always maintaining eye contact with your fellow actors. (See *Not enough cheating, and the curse of eye-to-eye contact* in *Time codes* at the end of this chapter, and read more about this in Chapter 11, "Directing actors for the screen.") You can't even trust the scenery, as they will only build what the camera can see, and you are often acting on a partial set that feels very wrong indeed. (See *Set and camera cheating* in *Time codes* at the end of this chapter.)

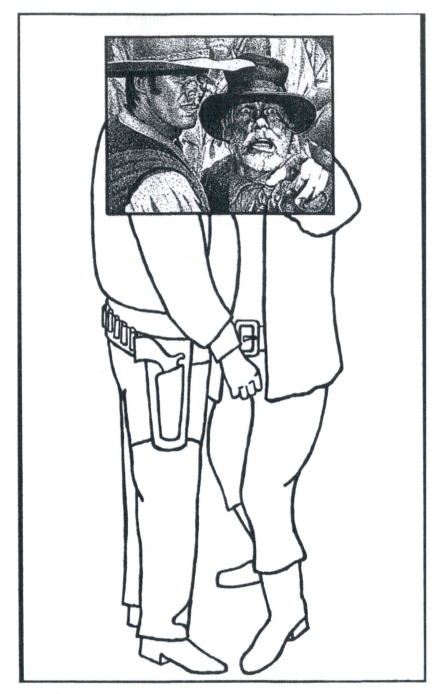

Screen distance

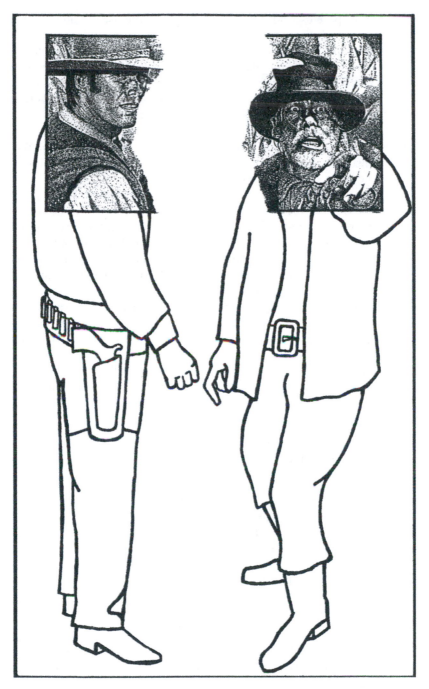

"Proper" distance

Not only is space expanded or contracted, but time itself is altered when a frame is put around things.

If someone asked you to come over and open the door, you would naturally wait until you heard the request before moving. But there can be screen situations where – because the actor making the request is shot in a medium close-up – it would seem to take too long for you to arrive. So the director might tell you to move **before being asked** by the other character, in order that you arrive on screen at a time that **appears** right. With the frame around, audiences expect people to be able to appear sooner, and so they do. Watch the screen again for examples of people being able to rocket from one side of the set to the other – you will find them!

A lot of the mini-notes you get on the set will have to do with the **picture** looking right: not just the artistic composition, but how your character comes across by the way you present it on the screen. To understand why you are asked to do these little "cheats" – to be able after a while to predict them and automatically put yourself in the correct positions – makes you a valued collaborator in this most demanding craft. You can then enjoy contributing, rather than feeling that we are all out to get you, to prevent you from giving your best.

Modern high speed filming has revealed that our faces are so expressive that micro-expressions chase across our faces very fast, and that sometimes one side of our face is showing one thought and the other side a different one. This is the reason why it is better to get your full face on screen (so the camera can read the maximum information from both sides of your face), and why it is so useful to cheat your face round to the camera, and not get caught up in eye-to-eye "truthfulness." (See *Face cheating* and *Not enough cheating* in *Time codes* at the end of this chapter.)

Secrets of what the frame does

- It gives everything within it significance.
- It changes distances.
- It changes the impression of time.
- It gives an aspect of truth – not truth itself.
- It breaks the link between what you are feeling and how you are acting.
- It encourages the left shoulder forward.

Group exercise

If you are in a group, look around the room and see what messages and moods you get from seeing everyone full length. If you now shoot everyone in close-up, zooming the camera in and moving it from person to person, then play back the results, you will be aghast at how much is **lost**. When you can only see someone in close-up, look how much is not there – all the information that comes from what clothes she is wearing, from how she has crossed her legs, from her bodily posture: all gone. **This** is why I can boldly say that in a close-up, you sometimes need to do **more** than you would ever do in real life or on the stage, because the only acting instrument you have for this shot is your face, and **it** has to do what you would normally use your whole body to do.

An actor speaking confidently, but anxiously drumming her fingers by her side, gives a message that would be lost if she were shot in close-up, the jumpy fingers unseen. She would have to do more with her face to compensate for having no other elements to act and communicate with, if she wanted the screen audience to receive the same message that a stage audience would have.

Best shoulder forward

A lot of our casting photographs make us look like criminals or lunatics, and the common factor is that we are facing the camera with our shoulders square on. Set up the camera for such a shot, and then try moving one shoulder forward, still facing the camera, and see the difference.

If a character is facing us with her shoulders, and she turns away from us, we might feel rejected. She **ought** to be facing us. But if a character is **not** facing us with her shoulders, and she turns toward us, it is her choice and makes us feel good. And if she turns away, well, that is the way she ought to be looking, anyway. So an actor doing this makes the audience feel good about her. Also, if your shoulders are slanted, the camera can get a tighter shot of you without losing the edge of your body, and we know that larger shots mean a better chance of affecting an audience with our faces and feelings.

So, angled shoulders often work better than square-on ones, and that is why so many models and starlets flounce onto the screen, then immediately angle their shoulders. (It also emphasizes their bodily profiles.) It just feels better, too, so the next time you are facing the camera for a photo, put your **left** shoulder forward, and you will get a better shot. Unfortunately, passport photos demand the full face position, so we all end up looking a bit furtive. (Why is it the left shoulder? It all has to do with the fact that we scan pictures from left to right, and that is dealt with more fully in Chapter 11, "Directing actors for the screen.")

Wide screen frame today

Film has for many years used the wide screen, with (in general) correspondingly looser shots than those used by television productions, but the advent of wide screen television is altering all that. Whereas before television dramas were content to intercut between an MCU of one character with the MCU of another, today the MCUs look empty up on the wide screen. The solution is either to shoot much tighter in a BCU (with the need for the actors to change their acting accordingly), or to shoot them as matching over-the-shoulder shots (with the actors having to get much better with their head to head continuity). Some directors solve this by framing the actors so that their noses are almost at the edge of the frame (which puts a lot of empty space behind the actor's head); others, remembering that screen dramas can now be watched on the small screens of a smartphone, shoot some very tight shots indeed. Either way, the wider screen and the smaller screen have changed the way the actors need to respond. (See *Set and camera cheating* in *Time codes* at the end of this chapter.)

Chapter 3: Time codes for the frame

(Rounded up to the nearest 5 seconds)

Face cheating

Cat on a Hot Tin Roof (Paul Newman and Elizabeth Taylor swap around)	00:09:45
Close Encounters of the Third Kind (Richard Dreyfus is not looking at the television set)	
Theatrical release 01:11:50; Special edition 01:07:45; Director's cut 01:15:40	
The Magnificent Seven (Steve McQueen brings his face round)	00:47:10

Noses too close

Before the Devil Knows You're Dead (Philip Seymour Hoffman and Ethan Hawke)	00:43:30
Carlito's Way (Al Pacino and John Leguizamo)	01:05:50
Notorious (Ingrid Bergman and Cary Grant)	00:22:05
The Sopranos (James Gandolfini and Michael Imperioli), season 1, #1	00:55:55

Not enough cheating, and the curse of eye-to-eye contact

Carousel (only profiles for the audience to see)	00:49:15
Carousel (lots of backs of heads)	01:55:25; 01:58:30; 01:59:15
Words and Music (Janet Leigh and Mickey Rooney; he brings his face round to camera ten times; she never does)	01:20:00

Position cheating

An Education (Carey Mulligan holds her book up very high)	01:29:20
The Ghost (the background guard runs from side to side to keep in shot)	00:18:35
Gone with the Wind (is Clark Gable on a box or is Vivien Leigh bending her knees?)	01:25:40
GoodFellas (cheated chairs so we can see them all round the table)	00:55:30
The Guns of Navarone (Anthony Quinn holds his hand very high)	01:31:55
Paint Your Wagon (far too close for Clint Eastwood and Lee Marvin)	00:36:50
Panic in the Streets (the group adjusts so the camera can see them all)	01:13:00
Panic in the Streets (three people changing position, but always to be seen)	01:17:45

Set and camera cheating

Day for Night (La nuit américaine) (a false window for Jaqueline Bisset)	01:20:25
The King's Speech (Helena Bonham Carter and Geoffrey Rush framed so only one is seen at a time)	00:09:15
Side by Side (Disc 2: James Cameron and scenery)	00:20:10

Talking to the back of the head

The Blind Side (Tim McGraw talks to Sandra Bullock's hair)	01:44:20
Cat on a Hot Tin Roof (Paul Newman and Elizabeth Taylor)	00:19:00
Heat (back-of-head acting in the diner by Dennis Haysbert)	00:39:35
Men in Black 3 (would you stand in an elevator with Will Smith like this?)	00:24:45
The Wizard of Oz (what can Billie Burke see of Judy Garland? Just hair?)	01:34:35

The complete list of films, dates, and directors is in the *Index of films* at the end of the book.

All the time codes are taken from my DVD player in London, with the DVDs bought in the UK, so you can know how many minutes and seconds the clip is from the start of the movie. Where I can, I have noted the different versions of the films.

There may well be variations in the time for different machines and formats, but these should be consistent for your download, DVD player, or computer, and so once you note the differences, you will know where to find each of the above clips.

Marilyn Monroe and her love

4

THE CAMERA

The camera is your Audience of One. It will almost certainly be more expensive than you, and probably more temperamental. Loving care and attention is lavished on it, and quite rightly, too, for without the camera there is no show.

A camera can pan, tilt, or zoom. It can be put on tracks to dolly in and out or follow along; it can crane up and down. In a multi-camera studio, it can do most of these most of the time. With single camera work, especially on location, it can do all of these – at a time price. I can easily explain the technical terms.

pan	rotating the camera through an arc: "pan left; pan right"; named after the long shots in the early movie days that slowly looked round the scenery: a panoramic view – hence a pan.
tilt	tilting the camera to look up or down – just what you would expect.
zoom	changing the size of shot by making it tighter (or looser) in a continuous way; it works by using a complex lens system that can continuously change its focal length.
track	moving the camera on a set of rails, or on a smooth floor; it is great fun to use, and directors use it to creep closer, back off, and crawl around actors.
dolly	can have the same meaning as **track**, but also refers to the carriage that the camera sits on when tracking.
crane	moving the whole camera up or down, often as an actor gets up or sits, so that the camera can remain at eye level.
left and right	the camera's left and the camera's right, as seen by the camera operator; because an actor's left and right are wholly dependent on the direction they are facing, we must use the camera's left and right, and this has the advantage that these are also screen left and right.

45

But all these terms only refer to what the camera **does** in a technical sense, and that is not what this section is about.

Now for what the camera does that affects the **acting**.

An imaginary acting exercise

Here is an exercise I do with actors and students, either new to the camera or with experience behind them, **after** I have introduced them to the secrets of screen acting – both the ones you have come across so far and ones you will come across in later sections.

I ask an actor to sit on a chair and act for about twenty seconds while I record the results. He can speak either something he has previously performed or something he knows by heart like a nursery rhyme or song, or improvise something. The person he is talking to should be just to the left side of the camera. (This is a good chance to test whether he understands what "talk to someone camera left" means.) I use the microphone on the end of a boom to get sound, and I set up the camera to record a medium close-up of everyone.

I then charge through the exercise, being rather brusque and demanding (just like an unsympathetic assistant director). I ask that the boom be brought nearer, or put farther away, then rush the next person in after the first has finished (just like busy crews do to actors when they are trying to finish a shoot on time).

(You can do it yourself now, or imagine that you are doing it. Go on – twenty seconds for the camera.)

I then play back the results. Oh dear! They all forget everything I have told them and go back to what they know – stage acting. Except that they are all rather stiff and formal. The vast majority of performers sit or stand there like butterflies stuck in a display cabinet. There is minimal movement, the head is rigid, and if anything of interest **is** going on, it is often in the hand gestures that, alas, are out of shot. To remind yourself about where the gestures should be made, go back to Chapter 3, "The frame."

When the footage is played back, you can see that many of these performers' faces are active only in the small area between the moving mouth and gesticulating eyebrows. The actor is only using about 10 percent of the screen to communicate with the audience. They tend, in fact, to do all those things they **think** screen acting is, the ones they have told me about at the beginning of our acquaintance (do less; be still; keep it all on the face; etc.), and it is all very bad and very boring.

Whenever a camera is recording your performance, think about how much of the camera's view you can fill with good, interesting, and entertaining information. It is surprising how many performers give themselves restrictions that are not there, as in the above exercise.

In real life if you have something important to say to someone in a room, you don't say it from the hall outside the door; you go inside to give yourself a good position to deliver your message. In a similar vein, a stage actor does not deliver his best lines from the wings, or from behind a sofa or another actor. No, often the only place for the actor is right in the center of the audience's attention.

The camera should be dealt with in the same way. If you have something good to do or say, make sure it is on camera. (See *Good moments* in *Time codes* at the end of this chapter.)

If you feel that this is such a truism that it is barely worth stating, then read this next bit.

When two people are on camera speaking to one another, and the shot is a two-shot (that is, both people are in the shot), it often happens that one of the actors cannot be seen well, because he is looking toward the other actor. I could, of course, also put the camera on the other side of them and get a **reverse matching two-shot**, but this takes extra time and effort that would be saved if the first actor had simply **cheated his face toward the camera**.

Cheating

As discussed in previous chapters, there is a lot of cheating that goes on in front of the camera. Those who do it well know that it is necessary and do it even before being asked. They also provide a motivation for the "cheating" so well that the audience thinks that it is the **character** who needs, at that moment, to bring his face to the camera, and so the "reality" of the scene is maintained.

Two pictures follow. One is of two people talking where the person nearer the camera is not cheating well. The result is that we cannot see her face clearly, so either we have to put in another camera shot – extra time and effort – or we are going to miss all that is happening on her face. Next is an example of a well cheated face. Here you can see that although the impression is still given of two people talking together, the one nearer the camera has cheated her face round so we can see both faces, and so get messages and information from both expressions as the scene is played. To be able to do this, and to do it so well that no one notices any artificiality, is the hallmark of a good and useful screen actor. (See *Position cheating* in *Time codes* at the end of this chapter.)

This idea of providing a motivation for the camera is quite easily understood when you think in terms of stage moves or gestures. A necessity (for example, a character needs to get away from the door to clear it for an upcoming entrance) must be disguised – **cheated** if you like – as a character move, such as the character "discovering" that he needs to cross away from the door to examine a picture on the wall **just** before the other character comes through. The technical necessity is **motivated** so as to appear to be a character need. If you are cheating, then, it is necessary to make it appear that whatever it is you are doing is **exactly** what your character would want to do at that time. So in the picture the actor is disguising the fact of bringing her face to the camera by looking at her tea cup: She has **motivated** the cheat – and she has also allowed the camera to see her "secret thoughts."

47

The camera also "needs" a motivation to move. For example, if the camera is looking at one person, and pans to another person, then it looks a bit odd if the camera suddenly charges off on its own. Instead it looks much better if the first person gives a little look with the eyes or moves his head, to **motivate** the camera to pan from one face to the other.

The actor will often be asked to do these little camera-motivating moments. During a discussion between several people, the camera will repeatedly go from one person to another, and it works better if the cut occurs as the actors give an "eye-flash" to the other speaker. (See also Chapter 14, "The editor and editing.")

Often, the director will want the size of shot to be changed, say, by zooming in to a close-up of a face for a climactic moment, but will not want the zoom to be so blatant. (They do not seem to mind about this so much in daily soap operas.) One way of doing this is to have a character crossing the shot (for example, a maid with a tray of drinks) **just** as the camera is zooming, so the actor's move **motivates** the camera to zoom in or zoom out, and the camera shot size changes as the actor moves, and this change is hidden by the motivation of the movement.

Mirror shots

How many times have you seen on screen an actor facing a mirror, his face reflected in it? Many, many times, we directors, I am afraid, find mirrors completely irresistible. We are always arranging it so that the actor can be seen in many different angles and ways. But think about it for a moment. If the camera can see the actor's face, then the actor is not seeing his own face, but **is seeing the camera!** So all those loving looks and gestures into the mirror are **not** real, **cannot** be real, but are the usual cheats I have been talking about that make screen acting so very different from the realism some thought it was. Every mirror shot is by definition a cheat, and the actor has to pretend to be seeing himself; sometimes you can see wildly angled mirrors that are held or come away from the wall (a matchbox behind the mirror can bring it out to get the correct angle). You can now see it looks so silly, but the job is to make it look real, to provide a motivation so that it appears that it is the character, your character, who wants to hold the mirror that way and allow the camera to see your face in the reflection.

During that lovely moment in *The Apartment* when Jack Lemmon's character looks at himself wearing his new bowler hat and recognizes the crack in the mirror, he was **not** looking at himself but was actually looking at the camera, **pretending** to be having an emotional moment of seeing his new hat and then the cracked mirror: screen acting, **good** screen acting. (See *Reflection cheating* in *Time codes* at the end of this chapter.)

If you have a camera, try it out now, with the camera doing certain moves, and work out how the actors can help to motivate it.

A badly cheated two-shot

A well cheated two-shot

A useful screen actor is one who understands the need to motivate camera moves and gives to the camera (all right, gives to the director, the editor, actually gives to **himself**) those little moments that allow the program to be cut together well (and so giving himself more screen time). (See *Position cheating* in *Time codes* at the end of this chapter.)

Speed of movement

A very common technique in starting a scene is to present a picture of a cup of tea (a glass of wine, a mug of beer) and tilt up with it as the speaker drinks, to reveal the scene. If a camera tilts (or pans) too rapidly, the effect is unsettling to the audience, so the actor will be asked to slow down that particular move. This leads to another "rule." Slow down **moves** so that the camera can follow them without bringing attention to itself. There is such a thing as a "filmic rise," when, to get out of a chair, instead of doing it normally – the natural thing is to lower your head as you start to get up – you put one leg under the chair and use it to sort of smoothly glide up and out of the chair. This allows a camera that is on your face to follow you easily as you get up. Watch how Commander Riker in *Star Trek: The Next Generation* sits down and gets up – by swinging his leg over the back of the chair. Why would he do this? Well, look at his face, and you can see that his expression, his eyes are never dipped out of view as he keeps his body straight by his unusual leg-swinging – you can see this in *Riker sits down* on YouTube, posted 2013.

This changing speed of movement is particularly applicable when walking past the camera, since the camera must not pan too fast or the scenery rushes past on the screen in an unnatural way, and attention is brought to the mechanics rather than the drama of the moment. This means that the actor is often asked to walk at a normal pace as he approaches where the camera is lurking, but to slow down just as he passes the camera. **Be very careful that in slowing down your moves you don't slow down your speech**. The rubric is:

Talk fast and move slow

This is quite difficult if your character is in a fast mode, such as being very angry. It really **feels** so odd to walk slowly across the room to grab your antagonist while words cascade out of you. Yes, it will feel most peculiar but **look** natural and wonderful – they may even say that the camera "loves you."

This love that is ascribed to the camera really, of course, works the other way around. Those actors who really love **the camera**, who play everything to the **Audience of One** that they know the camera to be, are the ones who understand the true nature of screen performance. Don't be confused, do **not** play to the camera operator **or** to the director, just to that friendly little lens that soaks up all your best moments and is your gateway into the hearts and minds of your eventual audience. Just imagine that your Audience of One is nearer or farther away from you according to the size of shot, and **then** act naturally.

Secrets on faces

In real life, we do not let other people see how we really feel – all those times our parents told us, "Don't let them see you are afraid . . . you fancy them . . . you are desperate for the job," and so on. Society could not work if we all went around showing on our faces how we really felt about everything – and yet that is precisely what really good screen actors do, and they achieve this by understanding that when the camera is only showing your face, you can indeed show your secret thoughts because the audience watching it feel that only they can see them. See Chapter 14, "The editor and editing," for more on this. (See *Good moments* in *Time codes* at the end of this chapter.)

Secrets of the camera

- It is your Audience of One.
- It wants you to cheat for it.
- It needs to be motivated.
- It needs you to talk fast but move slow.
- It has an invisible red carpet stretching out in front of it.
- It can show your innermost thoughts without the other characters seeing them.

Because you are acting to the special Audience of One, even when you are on a set, you cannot always see what a fellow actor is doing. Even the director cannot be sure. There are many stories from the business, like how, for instance, Laurence Olivier thought Marilyn Monroe was giving a nothing performance in the film *The Prince and the Showgirl*, which he was directing. He watched her performance from sitting under the camera, could not see what she was doing and so thought her performance inferior. However, when he went to watch the rushes, all her wonderful talents were to be seen, and he realized that her skills included putting into her close-ups all those extra moments and thoughts that stage actors expect to express with their bodies. (In an earlier publicity shot of new starlets, you can already see this camera-loving quality: of all the starlets who were posing for a group of photographers, only Marilyn was quietly, confidently smiling right into the camera lens.) (See *Secrets* in *Time codes* at the end of this chapter.)

Red carpet treatment

Because it is only an Audience of One, the camera has a very narrow view of life, and the camera sees in depth, not in breadth. The problem here is that all actors who have had anything at all to do with stage acting think in terms

Real people talking

Screen people talking (on the red carpet and cheating)

of breadth, of moving apart to allow the audience to see another character, to make room for the other actors to "breathe." For a camera it is all different. Imagine that there is a red carpet stretched out from the camera and all you have to do, wherever you are, is **keep on the red carpet**. In real life and on stage when the group gets bigger we sort of stretch out sideways; for the camera, stretch out lengthwise – always keeping on the red carpet.

Try it out now as an exercise. Place three people next to each other, and look at them side by side on the screen. Then get them in a line, have the camera look down the line, and see the difference.

Experiment with positioning, and you will find that to get, say, four people on the screen in reasonable proportion, we need to stretch them out in a long line (all on the red carpet), or at least compose them in depth, so that the camera can see them all, nearest to farthest.

People stretched out sideways demand such a wide shot that we can barely see who's who. People stretched out in depth can **all** be seen well, the only difficulty being that the person nearest the camera has to cheat to make sure we can see his face when talking to the others. (See *Keep on the red carpet* in *Time codes* at the end of this chapter.)

Look again at the screen people talking (on the page opposite), and see how the two nearest the camera have cheated their faces around. This has been made much easier for them because they have brought their **shoulders** round as well. Bringing your shoulders round to camera, even if it means having your back to the person you are talking to, means that you can glance over your shoulder to the person you are talking to, but can very easily bring your face round for when you want the camera to see it, and it does not look like cheating at all – the secret of cheating is to **get your shoulders round**.

For more of this, see Chapter 10, "Rehearsals and technicals."

Chapter 4: Time codes for the camera

(Rounded up to the nearest 5 seconds)

Good moments

The Fifth Element (Ian Holm and Gary Oldman are both camera experts)	00:51:05
Gentlemen Prefer Blondes (Marilyn Monroe always loved the camera)	01:23:00
Layer Cake (Daniel Craig and Kenneth Cranham both play for the camera)	00:09:55
Sexy Beast (lots of swearing by Ben Kingsley – but he makes sure the camera captures it all)	00:06:40

Keep on the red carpet

Accident (all fighting to find the camera)	00:52:35
Bridget Jones's Diary (Colin Firth finds the camera)	01:05:25
Cat on a Hot Tin Roof (five people crammed into shot)	00:39:50
Cat on a Hot Tin Roof (composition in depth)	00:41:55
Cat on a Hot Tin Roof (four then five people adjust for the camera)	01:14:50
The Ghost (background man between Olivia Williams and Ewan McGregor)	00:18:35
The Graduate (Richard Dreyfus makes sure he is seen)	01:19:15
Panic in the Streets (man at the back makes sure the camera can see him)	01:13:00
Room at the Top (lots of people making sure they are seen in group shots)	00:09:40

Position cheating

An Education (Carey Mulligan holds her book up very high)	01:29:20
Gone with the Wind (Vivien Leigh is not so much shorter than Clark Gable)	01:25:40
GoodFellas (cheated chairs so we can see them all)	00:55:30
Panic in the Streets (three people changing position, but Zero Mostel at the back is always to be seen)	01:17:45
Star Trek: The Next Generation (Jonathan Frakes), 2013 YouTube clip: *Riker sits down*	
The Third Man (Bernard Lee holds the letters up unnaturally high)	00:26:50

Reflection cheating

The Apartment (cracked mirror for Jack Lemmon)	00:50:40
The Artist (shop window for Jean Dujardin to look into)	01:23:00
The Blind Side (car window reveals Sandra Bullock)	01:55:45
An Education (Carey Mulligan and a long mirror)	00:36:20
An Education (and a small mirror for Rosamund Pike)	00:36:50
The Graduate (a reflection starts the Dustin Hoffman and Anne Bancroft scene)	00:27:35
Heartburn (bedroom and mirror for Steven Hill and Meryl Streep)	01:02:00
The Lady from Shanghai (multi-mirror finale for Orson Welles, Rita Hayworth, and Everett Sloane)	01:19:00
Runaway Jury (investigator Nick Searcy is confronted by mirrors)	01:46:10

Secrets

4 Months, 3 Weeks and 2 Days (4 luni, 3 saptamâni si 2 zile) (family meal and Anamaria Marinca's thoughts)	01:14:00
Bridget Jones's Diary (Renée Zellweger's reactions to Colin Firth)	00:52:10
Bridget Jones's Diary (and now her MCUs)	00:52:40
Cat on a Hot Tin Roof (Elizabeth Taylor's private thoughts about Skipper)	01:01:00
Hanna (Cate Blanchett's inner character)	01:36:10
Hugo (Ben Kingsley's reactions to the drawings)	00:05:35
Last Night (Keira Knightley's thoughts about her rival)	00:04:55
Magnolia (Tom Cruise trying not to answer questions)	01:24:25
The Prince and the Showgirl (close-up of Marilyn arriving)	00:14:15
The Prince and the Showgirl (big close-up of Marilyn toasting the President)	00:24:40
The Prince and the Showgirl (close-up of Marilyn flirting)	00:32:25
Rain Man (Dustin Hoffman can never show intelligence)	00:36:05
Rain Man (but Tom Cruise can)	01:21:15
Singin' in the Rain (Jean Hagen would not really let her beloved audience see how upset she was – unless only the film audience were seeing it)	00:11:45

The complete list of films, dates, and directors is in the *Index of films* at the end of the book.

All the time codes are taken from my DVD player in London, with the DVDs bought in the UK, so you can know how many minutes and seconds the clip is from the start of the movie. Where I can, I have noted the different versions of the films.

There may well be variations in the time for different machines and formats, but these should be consistent for your download, DVD player, or computer, and so once you note the differences, you will know where to find each of the above clips.

Laurel   and Hardy

Full of reactions – and doing lots of business

5

REACTIONS AND BUSINESS

Screen acting is as much about **reacting** as it is about **acting**. (I think it is probably more, but there is a limit to the amount of aggravation I should cause you at this point.) Listen to Steve McQueen: "Movie acting is reacting. Silence is golden on the screen."

In real life, when a group of people are talking, their eyes tend to go toward the person who is talking at the moment. Often the person who wants to speak next tries to give visual signals (such as raising a finger, leaning forward with the body) to get the others' attention and so get to speak.

In stage acting, the audience spends most of its time watching the actor who is speaking. If another actor draws the eye during a speech by a fellow performer, it is called **upstaging** and is not usually welcomed. (I once directed a stage actor who would mop his brow vigorously with a green silk handkerchief during the funny lines of his fellow actors, preventing them from getting a laugh from the audience. I thought this was a little peculiar – and so would you, since they were all in a play **written** by the green handkerchief waver.)

On screen, when there are two actors on the screen, one talking and the other listening, I believe that the audience watches the **listener** more than the speaker. In real life, or in stage acting life, we will watch the speaker, because, although her voice may be indicating one thing, the story and message from her body language may be telling another. On screen, since we are often shooting so tight that we cannot **see** the body language, we will concentrate on the main unknown – what the **listener** is thinking – and that means watching her **reactions**.

Look at the picture on page 112 – you can see that it is the combination of the talker and the listeners that make it such a powerful image. This is quite logical, if you think about it, since we can tell from the sound of the voice more or less what is on the face of the speaker – what we do **not** know is what the listener is thinking or feeling, and so we watch **that face**. And the listener is often reflecting what **we** the audience should be thinking and feeling.

Acting exercise

Remember the imaginary acting exercise in Chapter 4? Do you want to try it again? Twenty seconds of acting for the camera?

There is another fascinating result that almost always occurs: Nearly everyone who does the exercise speaks, prattles even, for the full twenty seconds. Nonstop verbiage cascades into the camera. They all seem to equate **acting** with **speaking**, for given that they had only twenty seconds, they pack it with twenty seconds' worth of words.

They could have scratched their heads, ummed and ahhed, started and stopped, drawled a few words out, or given lots of reactions and few words. They could, in fact, have presented what they have watched **thousands** of times on the screen; but no, what usually happens is that they present uptight, word-heavy performances that represent nothing that they have either seen on screen or experienced in real life.

How did you do in that exercise this time?

Golden rule – react before you speak

In real life, our faces tend to reflect what we have just said. We tell of a sad event, and our faces are then full of grief. We tell a funny story, and at the end we sometimes laugh more than our audience.

This is all very fine for real life; it even works well for the theater; it is **no** good for the screen.

On screen, a picture of one character speaking will be followed shortly by a picture of another character. The viewer does not want to know how the first person feels about something she has just said; they want to know what the **other** person feels about it. Since this is the unknown in the scene, directors and editors will usually cut away from a speaker **just before she has finished speaking** in order for us to see the responder **just before she starts to speak**. This means that much of what an actor does **after** she has finished speaking winds up on the cutting room floor. This footage cannot be used, for to stay on someone's face after they have finished talking would slow down the drama.

In the theater, this is the equivalent of doing any stage business **after** your final line and **before** you leave the stage. It never works, for it slows down the pace, and nothing else can happen until your character has exited. The golden rule for theater: Nothing should happen after the exit line but the exit itself.

If the actor wants to convey extra information to the audience with a facial expression, the best time to do this is therefore **before** the speech. (See *React before you speak* in *Time codes* at the end of this chapter.)

Reacting exercise

Imagine that I have a simple speech to say. "I am very happy I was able to meet you. Unfortunately, I must go now." Putting my facial reactions in **naturally**, it might turn out like this:

A picture of my neutral face

"I am very happy I was able to meet you." (*Big smile reflecting that happiness.*)

A picture of my happy face

"Unfortunately, I must go now." (*Downturned mouth shows the sadness.*)

A picture of my sad face

So – we saw a neutral face, heard the first part of the line, then saw a happy face, heard the bad news, then ended up with a sad face.

Here is a **screen** version of the same speech.

(*Face breaks into a great big smile.*) Editor/director can cut to your face during this, so the audience already knows your mood, wonders why, and can concentrate on your words.

A picture of my happy face

"I am very happy I was able to meet you." (*Face shows sadness.*)

A picture of my sad face

Audience wonders what on earth has happened and so sticks around for the next bit.

"Unfortunately, I must ..."

The shot has already changed to someone else

The editor/director has already cut to the next speaker, "... go now."

Audience can now see how the **next** speaker feels about all this.

So you have hooked your audience into your upcoming thought – you have made them **want** to watch you. First of all they saw a happy face – wait, why are you happy? Then they heard the line, and your face went sad – why? They had to listen to your next line to find out why. Dramatically more interesting, eh?

Yet again, I beg you, **do not believe me**. Instead, watch some more dramas on the screen to see what actors have been doing for ages but you have perhaps only now started to notice. Spot the reactions; notice the reactions before they make a speech; see how reactions can be more important than the speech itself. Stars have been known to give away lots of their lines to other characters, quite happy for someone else to lay out the plot. What **they** want to do is react to it all!

A really excellent example of this is the famous scene between Robert De Niro and Al Pacino in *Heat*. Both of them seem to react for a long time before each of their speeches – almost as if they were in competition with each other. What is really astounding, however, is that the same director directed the same scene in his earlier movie *L.A. Takedown* (which was remade with these more famous actors as *Heat*). Much less well-known actors played those same two roles, and viewing both of the scenes shows you that De Niro and Pacino do **lots and lots more** than the unknown actors. No question of "less is more" with them – it was "more is more," and quite right too, since they are both wonderfully effective: wonderful examples of reacting before speaking.

But did you read somewhere about how "real" this scene was? Watch it again on a download or DVD, and notice that halfway through this scene set in a busy restaurant, the sound effects of all those chattering people are completely faded out, leaving us just to listen to the quiet voices of Bob and Al with atmospheric music added, with the chattering being faded back up and the music out just before the end of the scene. Not a real thing about it – just the **appearance** of being real. (See *React before you speak* in *Time codes* at the end of this chapter.)

React showing feelings? Or your thoughts? Or just react?

Here is a very **worrying** observation from a worrying exercise.

Choose a simple reaction, like swallowing.

Ask someone to do this whenever you click your fingers, regardless of what they are thinking or feeling. In particular, she must not listen to what you say but just swallow when you click.

Film the results, and then play them back, speaking the extra dialogue just before each swallow so the audience sees the pictures you have filmed and hears your voice saying such things as:

"I'm arresting you for drug smuggling."	**swallow**
"I'd like to invite you out for dinner."	**swallow**
"You've just won the lottery!"	**swallow**

The audience will be very impressed with what wonderful, truthful, and subtle performances you have put on the screen, and so will you, even though you **know** the person swallowing was not feeling a thing – except perhaps a little foolish.

This is only an adaptation of an exercise conducted by the Russian director Lev Kuleshov in the 1920s, when he cross-cut between a close-up of an old man and pictures of a coffin, back to the old man, to a skipping child, to the old man, to a plate of soup. Viewers admired the subtle changes in the man's face – in fact, it was all the same shot of the old man who had been asked to think of nothing, but the **context** of this shot determined the changes, not the actor himself.

In our context, a reaction is in relation to what goes before or what follows and is therefore linked not necessarily with what the actor would truthfully do at that moment, but with the whole series of events. In any case, many a reaction that is put on screen is not, in fact, done in real time but quite some time afterward. When Gregory Peck takes his last look at Audrey Hepburn in *Roman Holiday*, and she goes off, he swallows. Now, when they filmed the shot of him it would have been some time before or after (if not another day altogether) the moment when she did, in fact, go off. So, was he "acting," going through all the thoughts his character would on losing his new love, or was he simply responding to a cue?

You see, it does not matter which is true; what matters is whether the **moment** was truthful and effective for an audience, **not** what the actor felt when it was shot. Another example from the same film came early on in the shooting. It was a night shoot, and the director William Wyler was despairing of getting a performance from Audrey Hepburn. (It was the scene in the car where she has to slip away back to the palace.) Finally, he bawled her out in front of the crew, reminded her that the job could be taken away from her and set the cameras rolling. We see in the movie her tear-stained face as she turns toward Gregory Peck for her final goodbye. Was **this** acting the moment in the script or a reaction to what the director had just told her about her personal prospects in the film world? (See *Reactions* in *Time codes* at the end of this chapter.)

The movies are full of examples of "right" reactions derived from "wrong" motivations. But how can they be wrong if they work? They are only wrong if you still cling (are your fingers letting go yet?) to the belief that the actor's real feelings **have** to match those of their characters. In *Casablanca* when Humphrey Bogart gave the nod that started the confrontational singing of the national anthem, he had no idea what he was doing. The director was collecting general reactions from him and one of them was a nod, and so he did one. It was only when the film had been edited together that he understood why. Should that ruin our appreciation of his wonderful performance? (See *Right or wrong* in *Time codes* at the end of this chapter.)

Listening

Much of screen acting is listening, and more is said about it in Chapter 9, "Auditions," and Chapter 14, "The editor and editing." I just want to add a little exercise about it here.

I was working with an "elite" group of actors (that means they were all employed, and their names would be known by many outside the business). I was talking about positive listening. One actor was particularly upset by this, claiming that she hated watching actors pull faces and that the listening we do on screen should be what we would do in real life.

I immediately got her up to "listen" while another actor talked, and I recorded the result as a two-shot. When it was played back she was quite pleased with her good listening reactions. I then asked her to do it again, but this time not to listen to what the other actor was actually saying, but to spend her energies in giving a whole range of expressions. She did this, and I again recorded the result. Before playing it back, I asked, "How was that?" "Well, it was **terrible**," she replied, but we all – the other actors and I in chorus – went, "It was **wonderful**!" Which it was. She was quite upset – "But I felt awful doing all those faces" – and she was only comforted when I pointed out that **because she did them so truthfully and well**, they all worked, and it made for a stunning piece of screen acting.

I wonder if she had the nerve to do this again. And will you? Don't forget, the reactions must **appear** truthful and motivated, but they don't actually have to be so. The wonderful Romanian actress Anamaria Marinca put it best when she said, "I think acting is about being much more real than in real life. It's about forgetting about the mask that we constantly put on to go out and face the world. I'm much more real when I'm playing a character, I'm more vulnerable, and you can see me more than maybe meeting me on the street." (See the section on *Secret thoughts* in Chapter 4, "The camera," and see *Reactions* in *Time codes* at the end of this chapter.)

Another way of showing and experiencing this is the Alone on Stage exercise. Get two people (yes, you can be one) to act in front of the group or audience, with one doing all the speaking, and the other listening. Then get them to repeat it, but this time the speaker must be offstage – the audience must not see them, but only the listener. Does this change things? Of course it does, for the listener, knowing now that the audience can only see her, will do more with her reactions to keep the audience informed of what is going on. This is the same as being in a single shot on camera – pretend that you are alone on stage, and that the speaker is in the wings, and react accordingly.

Business (biz)

Business means any gesture or action usually involving a property. Actors often use these occasions to let the audience understand another aspect of their characters, or to mark where a thought is changing. Although it might on the surface be what they would do naturally (pick up a telephone, open a newspaper), the **way** they do it lets the audience know what the characters are really feeling.

There are some schools of acting, particularly on the American side of the Atlantic, that feel that this is not "truthful," and they advise actors not to do it. What a mistake! You see her, the poor actor on screen, desperately wanting to show emotion, and, having nothing to hand (literally), she pushes out her own hands as if in supplication – "Please give me a prop!" You can see her "I've got an idea," as she brings her hands up to her head. "Let's put on a show!" and her hands stretch out full of impotent energy and longing. (If I see such a thing on a set, my immediate reaction is to give the actor a prop to play with.)

In *Game of Thrones* Charles Dance has a scene criticizing his son's lack of initiative – and as he acts he is skinning a deer, with the cutting and ripping (and pausing) adding to the sense of the scene. Yul Brynner complained to the producers of *The Magnificent Seven* that Steve McQueen was always doing business when he was talking, and if he didn't stop, he himself would do business. The result of such a "business competition" is a delight to see. (See *Business* in *Time codes* at the end of this chapter.)

Contrasts and the theory of opposites

You open a letter and find it contains good news. It is difficult to show your new feelings to the camera if you are already smiling – and of course if you already have a sad or neutral expression on your face it is very hard to show sadness at bad news in a letter. If you are looking sad or concerned as you open the good news letter, then your subsequent smile will light up the camera. And if you are smiling at someone in the room when opening the bad news letter, then the sudden change in your expression will be all the more clear and effective. This is the Theory of Opposites – whatever you are about to show, do the opposite first. I had already found this to be effective before finding out that Alfred Hitchcock had been doing this long before me. (See *Contrasts* in *Time codes* at the end of this chapter.)

Properties

Let's talk about props. Think of a pencil. Now, it is not going to change a lot in the next few minutes. It is an unchangeable object, but if you pick it up, it becomes a way of allowing the audience into your thoughts; it allows us to see how your character is feeling. If you pick it up delicately or grab it, this would show two different emotions and attitudes. If you wobble it about gently or stab it into the sofa, this would show two more. If you throw it on the table or break it in half, you have given more messages still. As you can see, a useful

65

exercise is to see how many different things you can do with a pencil, all to help the audience understand and believe more.

Some years back, directing a simple scene with three roommates, I suggested that the stay-at-home should be drying her hair (after having just washed it) when the other two returned. This led to immediate professional jealousy: "Biz! We want our biz!" the other two shouted. Can you see the scene?

Actor with the wet hair (entering and drying her hair vigorously with a towel): "Hello you two." (Toweling the hair slows down to a sensual level.) "How were your dates?" (Drying the hair with the towel now speeds up.) "I didn't want to go out myself anyway." She was able to use the business (drying hair) to convey her inner thoughts (the subtext).

Business (or biz) is useful for pointing up a performance as long as it does not junk it up. Here is another scene, where two staff nurses were scripted as having a fierce discussion – the one telling the other to stay away from her husband. How was I to shoot this? I set it in the small cupboard where the medicines were kept and did the scene all in one shot. The entire scene, with its back-and-forth dialogue and emotions, was punctuated at the appropriate times with counting pills biz, opening pill boxes biz, counting the pills in them biz, and swooshing them back into the box biz. The actors, both experienced and excellent, loved working out how to time which activity would match what emotion at any particular moment.

I feel sometimes that actors on screen should never be still, for the screen needs to be continually drawing the eye to its performers. Don't get me wrong, I am not talking of large gestures and moves, but very, very small, subtle, continuous activity. If you look closely at so-called "static" actors, you will see that they are not, in fact, completely static, but there is a little move here, the eyes twitch there, the jaw muscles tighten there – loads of little movements that keep that flat screen image alive. Look at Bob Hoskins as he realizes he is about to be killed in the last shot of *The Long Good Friday*, or Meryl Streep in *Heartburn* at the hair salon as she realizes that her husband is cheating on her.

When we wave someone goodbye at the airport or railway station, we do not hold our hand up and leave it there. No, we wave it – and wave it for as long as the recipient can see us. It is as if we have to keep it moving to prove that we are still there, that we still care. In a similar way, reactions have to keep happening on a face – little shifts, little twitches of the jaw muscles – and it is as untrue to leave the face stationary as it is to have an unwaving farewell.

I had finished a screen acting workshop in California, and some of the acting students were still a little unconvinced that this was true (still hoping for that "just think it and the camera will reveal all" philosophy?). As I switched off the large monitor screen showing the output of the camera, it happened to switch to a local channel that was showing an old episode of *Police Woman*. As we watched (sound off, of course) you could see that even though she was not speaking, her character was never still for a single moment – she was always on the move, turning down a collar here, straightening a belt there. The laughter in the class showed that they had finally taken the point.

Silent movie exercise

This is for those who want better proof of how reactions can inform an audience, rather than just relying on the reactions your character might "naturally" do.

Select a student to act out a scene as if it were a silent movie. Something nice and melodramatic – like standing on the castle ramparts as the villain besieging the castle shouts up that, unless she throws down the keys to the castle, he will put out her husband's eyes; she refuses, and so he does put out her beloved's eyes.

Get her to act it, and record the results.

Now, repeat the scene, but this time have the actor just obey the director's voice, and have the director (you?) give a continuous stream of commands: "Look down; clap your hands over your mouth; shake your head; suddenly look up; press your fists to your eyes; look down then up to the skies; scream; now slowly look down," and so on.

Record this, then play back the two versions. It is almost **embarrassing** how much better the "directed" version can be than the "realistic" one. It shouldn't surprise us too much; after all, this **is** what happened in the silent movie days. And **why** was there a need for a director to behave this way? (In the early days of film it was thought that this talent of "getting a performance out of an actor" was the prime directorial job.) The reason is that, in reality, events happen too slowly and too subtly to communicate on the screen. Actors need to do **more** and **in a shorter time** in order to give an impression of "truth."

Reaction secrets

- React before you speak.
- React while others are speaking.
- The context gives a reaction significance – not necessarily the actor.
- Reacting can be more important than acting.
- The use of properties makes reactions easier, and easier to understand.
- Speed up the gap between reactions.
- Practice your reactions – in a mirror.

For a recent commercial, an actor was required to give five distinct reactions in three and a half seconds, and she managed wonderfully well. It was not what she would have done in real life, but was a speeded up version of "naturalism." (See also Chapter 9, "Auditions.")

You see, true human reactions can take between one and a half and two seconds as we think things through. This does not apply to instinctive actions, such as playing tennis, for there is no time for a top tennis player to think for even a fraction of a second before rocketing the tennis ball back to the server. These tennis reactions are only made possible by training, and the same should apply to acting reactions. What might take the actor a while (because she has to think it through) will take a much shorter time for the real person in the thick of it. For an actor to reproduce what the real person does (to reproduce sport stars' lightning reactions?) she must abandon **thinking** and go for instinctive reactions.

Because we are not trained or practiced in some of these fast reactions, we sometimes have to do them on cue, such as having a director talk us through a series of reactions very quickly (or shout through a megaphone). Although it will not be real to us, the rate of reacting **would** be real for the instinctive moment we are aiming to portray.

In the Massachusetts court case involving the English nanny accused of causing the death of her charge, the verdict was broadcast live – and when she was told she was guilty of murder, she did absolutely nothing for eleven seconds (I timed it), and **then** collapsed into tears. A real reaction of course, but totally unusable on the screen, where an instant reaction would be called for. Real life just takes too long – we need the "reality" of condensed emotions in condensed time.

Practicing gestures

To achieve these sorts of skills and results, you have to get good at them – and that means research and practice. Research means watching yourself in real-life situations and finding out what **your** vocabulary of moves and gestures is. Watch other people in the subway, in shops, at parties: What do they **do** that can be added to your vocabulary? Then watch screens, see what other actors do, see which bits you can steal – I mean adapt – for your own use.

I have never forgotten working with an actor who wore glasses when sitting in class but took them off to act. He did this in such a smooth way, rising up from his chair and slipping his glasses off his face and into his top pocket, that you forgot he wore them at all. This piece of business was obviously one that he had perfected over the years – and it said something about him. I am on the lookout for where I can give this lovely piece of business to an actor as an appropriate choice for a particular moment. (And I challenge any actor to reproduce this speed and efficiency just by thinking about it.)

Humphrey Bogart was known for his sneers. He did them well; they were part of his actor's equipment. Did you know that he spent many hours practicing them, so that eventually he could sneer with any part of his lip he wanted? You see, he understood about reactions and business and made it his job not just to be good at them, but to be **excellent**.

Chapter 5: Time codes for reactions and business

(Rounded up to the nearest 5 seconds)

Business

A Few Good Men (Tom Cruise never stops doing things)	00:10:30
A Few Good Men (Tom now eats an apple, and keeps his hand gestures up)	00:11:20
Game of Thrones (Charles Dance skinning a deer), season 1, #7	00:01:55
The Magnificent Seven (Steve McQueen and Yul Brynner at the fence)	00:17:35
The Magnificent Seven (Steve and Yul into competition time)	00:11:55
Margin Call (Jeremy Irons eating and acting)	01:30:20
Margin Call (Jeremy Irons speaks and moves)	00:44:25
The Secret in Their Eyes (El secreto de sus ojos) (Soledad Villamil only stops doing business at her desk when her thought changes)	00:06:50
Stage Fright (Marlene Dietrich moves all the time, stealing our attention)	01:36:00

Contrasts

The Artist (contrasts on and off stage)	00:06:00
The Fifth Element (Ian Holm's contrast)	01:40:25
The Fifth Element (Gary Oldman's contrast)	01:32:20
Marnie (Bonus Material: Documentary: Hitchcock's note on contrasts to Diane Baker)	00:33:35

React before you speak

All That Jazz (if the chorus line had reacted before speaking, they would have been given better moments in the movie)	00:05:45
Before the Devil Knows You're Dead (Marisa Tomei's reactions)	00:38:35
Bridget Jones's Diary (Renée Zellweger does it right)	01:22:25
Clear and Present Danger (lots and lots of reactions from Donald Moffat)	02:07:00

Heat (Michael Mann wrote, directed, and produced – with Al Pacino and Robert De Niro facing each other over the table and both doing lots before they speak) — 01:25:15

L.A. Takedown (earlier version with the same script, director, producer – and the two less well-know actors: Scott Plank and Alex McArthur) — 00:54:35

The Magnificent Seven (Steve McQueen and old man) — 01:04:40

The Magnificent Seven (Steve McQueen and farmer) — 01:19:10

Margin Call (Kevin Spacey and Paul Bettany react before speaking) — 00:10:50

Presumed Innocent (Sab Shimono makes the most of his court appearance) — 01:37:10

Six Days Seven Nights (both Harrison Ford and Anne Heche do lots) — 01:05:05

Reactions

4 Months, 3 Weeks and 2 Days (4 luni, 3 saptamâni si 2 zile) (Anamaria Marinca puts her thoughts on her face listening during the meal) — 01:14:00

Before the Devil Knows You're Dead (good reactions in the car by Philip Seymour Hoffman and Marisa Tomei) — 01:17:45

The Graduate (wonderful reactions by Dustin Hoffman's parents, William Daniels and Elizabeth Wilson) — 01:09:20

Heartburn (as Meryl Streep slowly realizes her husband is cheating on her) — 00:46:15

Last Night (Keira Knightly the wife and Eva Mendes the rival) — 00:05:20

The Long Good Friday (Bob Hoskins's final shot, just facial reactions) — 01:45:20

Love in a Cold Climate (twenty-two seconds of reactions between Sheila Gish, Anthony Andrews, and Megan Dodds) — 01:12:20

The Magnificent Seven (Steve McQueen looking at food) — 01:01:10

The Magnificent Seven (Steve McQueen looking at women) — 01:02:40

Master and Commander (Paul Bettany operates on himself, reacting a lot) — 01:27:30

Prime Suspect (Prime Suspect 1: A Price to Pay) (Zoe Wanamaker steals the scene from Helen Mirren) — 03:00:10

Rambo: First Blood Part II (Sylvester Stallone's face writhes with emotion in his last speech) — 01:27:45

Roman Holiday (Gregory Peck swallows)   01:51:30

The Shining (Jack Nicholson smiles during   US 00:05:10; UK 00:04:50
every shot – except one)

Right or wrong?

Casablanca (Humphrey Bogart just gave a nod)   01:09:10

Close Encounters of the Third Kind (Cary Guffey's look of wonder)

         Theatrical release; Special edition; Director's cut 00:12:25

Close Encounters of the Third Kind (Disc 2: Documentary: 00:40:45
child looks around)

Close Encounters of the Third Kind (Cary looks up)

   Theatrical release 00:45:25; Special edition 00:47:30; Director's cut 00:47:20

Close Encounters of the Third Kind (Disc 2: Documentary: 00:39:40
child looks up)

Roman Holiday (Audrey Hepburn is upset – is she acting,   01:34:00
or is it real?)

The complete list of films, dates, and directors is in the *Index of films* at the end of the book.

All the time codes are taken from my DVD player in London, with the DVDs bought in the UK, so you can know how many minutes and seconds the clip is from the start of the movie. Where I can, I have noted the different versions of the films.

There may well be variations in the time for different machines and formats, but these should be consistent for your download, DVD player, or computer, and so once you note the differences, you will know where to find each of the above clips.

Richard Burton and Elizabeth Taylor

Her vocal level pretends he is here

6

SOUND AND VOCAL LEVELS

The most important chapter in the book.

This, you might think, seems a bit strange, since this book is about screen acting, and you would expect the main thrust to be about the **look** of things rather than the **sound** of them.

I put this as the most important because, in my experience, the main reason why good actors are **not** good on screen is that their vocal levels are wrong. Time and time again, I see a good performance (or a potentially good actor) ruined by speaking too loudly, and the performance coming across as "too theatrical." In that twenty-second acting exercise that you did in Chapter 4, you also got the sound level wrong, didn't you? You broadcast your performance loudly to the whole group, rather than to the microphone. Why do you think I kept moving the microphone during the exercise? It was reminding you of what it was doing, and how close it was.

Again, we need to go back to the basics.

In real life we vary our level of speaking according to how excited or passionate we may be, **and** how far away the person is that we are speaking to.

On stage, we do the same, but also incorporate how far away the furthest member of the audience is.

And on screen? Here, although the person we are speaking to may be on the other side of the room, the **effective** distance we should project to varies according to the **size of shot**.

When an audience looks at an actor on the screen, it is as if the person he is speaking to is just beyond the frame. So if it is a long shot, it is as if the person he is speaking to is about twenty feet away. If it is a medium close-up, it is as if the person is ten feet away. And if it is a close-up, then it is as if the person he is speaking to is only a few inches away.

Before you start to panic and think that you have to work out what size shot you are in, and what level of projection that should require, let me introduce you to your best friend and helper. It is not, of course, the director – it is the boom, at the end of which is the microphone.

The microphone

In most dramas, the boom operator will vary the distance from the microphone to the actor according to the size of shot, to ensure the production has correct "sound perspective." This simply means that when we see an actor in long shot, we expect to hear his voice as from a distance (and have a bit of echo or reverberation about it), while if we see an actor in a tight close-up we expect to hear the sound in a very intimate way. These effects are achieved by varying the distance between the actor's mouth and the microphone.

As a rough rule of thumb, then, if you project to the other person **as if he were as far away from you as the microphone on the boom**, then you will be projecting at the right level for the size of shot.

How simple, how easy, thank you very much.

Does it surprise you to learn that it is not quite as simple as that? For a start, if you are using very little volume (for a tight close-up, say) then there is a danger that you will slow down your delivery, reduce your reactions, lack energy, and come across as very lethargic and downbeat. You must therefore **keep** your energy and attack, but **reduce** the actual volume, and that is not very easy at all. It is quite unnatural – but by now you should be reconciled to the thought that screen acting is not necessarily going to make you **feel** good, only **come across** as good.

Normally, the faster you speak, the louder you will get. ("How dare you – get away from my door!") If you take your voice down to a very low level, you will also be speaking slowly. ("Well, hello stranger. Can I buy you a drink?") To vary your projection level without varying the speed is so unnatural, it is hard to believe that this is what actors do, but watch a downloaded movie, or turn on the television set, turn up the sound, and listen to what they are actually doing. A lecturer who talks enthusiastically and loudly, energetically waving his arms, will come across on screen as a theatrical ham. If he wildly reduces his volume level, but **keeps** every bit of energy and enthusiasm, he comes across as a television personality! Listen to a fast-speaking character in a close-up in a drama, and notice that he is not actually booming his lines, but hissing them – but beware of whispering, of which more later. (See also Chapter 1, "Screen versus stage," and Chapter 3, "The frame," and the **talk fast move slow** thoughts in Chapter 4, "The camera.")

As a further rule of thumb, the microphone will be where the edge of the frame is, and during the camera rehearsal the boom operator will be dipping in and out of the shot to find the edge. Do not always blame the boom operator if you see a microphone in shot; it could be that the camera operator has framed the shot differently to the rehearsal, or the actor has gone to the wrong position, ruining the careful geometry between camera, actor, and microphone. (See *Talking quietly* in *Time codes* at the end of this chapter.)

Directors and vocal levels

I have found that many directors have no concept of this entire topic. They will criticize a performance for being "too theatrical" when it should have been criticized for being too loud for the medium. They have even said of an actor that he "pulled too many faces" when, in fact, all the actor had done was over-project his voice.

A friend I was talking to, telling her that in her last screen drama she was not so effective because she had always spoken louder than her screen husband, told me that they had had a lot of trouble with the sound on the shoot, and that "Miranda Richardson was very difficult – the sound man begged her to speak up, the director begged her to speak up, but she refused – she was terrible." Well, I had watched the show and thought that there was only one superb performance in it – Miranda Richardson's. She obviously knew what the director did not, that her voice should match the shot, not the circumstances.

When I watch certain films or television productions, I see actors talking to each other where the listener would not be able to hear the speaker at all – the speaker being very sincere, truthful, and **quiet** – and no one seems to notice! That is because it **seems** natural, even though it is one of the most untruthful things that screen acting does. I have yet to read or hear an actor talk about this very important aspect of his craft. They **do** it, but no one talks about it.

If you want some good examples of this, watch Kyle MacLachlan talking to Laura Dern in the diner in *Blue Velvet*, the aforementioned Al Pacino and Robert De Niro in *Heat*, or Harrison Ford in anything. In each case, the listener simply **would not have been able to hear** the speaker in real life, but in screen life it was just **fine**. The recent Oscar awarded to Anne Hathaway is a tribute to the fact that she sang in a way I have never heard before in film – she sang as if the audience were just inches away from her (singers usually can't wait to fill the air with their loud confident voices). She sang very intimately, yet keeping to the notes (this is very difficult to do), and came up with a winning performance. Although most of the film *Les Misérables* is sung, when the other characters **do** speak, they speak very softly indeed. (See *Talking quietly* in *Time codes* at the end of this chapter.)

In *A Few Good Men* Tom Cruise has a nice scene when he is talking of how his father would have liked to have seen him graduate from law school. He starts off in a normal voice, in a medium shot, and as the camera dollies in closer to him, his voice drops until at the end – and in a close-up – he is speaking very quietly indeed (and his listener could not have heard him at all by then). He had adjusted his vocal level completely to the changing size of shot. Gregory Peck developed the useful technique of waving his arms vigorously when angry, rather than raising his voice. (See *Changing as shot changes* and *Gesture instead of shouting* in *Time codes* at the end of this chapter.)

When Sean Connery left the scene as James Bond, they replaced him with George Lazenby. Everyone concerned with the project, and certainly

George Lazenby himself, wanted this new look 007 to be a success – but alas, the audience did not take to him and he was soon replaced with Roger Moore. There are many comments flying around as to why he was not a success, but if you look **and listen** to what he does in his first (and last) Bond movie, *On Her Majesty's Secret Service*, you will discover that his simple problem was that for the entire film he spoke too loudly – every shot. If only one person on the production team had noticed, if only they had given me a phone call . . . (See *Getting it right* and *Getting it wrong* in *Time codes* at the end of this chapter.)

Practicalities

The actual sound level "style" will vary from production to production, and from medium to medium, so a good rule of thumb here would be **never speak louder than the star** (especially if it is Miranda Richardson!). Find what the standard is and work around that level. A situation comedy is usually delivered with more actual vocal level than an intense family drama, but you should beware if there is a studio audience of projecting to **them**. They will be hearing the show via the loudspeakers hung around the studio, and so you should **still** be aware of where the microphone is.

Funnily enough, as the shot gets tighter and the vocal level needs to get more intimate, there is less of your body showing, so the only medium left to communicate with is your face. I believe that in certain scenes this means doing **even more** with your face than usual (because it is the only acting thing left to be seen), and even less with your voice (because the shot is so tight).

So in the picture at the beginning of this chapter (page 72), Elizabeth Taylor should speak to Richard Burton **as if** he were sitting on her shoulder, and that is what you find she does.

I was shooting a dramatic moment in which one character fires a shot over the head of another character, who then dives to the ground. I had him fall into shot in close-up, with the first character seen in long shot over his shoulder. They exchanged a few words, and I had to give a cue to the distant actor as to when to speak, because he could not hear a single thing said by the actor on the ground (who, being in close-up, was only projecting to that level). They were acting away, and I was waving my arms whenever the standing actor had to speak, while he was pretending he had just heard what was said to him. Yes, filming is indeed a funny business.

Try this as an exercise. Give a speech that starts calmly and ends up with you in a raging temper. Put this speech on camera, and have the camera person start the shot as a long shot, and slowly zoom in so that the end shot (and the end temper) is in close-up. If you have a boom, this will mean that the microphone will start some six feet away from you and will sink to within a few inches of your head during the speech. After a few attempts, you will start to learn the trick of building emotionally as you get softer with your speech. But it **does** feel odd, doesn't it?

One of my ex-students phoned me in delight. Six months after graduating she had landed a part in Germany in the latest Claude Chabrol film, and she wanted to thank me for making it possible. (Such phone calls are most welcome!) A few days later she phoned me in despair. "The sound man says I am speaking too softly, but I think it is right for the size of shot. What should I do?" My dangerous advice was "What does Claude Chabrol say?" You see, there are some technicians who, to make their lives easier, will ask you to speak up, but it is **not necessarily best for you**. It just saves them the bother of getting correct sound. So, although you must want to cooperate with your co-workers, on this one I would suggest that as long as the director is happy, you give a cheery acknowledgment to the sound person and – er – carry on as before. If it really is too soft, they can do things about it, but too loud leads to you coming across as harsh and unconvincing.

I beg you, **don't believe me on this one**, but watch the acting on a screen at home, go out and watch your favorite movie star at a cinema, and listen to **exactly** what he is doing. I promise you will be amazed at the low levels used.

I was making this point to a regular director on a New York daily drama. She strenuously denied that her actors did such a thing: They just reacted to each other normally, she told me. I stayed on the floor to watch the recording of an episode (and here the actors have to do a one-hour episode each day of a five-day week). In each scene as the climax arrived, my friend the director (in her soundproof booth) was having the cameras get closer and closer shots, and – yes – the actors were building in intensity and **actually getting quieter**. At the end of the recording, my friend and I both claimed that what had happened was what we expected. She **still** believed that her actors' vocal levels were not changing, because to her, in the booth, that was what they **appeared** to be doing. **I knew** that the actors had, through instinct or experience, varied their performances, and in particular their vocal performances, according to the size of shot, because I was on the set listening to them.

A small addendum here, especially for those in quickly made daily dramas: It is not a good idea in these fast soap operas to use the distance of the boom to guess the size of shot. Because the shows are shot so very quickly, most boom operators use long condenser microphones, and leave the boom at the top of the ceiling to avoid the dreaded "microphone in shot, we will have to go again" syndrome. So the microphone is the same distance away for a close-up as it is for a long shot.

Radio mikes pose no problem at all for vocal levels. Just ask yourself, "How far away from me is the microphone?" And as the answer will be "about six inches," then you speak as if the person you are talking to is **that** far away from you!

Always speak loudly at least once in a screen drama, so that the audience know your soft speaking is an acting choice, not the regular way you speak.

Al Pacino always seems to do this. Be careful that if you get in the habit of soft speaking, you do not end up with **all** your speeches being soft – in long shots as well as close-ups. This may indeed encourage the director to shoot you only in close-ups, but it means that in your long shots your body will seem to hang under your head like a sack of potatoes – unmoving and uninteresting. (See *Being loud* in *Time codes* at the end of this chapter.)

Intimate speaking exercise

Here is a very good exercise that everyone should try. Find a partner, sit about three feet apart, and have an ordinary conversation with him.

Now put your faces about six inches apart and have exactly the same conversation, but only speak as loudly as you would to someone that distance away from you. **Now** sit three feet apart again and have the conversation again **at the vocal level needed for the six-inches-apart position**. You have now spoken correctly for a close-up.

I do a variation of this when I am rehearsing actors, and they speak too loudly. I just let them continue their performance, but I shove my face in and watch it from a distance of six inches. This soon brings their volume down. (And maybe **this** is why all good screen actors use breath fresheners!)

As a wonderful bonus, whenever low vocal levels are used with normal speaking rates, because the actor now has less going on with the projected voice, much more happens with the face. Eyes light up and sparkle, the face becomes more interesting and animated, and character and attitude **pour** out of the face when the vocal level is fast and low.

We can now see that a main difference between acting for the camera and acting on the stage is this – for the stage we push our performance **out** to the audience (especially with our voices), but for the camera we (with our intimate vocal levels) pull the audience **in.** It is a totally different transaction, and thinking in these terms will help you understand why it is that you knew there were differences in acting between the two mediums, but did not know what they were.

Film speaking

There is another major difference between television and film, and it belongs in this chapter because it is all about vocal levels.

A movie actor will do a scene many ways, not just because it is shot many times (as in going for another take), but because each moment will be covered from different angles, **and with different size shots**.

A scene between two actors could typically be covered in the following ways:

- Wide two-shot of both of them
- Loose, over-shoulder two-shot favoring one

- Tight, over-shoulder two-shot favoring one
- Medium close-up of one
- Close-up of one
- Loose, over-shoulder two-shot favoring other
- Tight, over-shoulder two-shot favoring other
- Medium close-up of other
- Close-up of other.

Now, moments will have been recorded in at least nine different ways, with many different takes of each way. The director and editor will choose the most effective, and that means choosing the most effective size shot that matches the actor's performance **and** vocal level. In other words, the film actor can do what he instinctively feels is right or what he judges to be right, but the **size of shot** chosen and used by the editor/director might well depend on how loudly or softly the actor has spoken.

There are some actors (Marlon Brando was one) who tend to work better in medium shots; others (Harrison Ford for example) work best in close-up. As long as they are working in film, where there are choices, then the actor can "act naturally" and the shot is chosen in which the performance is seen to be the most effective. Sylvester Stallone, at the end of *Rambo: First Blood Part II* in his climactic speech, "I want what they want – and every other guy who came over here and spilled his guts and gave everything he had wants," was not shouting at all, even though he was some distance from the person he was talking to, but his face writhes with intensity as he delivers the lines, as he puts his energy into his face and not his voice. (See *Getting it right* in *Time codes* at the end of this chapter.)

Again, go on – try to do it yourself. It is really difficult to approximate what screen actors do. It just feels so **silly** whispering, "and spilled his guts and gave everything he had" as you seemingly "pull faces." But it **is** effective, and until you try to replicate what you know they do up on the screen, you will be forever held back by an incorrect opinion about what "feels" right.

The unfortunate television actor, however, is often given only one size shot for a particular moment and has to make **that** work, whatever he feels he wants to do. In fact, I believe that it is the **television** actor who needs to know and adjust his vocal levels more accurately than the film actor.

Whispering, mumbling, and talking too softly

In the twenty years since I started work on the first edition of this book, it is noticeable that actors have stopped shouting so much on screen – but unfortunately some have gone too far, and because they know they must not be too loud are now only acting in whispers.

Actors who have given wonderful filmic performances in the past have also picked up this annoying habit – such as Liam Neeson in *Non-Stop*, Christian

Bale in *American Hustle*, and Geoffrey Rush in *The Book Thief* – and consistently whisper throughout these movies. Whispering is a sign that you do not want outsiders to hear, but to do the whole part this way gives it an unreality and becomes a style in itself. If you are talking normally to someone else, and the audience listening to it is only inches or centimeters away – well, you will not speak very loudly at all, but **you won't whisper!** Only project to where the apparent audience is, and only whisper when it is a line that actually **needs** to be whispered.

A critic wrote "It has become fashionable of late to whisper everything, because apparently this is subtle. Subtle often masquerades as naturalistic, but that is not always the case. To whisper everything is as lacking in reality, as devoid of light and shade, as to boom it all." Quite. (See *Whispering* in *Time codes* at the end of this chapter.)

- Close-up = the audience is only inches away (think centimeters)
- Medium close-up = the audience is only feet away (think a meter)
- Mid-shot = the audience is only yards away (think meters)

Even some of my favorite actors, such as Harrison Ford, sometimes speak inappropriately softly. In *Morning Glory* he, as usual, talks at a close-up level, but sitting on a bench with his co-star when the director cuts away to a wide tracking shot, Harrison maintains the very low level of speaking – he commits the crime of consistency – and it just does not work. In the same movie, playing a TV news reporter, he speaks the way no journalist has ever spoken on location, with his consistent quiet voice, and again it is inappropriate and does not ring true. I was watching a period drama, and found one performance particularly boring, even though he was a good actor. I then realized that he was suffering from the **crime of consistency** – that is, he delivered his lines in a very low monotone, with the same lack of volume for the wide shots as for the close-ups. The overall effect is to dull the audience, to create the feeling that nothing is happening – consistency of volume is **not** your friend, even if the director has asked for soft speaking from all. But didn't you earlier talk of a director who wanted everyone to speak louder? Yes – it is a tricky problem, solved by varying your volume according to the size of shot, and avoiding the crime of consistency. (See *Getting it wrong* in *Time codes* at the end of this chapter.)

Mumbling is also a growing problem, caused by actors correctly understanding that screen acting requires much less voice – but I cannot be the only person who prefers to record a drama on television as I am watching it, so when I cannot understand what they have said, I can rewind, switch on the subtitles, and then find out what it was they were saying. There have been times when I defy even the most acute young ears to understand what has just been said. Remember, audiences need your lip shapes to help them hear what you say, so if you are not being shot in full face – in a profile or three-quarter shot – then you must be aware that your consonants need to be picked out more strongly than if you are in full face. The information is in the consonants – the emotion is in the vowel sounds. As I write this in 2014, the BBC has just shown a new version of *Jamaica Inn*, and has been inundated with complaints that the audience could not hear what the actors were saying. They pretended it was a technical problem with sound (why does the sound department always get blamed?), but the real problem was that the director/actor combinations had produced something that was unacceptable. Viewers complained the next day: "Incoherent mumbling from all cast members – dreadful," said one; "I was looking forward to watching this new drama but after only a few minutes struggled to even make out most of the mumbled conversations," was a typical response. "I'm not hard of hearing but I had to turn the subtitles on to understand what was being said. This program contained the poorest diction I have ever come across," said another. The sound department can only do so much – reduce the background music and sounds, and boost the actual speaking levels – but if the original material is faulty then the only solution is to re-record all the dialogue, or employ actors who remember that their first task is to communicate with an audience, even if it means softening a given accent. After all, some of the cast of *Jamaica Inn* **could** be heard and understood perfectly, even when doing the correct accent – but with good diction.

Accents

It is a strange phenomenon that when an actor acts with an accent that is not their own natural one, they tend to speak too loudly (if only this mistake had been made by the cast of *Jamaica Inn*!). I suppose that the effort to keep to the new vowel sounds and intonations can push the voice into incorrect levels – even the greats such as Johnny Depp and Daniel Craig have fallen into this trap (but never, of course, Meryl Streep). Be sure that this does not happen to you. (See *Accent problems* in *Time codes* at the end of this chapter.)

Overlaps

One of the most common reasons for a shot to have to be taken again is "No good for sound!" A prime cause of this is overlaps.

To explain: If I am shooting two people talking to each other, I can set the camera up to get a nice tight shot of one of them, and the microphone can come in over his head to give me good sound. When this person speaks, I get a nice "intimate" sound, and when the other person speaks, a nasty distant sound. But that does not matter, for I will shortly move the camera around to get a nice tight shot **and** sound of him, and I will use **this** sound whether it is the shot of him or the shot of his friend. Problems arise when one actor overlaps his dialogue with the other actor, for this now means that I have nice "intimate" sound mixed up with nasty distant sound, and it is unusable. If an actor, then, has to overlap or come in on cue very quickly, he must leave a little gap between the end of the other person's speech and his own, and **in the edit** I will mix it so it will **appear** as if they had overlapped.

Sound secrets

- Project only as far as the microphone.
- Adjust vocal level to size of shot – beware of the crime of consistency.
- Never speak louder than the star.
- Only whisper for secret moments.
- Do not slow down or lose energy when speaking at a low level.
- Do not overlap unless specifically told you can do so.

In other words, don't keep talking until you get interrupted ("Going again for sound!"), but leave one word floating in the air with the next crashing in after a mini-pause. Yet again, it will feel more than odd but will sound great in the final edited version.

Of course, it is absolutely necessary for the actor to know whether the shot that is about to be taken is to be cut into (in which case there must be no overlaps), or if it is going to be a contained shot (in which case it can be possible to overlap and be more "natural"). It is entirely professional to ask for this information from the assistant director. ("Is this a contained single, or are we cross-cutting?") I always tell my actors if it is a scene where they **can** overlap, for I find that most experienced actors have trained themselves never, ever, to come in over someone else's line unless they are expressly told they can do so.

Wild tracks

This is another name for sounds like footsteps going upstairs or someone turning the page of a newspaper. They are often recorded after the main acting has taken place. When they need to be used, it is all due to the **low** vocal levels that work so well on screen.

Because the actor is speaking nice and intimately and **low**, all the other sounds getting picked up by the microphone seem too loud – the sound department's nightmare is a scene where characters are eating cornflakes, or vigorously examining a newspaper. Actors are often told to mime certain events (**pretend** you are doing the washing up) so that good sound of their voices can be taken, and the sound effects recorded as a **wild track** at the end of the scene, and added in during the dubbing session. Again, going back to the scene in the diner in *Blue Velvet*, or the restaurant scene in *Heat*, you will be astounded at just how soft the background effects of cutlery, talking, and other eating sounds are: completely unnatural, but just right as a background to the intense scene between the two lovers, or the two adversaries.

Dubbing

Especially for the movies, but sometimes even for films made for television, the dubbing session sometimes involves actors re-recording their lines. It is, as an experienced actor claimed, your last chance to improve your performance. It certainly allows you to gear what you are saying to the way you now see the shots have been cut together. Again, it is the lucky film actor who gets this privilege (and can so make the vocal levels correct at last), rather than the television actor, whose voice will tend to be whatever he did on the shoot.

The problem here can be where the degree of intimacy with the microphone does not match that of the faces up on the screen. Actors often ask me why we can't just turn the volume down if the actor is speaking too loudly. Well, we can, but it is the **performance** that suffers if the volume is wrong. When an actor is projecting to any great distance, his face becomes a bit harsh and stiff. When very little volume is being used, then his face becomes very much more alive, the eyes become more active – it is as if the actor, not being able to project his voice, is now projecting his personality. **That** is why it works so well. That is also why turning down the volume of the sound recording would leave the face stiff and hard, but for the actor to take the volume down opens up a whole world of sincere, vulnerable, and effective moments.

Chapter 6: Time codes for sound and vocal levels

(Rounded up to the nearest 5 seconds)

Accent problems

The King's Speech (putting on a Churchill voice defeats Timothy Spall)	01:05:00
Munich (Daniel Craig's South African loudness)	01:39:30
Sleepy Hollow (Johnny Depp speaks louder than his co-actors)	00:17:20

Sleepy Hollow (he still is speaking too loudly with his English accent)	00:37:50
True Grit (Jeff Bridges in court is hard to understand)	00:15:45
True Grit (the voice from the privy is very difficult to understand, so CollegeHumor have helped out with their own imagined sub-titles), 2011 YouTube video: *True Grit with Sub-titles*	00:07:05

Being loud

Heat (Al Pacino with his wife Diane Venora)	01:02:00
Heat (Al Pacino bullies Hank Azaria)	01:14:40
Léon (Gary Oldman shouts)	01:22:35; Extended 01:48:30

Changing as shot changes

Bridget Jones's Diary (Gemma Jones loud in two-shot, soft in MCU)	00:01:30
A Few Good Men (tracking in, Tom Cruise drops his voice)	01:43:40
A Few Good Men (walking back from a close-up, he does the opposite)	02:00:40
Game of Thrones (talking to the troops in a wide shot, Kit Harington changes his voice when it changes to a close-up), season 1, #9	00:46:15
The Lord of the Rings: The Two Towers (soft voice from John Back in the tight shot, loud voice in the wider one)	01:41:10
Master and Commander (Russell Crowe starts loud with whole crew, then quickly gets soft to match the close shot)	01:41:45
Minority Report (tracking out, Tom Cruise speaks louder)	01:42:00

Gesture instead of shouting

The Guns of Navarone (Gregory Peck waves his arm)	01:55:25
The Guns of Navarone (Peck growls, not shouts, at the climax)	01:58:40

Getting it right

Dr. No (Sean Connery's first words)	00:07:25
Dr. No (Connery with M)	00:10:10
Rambo: First Blood Part II (Sylvester Stallone puts his energy into his face, not into his voice)	01:27:45

Getting it wrong

On Her Majesty's Secret Service (George Lazenby's first words)	00:04:05
On Her Majesty's Secret Service (Lazenby with M)	01:53:50
Master and Commander (consistent speaking by Robert Pugh – alas)	00:31:20
Morning Glory (Harrison Ford being a reporter in an unrealistic way)	01:22:25
Morning Glory (he speaks consistently softly, even though the shot is wide)	01:22:55

Talking quietly

Affliction (Nick Nolte and Sissy Spacek)	00:41:10
Blue Velvet (Kyle MacLachlan and Laura Dern)	01:02:00
An Ideal Husband (American Julianne Moore and English Jeremy Northam share this transatlantic skill)	00:09:55
Last Night (Keira Knightley and Sam Worthington being soft)	00:14:50
Last Night (Eva Mendes and Sam Worthington in pool)	01:03:30
Layer Cake (Daniel Craig pitches it perfectly with Kenneth Cranham)	00:11:10
Les Misérables (Anne Hathaway singing)	00:26:10
Les Misérables (Hugh Jackman asking for help at the convent)	01:00:10
The Lord of the Rings: The Two Towers (almost whispering from Liv Tyler and Hugo Weaving)	01:35:15
Margin Call (Kevin Spacey and Jeremy Irons speak quietly)	00:53:00
Master and Commander (Russell Crowe shows Paul Bettany how to do it)	00:16:10
Master and Commander (Russell and eight others)	00:30:30
Six Days Seven Nights (farewell by Anne Heche and Harrison Ford)	01:24:10
Who's Afraid of Virginia Woolf? (Richard Burton and Elizabeth Taylor being quiet, although the two-shot at the start of this chapter did not make it through the edit)	01:50:35

Whispering:

American Hustle (Christian Bale talking/whispering to Jennifer Lawrence)	00:20:55
American Hustle (Christian Bale talking/whispering to Amy Adams)	00:31:50
American Hustle (Christian Bale talking/whispering to Bradley Cooper)	00:35:15

The complete list of films, dates, and directors is in the *Index of films* at the end of the book.

All the time codes are taken from my DVD player in London, with the DVDs bought in the UK, so you can know how many minutes and seconds the clip is from the start of the movie. Where I can, I have noted the different versions of the films.

There may well be variations in the time for different machines and formats, but these should be consistent for your download, DVD player, or computer, and so once you note the differences, you will know where to find each of the above clips.

Are they the right types?

Did you hit on the right type for the part?

Back row: Goldie Hawn (*Ditzy Blonde*), Paul Newman (*Romantic Lead*), Buster Keaton (*Silent Stone Face*), Katharine Hepburn (*Waspish Lady*), Bette Davis (*Tough Cookie*).

Front row: Marilyn Monroe (*Pouting Sensuality*), Arnold Schwarzenegger (*Action Man*), Humphrey Bogart (*Sneering Hero*), Spencer Tracy (*Craggy Integrity*), Dustin Hoffman (*Intense Character*), Jodie Foster (*Sensitive Waif*).

7

TYPECASTING

I started entertainment life as a Director in English rep, with a regular company doing different plays every one, two, or three weeks. The actors needed to be (and were) versatile and wonderful – so I entirely disapprove of this whole chapter.

It is here because, alas, I know it to be all too true!

Suppose that you went out to the movies right now. As you buy your ticket, you look at the poster in the foyer, and you recognize **all** the names of the stars in the film you are about to see.

How many of those performances can you predict **before** you see the movie? Most of them? **All** of them?

You see, I have not told you if the movie is modern or set in ancient times, whether it is a mystery or a comedy, whether it is set in Paris or outer space, whether it was written by a genius or a hack. Yet you **know** the performances (or most of them) by knowing the names of the actors.

This is what is known as typecasting.

Imagine a scene in a movie where the doorbell rings, the hero goes to open it, and there is the pizza delivery person, who says, "Here is the pizza you ordered." Imagine that the part is played by **you**. What will be the effect in the movie of you saying that line?

You might well reply that it depends on what you are acting, what you are portraying, what thoughts/emotions/memories are in your head. But you would be wrong.

Look in the mirror, and be firm and realistic. What message comes across from your face in repose?

Now **that** is what the message of your performance will be, and it will owe more to the packet of genes given to you by your parents than to the artistic/creative acting process you went through to prepare for the role.

Some people come across as sad (a naturally turned down mouth), others as cheerful (a naturally upturned mouth), as sensuous (a wide, wide mouth with pouting lips), as serious (thin lips), and so on.

Go on – which are **you**?

Now imagine that the same process is applied to your friends and acquaintances. What sort of message is given by **their** faces?

Now you can understand how typecasting comes about. In the scene I have just described of the pizza delivery, there is no more to the part than the line delivered at the door. In a stage drama there is usually some description before or after the introduction of an important character; each person will get some moment or other to establish her character and mood. But on the screen? "Here is the pizza you ordered"? There is just no **time** to establish anything else, so the director (or producer or casting person) will, if a "serious student" type is wanted, cast someone who **looks** like a serious student (even though the actor concerned could well have flunked all her exams). If the director wants a bimbo type, she will cast a bimbo-looking person (even though the actor herself might be indifferent to those elements of life); if a psychopath, someone who **looks** it (though she may never even kick the cat); and so on.

Typecasting examples

In the movie *The Guns of Navarone* there is a scene where Gregory Peck and his friends have been captured by the Germans and are being unsuccessfully interrogated by an officer. Then the door opens and another officer comes in. The director gives this newcomer a close-up, and we see the high cheek bones, the white-blond hair, the "traditional" Germanic looks. There is no need for any dialogue, scene, or descriptions: We **know** he is the Nasty Nazi **just** by the way he looks. You could say that his close-up **was** the performance.

The actor involved had no need for any inner life, motivation or such like; his looks told us the complete story. The director understood that the choice and type of shot, that is, a close-up just after he enters, comprised the actor's performance. (See *Cast for the way they look* in *Time codes* at the end of this chapter.)

There was a famous Austrian classic actor called Anton Diffring, who fled to England when the Nazi regime took power in the 1930s. Once in the UK, he got continuous employment in the film industry playing, no, not classic parts, but a whole series of Nasty Nazis, because that is the way he sounded and **looked**.

You see, in the screen world, time is at a premium, not just in the making of a drama, but in the telling of a drama. So you need a kind of shorthand, a quick way of conveying a whole range of information about a character, and the quickest and best way of doing this is, yes, typecasting.

I was once trying to cast the part of a doctor for a BBC play. Because I was still negotiating for the two leads, I did not know what was left in the budget for the part of the doctor, and agents were sending in suggestions every day. When it came to choose, my secretary handed me a list of over three hundred actors (including six genuine MDs who had given up medicine for acting) to consider for the role. I rejected all of these; after all, was I not a theater director with many ideas and contacts? I looked through my private file index for those actors who could do the role wonderfully and came up with forty-three names – again, far too many to be auditioned for what was only a smallish part. Then I realized that they were all males – so I cast an actress instead. "Why a woman?" asked my producer. "Why not?" was the only real reply.

Again, looking for two old men to play parts in a drama set in a geriatric ward, I refused the suggestion that I should interview up to fifty old actors. No, I narrowed it down to six, since I didn't want to have lots of little old men trekking across London with only a one in twenty-five chance of getting the part. Then a terrible thing happened: **Each** of the six who auditioned for me could have played **either** of the roles. They were all wonderful actors, some of whom I had seen years before in the West End theaters of London. So who did I cast? Who would you cast, and why? Not the best; they were **all** wonderful. So I ended up casting the short fat one and the tall thin one . . . "Aagghh! I have just typecast!"

There was a gathering of ambassadors in London to meet the Queen of England, and a photograph was taken of the huge group of them. An enterprising newspaper contacted several casting directors and asked them to send along actors to be auditioned for the part of "the Ambassador." They took a photo of **this** group of actors and published it alongside the picture of the real ambassadors. Among the actors were the little men with goatee beards, men with pot bellies, monocles, and sashes, all the stereotypes of "ambassador" – **and not a single ambassador in London looked like any of them.** You see, they were actors asked to play the impression of "ambassador," not trying to imitate life.

Toward the end of his life, Steve McQueen wanted to play an entirely different role, so he sank some of his own money into a film of Ibsen's *An Enemy of the People* with himself playing the lead part of the doctor, a sort of antihero. For this film, he put on a bit of weight, grew a beard, and sported very long hair. What did you think of his performance?

You haven't seen the movie? You haven't even **heard** of it? I am not surprised. The company making Steve McQueen's next movie bought it up and shelved it – no, not because his performance was so bad (in fact it is very good), but because they did not want an audience to see and remember him as any other than the crinkly-eyed, tight-smiling image that **they** had bought for their movie. It is called protecting your investment. That's the film business.

Robert Redford was once asked, in an in-depth TV interview, why he gave such an indifferent performance in his last movie. His answer was refreshing for its honesty: "I **could** have played the part very well, but I was paid all those millions of dollars to present Bob Redford." Oh. Michael York was fed up with only playing "nice young men," and was thrilled when he got the more villainous part of Tybalt in Zeffirelli's *Romeo and Juliet*. He performed it very well, but waited in vain for a similar role in the future – it was back to being nice after that. Steve McQueen himself said: "I am a limited actor. My range isn't that great and I don't have that much scope. I'm pretty much myself most of the time in my movies and I have accepted that." (See *Cast against type* in *Time codes* at the end of this chapter.)

Those actors who are really attractive need not do so much on screen, for the audience are only too happy to spend time gazing at their perfect features, but those of us (does this apply to you? – it does to me) whose features are more ordinary need to do more on screen to keep the audience's attention. Interestingly, some of those very beautiful actors whose features softened and changed over the years (such as Paul Newman) changed their acting as they got older to do more with their now not so wondrous faces. (See *Drop dead gorgeous versus more ordinary* in *Time codes* at the end of this chapter.)

We all admire and want to be those actors who **do** portray many different character types, even with different accents (Robert De Niro, Ewan McGregor, Gwyneth Paltrow, Meryl Streep), but we end up – **if we are very lucky** – playing the same range of roles as do Julia Roberts and Bruce Willis. It is simple economics: a film is so very expensive that the last thing the money people want is to take a risk with a performance, so they buy the performance that they already know the public likes. And it is these money people who make the major decisions: not the artistic people, but the ones who have to drum up all those necessary millions of dollars.

What if the star is incapable of portraying a very different role? No one will know, for the roles will be chosen (and rewritten) to fit the exact image that sells movie tickets by the millions. What if she **can** portray a very different role, and does so? The audience, expecting the same performance as usual, might stay away in droves. Far, far better to insist that the director (and the writers who construct the part) and the costume designers and the makeup people recreate the role that made millions last time in hopes of repeating the trick this time.

The megastars are famous all over the world. Action men such as Arnold Schwarzenegger and Sylvester Stallone pack them in in a host of different languages. Now let's think about that. Have you ever seen an American film with its stars' dialogue dubbed into Japanese, German, or Italian? Yes, there are all the familiar faces – and out of their mouths come these strange noises. Yet they are **still** stars, **still** popular, and **still** get mass audiences. This proves, does it not, that the attraction of the actors lies more in their looks – and what they do with them – than in their voices.

I was watching a scene from *12 Angry Men* on Italian television, and although I knew the faces very well, it seemed so different without the distinctive vocal timbres of Henry Fonda, Lee J. Cobb, and E.G. Marshall. What was interesting was that at the end of the film, there was a separate list of credits for the dubbers, recognizing their unique contributions. The actors in the movie – the American actors – were appreciated for their visual performances and for their visual screen presence: their typecasting!

Go back to the picture at the beginning of this chapter (pages 88 and 89). Now, how many of these actors were cast for their versatility, and how many were cast with their performances already known? Of course, because they are or were great actors, their performances are remarkable – but within their types, not outside them. (See *Cast for the way they look* in *Time codes* at the end of this chapter.) Hitchcock cast his daughter as the secretary in *Psycho* – but it was her looks he was after. Gus Van Sant cast the wife of a friend, who was much more glamorous than the lead actress, in his shot-for-shot remake of *Psycho* – and got a very different effect. (See *Different looks get different results* in *Time codes* at the end of this chapter.)

Inexperienced screen actors

I imagine that if you are reading this, you might well be in that large range of actors who have little or no experience in the techniques of screen acting. If I (or anyone else) were to cast you, we would **know** about your inexperience. So if we did cast you, we might find that your technique was a little lacking, or that you might react badly to the pressure; your **performance** might suffer. No matter. As long as you **look** right, well, nothing can take **that** away from you; at least **that** part of your performance will be there, regardless of other factors. So it is more than likely that for your very first part on screen, you will be typecast – even if you get to do different roles in the future – and so this chapter is particularly important for those of you new to the business.

In a soap opera or drama series, there can be many different writers and directors that may affect one particular character. The only consistent factor is the actor, and the one characteristic of the actor that will stay more or less consistent is the way she looks and comes across.

Interview exercise

Now you must try the most cruel-to-be-kind exercise of all.

Imagine that you have been interviewed for a small screen job by someone you didn't know – maybe it was me!

Imagine that the interview only lasted for thirty seconds, and, as you left the room, you saw me write a quick sentence on my clipboard just as the next person was walking in for her interview.

You know that I must have written a quick, short sentence about you.

What did I write?

Try writing it out yourself.

What did you write? What do strangers think when they see your **face**? What have friends told you they first thought of you when they first met you (before they grew to know and love you for yourself)?

Sit in front of the mirror, and look very hard. See the size of your eyes, nose, mouth, ears. See the complexion, the blemishes, the hairline. See the fat or the bone, the "character" wrinkles, or the baby-face smoothness.

And ask yourself, what would an audience think seeing this? What sort of character, what sort of message would they get from these, my special looks?

I am **not** saying you are doomed to play just the one type of part (although an amazing number of actors do seem to land only one sort of role). I **am** saying that, as a newcomer, you are **much** more likely to get employed for your looks than for your versatility. (David H. Lawrence XVII did not get the role of the Puppetmaster because he is drop dead gorgeous.) Most of the very big names have trouble enough getting variety into the roles they are offered, so further down the line it is all too difficult.

My advice then is: Use it or lose it. Use that nose, that chin, those ears – or get them fixed. Do not hope that they will not have an effect on what the camera thinks of you. Apart from the expected work on noses, chins, breasts, and so on, plastic surgeons can now alter your lips to **give** you a permanent smile. (No, no one chooses a permanent scowl.)

So, get known as good at your type, **then** with the experience you get, other roles can become open to you. But I am afraid that those siren voices that talk of range, growth, and variety – all valuable and wonderful things – are not really addressing the reality of what is required of a beginner in the time-pressured world of screen acting.

After all, the history of great actors is not always the history of great versatility.

In Shakespeare's day Richard Burbadge (his lead actor) certainly did not play the small parts played by the resident comic. Will Kemp (his clown) never got a chance to play the lead role in *Richard III*. In fact, in an Elizabethan play that has an audition scene, the playwright has Burbadge as a character judging what type of part the potential actor should play from the look of his face and body, and from the sound of his voice. Do these four-hundred-year-old thoughts sound familiar?

Back in the 1970s, we all enjoyed watching a ditzy blonde on *Rowan & Martin's Laugh-In*. We were sure that this was no performance – she just **was** the zany, scatterbrained person we saw. The subsequent film career of Goldie Hawn proves that she **always** knew what she was doing, and the first thing that she did was to get very, very good at playing her image of a zany blonde. The better parts came later when she was wanted, and therefore had more negotiating power. She adorns Chapter 13, "The shoot" (page 166), as a tribute to her considerable screen acting talents, and the way she used her typecasting to develop a wonderful career.

Humphrey Bogart still has retrospective film seasons devoted to his work. Why? I think it is because, as a stage actor – although he understood perfectly well what was required of him in being cast in a film – he also made absolutely certain that his performance in *The Maltese Falcon* was different from that in *The Big Sleep* and again subtly different from that in *Casablanca*. In other words, **within his type** he found his variety and his versatility, and this is what I believe makes him still watchable today. He never gives exactly the same performance, but each **is** within his typecast range (well, with the possible exception of *Sabrina*).

The father of playwright Eugene O'Neill played the part of the Count in *The Count of Monte Cristo* on tour all over America for over forty years! So no long moans please about how the modern actor, unlike her predecessors, never gets a variety of roles. I think in those days it was more often like today's casting methods than not. Only for the relatively brief period (in the whole history of theater) when repertory theaters were operating – from about 1920 to the 1960s – and actors were required to come in and play a different role every week or so, was the quality of versatility really required. Since this period is within living memory, and since many of the acting teachers on both sides of the Atlantic were trained to be ready for this style of acting, it is not surprising that they, in turn, feel that this is the "true" form of acting and gear their training toward this type of performance.

As John Wayne commented in a television interview: "You've got to **act** natural – you can't **be** natural, that would stop the tempo. You've got to keep things going along, to push your personality through."

On a happier note, British actor Daniel Radcliffe made his impact by appearing as Harry Potter, a self-confessed geek. After playing this for ten years, he has used this as a stepping stone to play varied and different types, in plays such as *Equus* and *The Cripple of Inishmaan* both in London and New York, in the musical *How to Succeed in Business Without Really Trying*, and in varied films including *What If* and *The Woman in Black*. He turned down all the similar Harry Potterish parts. The moral? Get known first, get wanted, **then** think about how to show us what you can do, and ponder where your career is going.

Film typecasting versus television typecasting

There has been a change in the last decade or so, and it is interesting to think about why this is so. In the old days, the wonderful stars were turning out films for their Hollywood masters as quickly as possible, yet an actor like Humphrey Bogart would still only be in three movies a year, giving a total of about five hours of screen work for his Audience of One.

A modern successful actor in a situation comedy on television, or better still in a dramatic serial or daily soap drama, will be giving many, many more hours of screen performances a year than a successful film actor did in the old days. This means that while Bogart could still give variations on a theme, the modern star of a television series is herself the theme, and of course no one expects or wants her to give anything other than the performance the audience already loves and appreciates.

Profiles

Here is another exercise – not so cruel, but with very interesting results. You can do it either with a digi-camera or with a friend.

Set yourself at right angles to the camera (or friend) so that we see your profile. Go on! So many actors are ashamed of their profiles and try to keep their faces straight on to the camera, not realizing that **we** who meet you see this side of you as well as your full front. Just because **you** nearly always see yourself full front in a mirror does not mean to say that we don't know about the double chin, the lack of one, the "interesting" nose, and so on.

At a signal, while thinking nothing at all, turn from profile to full face, and see what message is given. Yes, there **is** an implicit message, even when there is not any thought at all. If this is recorded with a series of people, then you can make it even more fun by adding extra dialogue when playing back the result, like, "Well officer, we picked her up for shoplifting," or "We caught him traveling without a ticket," or "She's under arrest for drug smuggling." You will find that some people come across as guilty, while with some, we all believe in their innocence. The look of individuals speaks a certain story, and you need to know what story your face tells. (Did they think **you** were innocent or guilty?)

The reason for different messages from different faces is quite easy to understand. A person with, say, an enormous nose would go from conveying a very forceful look – this huge nose cutting into the air, so to speak – to a softer image as the face comes around to the camera. A person with no chin changing from a weak-looking individual to one with, say, enormous eyes gives a completely **different** effect.

Now, there is nothing much you can do about all this, barring expensive plastic surgery, except **study** it and learn what your face conveys in full front, in profile, **and** in the change between the two. There are many actors whose most effective moments come when they slowly turn to camera, and now you can see why!

Try this as an exercise. Get in front of the camera, and goggle your eyes. Get everyone else to do this. Play back the results, and see the effect. Those people with enormous eyes must be careful, for if they goggle their eyes too much, it can look false. People with smaller eyes, however, can goggle to their hearts' content (maybe should goggle), and it just makes them appear more alive and interesting. Try the same exercise with licking lips, flaring nostrils, blinking – try all the variations of your facial movements.

From all this a simple truth emerges: There are no absolute rules of what to do with your face, for **it all depends** on what sort of face you have. So study it, get used to it, and get used to using **your** particular facial strengths.

Photographs

The very fact that you send out photographs is an admission that your **acting** can be judged by the way you look. I know that a great desire not to be typecast and to be seen as versatile leads some actors to send out "contrasting" photographs. I'm afraid that very rarely indeed do different photographs do that – they mostly just look like the same person being either happy or serious (the usual choices).

It is often true that people go into acting precisely to **be** versatile. After all, the actors they mention when asked who they most admire are nearly always those who are allowed to be versatile (as I think in each generation one or

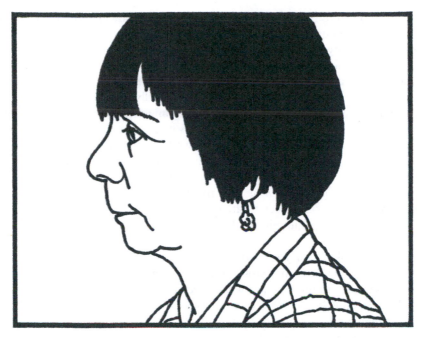

Profile view – one image

Full face – different image

two are allowed to be). I believe, however, that the vast majority of actors are expected to present one thing.

I am **certainly** not saying that is **my** position regarding acting. I **am** saying that this is the feeling of the profession. With all forms of drama getting prohibitively expensive, it is getting more and more difficult to take a risk – a risk that this person might not be able to present a totally different character. If you cast someone who looks right (so goes the argument), then even if the acting is only so-so, or she falls to pieces because it is her first time on screen and it all becomes a bit much for her, then at least we have got the **look** right. Performances can always be improved in the editing stage by cutting you out of shots, or having you just looking over your shoulder toward the other actors. As in the example of *The Guns of Navarone*, your major contribution to a drama, at least in the early stages of your career, is often the shorthand of getting the look right.

Photographs you send out should do two things:

1. If I am looking for you (and that means not only the way you look, but also the way you come across – the "you that we know and love"), then I must be able to find you just with a five-second glance at your photograph. Five seconds is generous. In some New York casting sessions, they flash through a stack of photographs as if they were a deck of cards, and your images go by at about four a second!
2. If I send for the person whose photograph I have approved, then **that** is the person I expect to walk into the audition. Why bother to remove all those wrinkles/double chins if I will see them when you turn up? Why bother to have the camera especially low when your photo was taken, to make you look really tall, if I call you in for a part that demands height? It makes me deeply unhappy – vengefully so – when I am looking for a nightclub bouncer and send for you on the basis of the hunky-looking photograph you sent me, and you turn up at five foot six inches tall.

Actors are often in despair trying to find a set of photographs that suits them. Here are a few things to remember:

1. Never forget that the photographer works for you. Don't let her dominate the session to the extent that you are a victim of her whims and style.
2. It is sad but true that most photographers make most of their money from failed or aspiring actors – let me explain – not bad actors, but actors currently not working, as well as all students out of drama training who immediately get a set of head shots. Whenever an actor thinks her career needs a boost, the first thing she thinks of is getting a new set of photos. Most agents when they take on a new client will demand, as a starter, a new set of shots. This often means that the photographer is used to making you feel good about yourself, and this can sometimes be at the expense of getting you the shots that you need to get work.

100

3. The photographer will also often hide those aspects of you that you most dislike, and these could well be the aspects that **give** you your individuality, that allow you to be most totally "you." I once wanted a teenager with acne, and had to scour the pictures for an actor who I had to guess had this skin condition, for no actors owned up to it in their head shots. Another time I was trying to cast a dying man and had to plough through all the tricks of photography to find an emaciated face. When he came for the interview he had a scar down one side of his face – wonderful! It had been hidden by a shadow in his photo, but it would have made me want him **even more** if I had seen it from the start. Vanity, oh vanity, is a fence to be leapt over. So please – because the "professional" beauties are already up there or are currently being **manufactured** by the plastic surgeons – don't compete with **them.** Present yourself, warts and all. (You see, maybe we are **looking** for warts.)

4. Different photographers have different styles, and it is entirely within your rights to ask to see samples of actors in your type and range they have photographed. In the course of your career, get used to what works best for you and, if necessary, insist on it. Too many "nice" photographs are only good for putting on your mother's piano for guests to admire – but will they get you **work**? Insist on at least six shots at the end of the session for you to do **your** thing, for you to present those aspects of yourself that you know get you work.

5. Often you will have a snapshot (it could be one taken many years ago) that you just love – or at least others around you love. Get this and take it into your photographer and say, "I want a professional version of this!" It will be a quick and effective way of telling your photographer what you want. I have nothing against photographers. They can be very nice people, and often their dominating ways have only developed because they have come across so many actors who do not know what they want, so they help out by giving **their** opinions.

The secrets of typecasting

- Most parts are cast with actors who have already shown that they can play that part.
- Your face already has a performance stitched onto it.
- The image of a type is not necessarily linked with real life at all.
- To protect its investments, the industry wants to keep actors within their types.
- Each generation is usually only allowed one versatile actor.
- Actors through the ages have usually been limited to their typecasting.
- Get regularly cast as your type – **then** branch out.
- If they send for you from a photograph, they expect that person to turn up.
- If they are looking for you, they must find you from your photograph.

6. I think that your photograph looks better if there is only one dot of light in the center of your eyes. It is possible, so if that is what you want, demand it.
7. Clothes tell an amazing amount about the sort of performance we can expect from you. A hint of a bosom "tells" us that you are well endowed; expensive earrings and a diamond choker "tell" us that you can play in an expensive environment; a torn T-shirt showing bulging muscles "tells" us you could play a street fighter, and so on.

The photograph exercise

Here is a nice exercise to conclude these thoughts on photographs. Take an actor's photo, and put it on an easel. Place a digi-camera in front of it so the image fills the monitor screen. Now, ask the actor to act a piece "in the manner of the photo." Everyone should join together in directing the performer. The instructions can be anything from "Make your voice higher, lower," to "Be more streetwise; have less intelligence," to "Act younger/older" – all these sorts of things. When it is framed up on the screen, a photo is astoundingly explicit in telling us what to expect from a performance. Finally (and it can take quite some time), the audience will be happy with the performance matching the photo. Now, and only now, is the actor asked if she likes the performance. If not (and it usually is not), then she could be using the wrong photo.

The whole process can be repeated with different photos from an actor's portfolio until a match is found between what her photo "says" and the performance that she feels is most naturally "her." By using this technique, it is very easy for the actor to find the "correct" photo for her to send out, and maybe – just maybe – what alternative photo to send for a different occasion or job.

A final word about typecasting. When we go to an art gallery, we sometimes take a foolish pride in recognizing an artist at a distance – **that** is a Rembrandt, **there** is a Magritte, and so on. It does not bother us that the body of work by such a great artist is recognizable **as** his work; we do not, in fact, expect a great artist to be versatile, but to be recognizable and wonderful, **within his own style**.

I believe the same applies to the artists of the screen and stage.

Chapter 7: Time codes for typecasting

(Rounded up to the nearest 5 seconds)

Cast against type

An Enemy of the People (Steve McQueen explaining to family and friends how the springs are polluted)	00:17:35
The Fifth Element (did you know Chris Tucker could go this far?)	01:08:25

The Fifth Element (Chris Tucker and Bruce Willis)	01:10:40
Romeo and Juliet (Michael York playing a villain – for once)	00:03:30

Cast for the way they look

Accident (Michael York as usual)	00:10:35
Barton Fink (were John Turturro's looks more important than his acting?)	01:04:40
Cabaret (Michael York arrives at the boarding house)	00:07:10
Donnie Brasco (Val Avery the same as when cooking in his kitchen)	01:01:05
The Guns of Navarone (typecasting of George Mikell)	01:25:50
Last Action Hero (too many beautiful girls for Austin O'Brien)	00:38:15

Drop dead gorgeous versus more ordinary

Bridget Jones's Diary (Renée Zellweger has to work much harder than Colin Firth)	01:22:25
Cat on a Hot Tin Roof (as does Burl Ives with Paul Newman)	00:47:25
Michael Clayton (and Sidney Pollack with George Clooney)	01:14:55
Road to Perdition (an old Paul Newman)	00:29:10
Road to Perdition (still doing more with his old face)	01:30:05

Different looks get different results

Gentlemen Prefer Blondes (Marilyn Monroe's version of the song)	01:07:50
Gentlemen Prefer Blondes (Jane Russell's version of the same song)	01:17:55
Psycho (1960 secretary: ordinary looking Patricia Hitchcock)	00:06:20
Psycho (1998 secretary: gorgeous looking Rita Wilson)	00:06:25

The complete list of films, dates, and directors is in the *Index of films* at the end of the book.

All the time codes are taken from my DVD player in London, with the DVDs bought in the UK, so you can know how many minutes and seconds the clip is from the start of the movie. Where I can, I have noted the different versions of the films.

There may well be variations in the time for different machines and formats, but these should be consistent for your download, DVD player, or computer, and so once you note the differences, you will know where to find each of the above clips.

Laurence Olivier and Dustin Hoffman

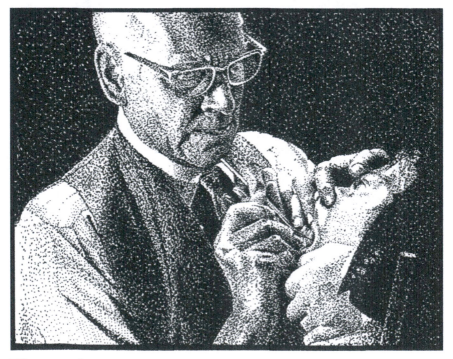

Whatever works

8

ACTING

You have to be a bit worried by now that I seem to have addressed a whole lot of technical problems, but have not dealt with the central issue of "acting."

This is not accidental, even though the book is called *Secrets of Screen Acting*. But before we get into acting, we have to discuss what good acting really is.

I acted as a student in England and trained at a Method drama department in the US. Since then I have directed theater and television productions in the UK and the US as well as Australia, Canada, Denmark, Germany, Ireland, Israel, Jordan, Kenya, Latvia, South Africa, and South Korea. Since 1975 I have been training and teaching actors on both sides of the Atlantic, as well as all over Europe. I have had access to, and knowledge of, a wide variety of acting and acting styles.

The result is that I find it impossible to define what a good actor should "do" in order to give a fine performance. I have known actors who believe and feel everything and who give stunning performances. I have known those who equally believe and feel everything who give rotten performances. I have come across those who have no idea what they are doing, who wow the critics and audiences with the truth of their acting – and, of course, the reverse, where the lack of belief and truth shows up only too well.

The one link I find is quite simply – **whatever works**. Here in the UK at the moment (2014) we have working on stage and screen some wonderful actors – Kenneth Branagh, Judi Dench, Michael Gambon, Helen Mirren, Mark Rylance, Emma Thompson. They **all** give stunning performances in both media, and all use quite different means to do so. The only link between them is that they are great actors. In the same way, I believe that his early performances showed Marlon Brando to be a great actor – no, not because he trained in any particular way, but just because he **was** a great actor. (See *Contrasting styles* in *Time codes* at the end of this chapter.)

In his last acting days Marlon Brando did not learn his lines, but had his secretary read his lines to him over a microphone to be picked up by a concealed earpiece. This allowed him to be completely spontaneous with each of his speeches (and it saved a lot of homework). Whatever works.

Laurence Olivier, pictured at the beginning of this chapter, had some slight difficulty with Dustin Hoffman wanting to improvise a lot while they were creating their roles in *Marathon Man*. On one specific occasion, when Hoffman came lurching in to makeup, exhausted after keeping himself up for days, and having run and run (just as his character was supposed to have done for the next bit of the film), Larry looked up at the exhausted, red-eyed figure and inquired sweetly, "Wouldn't it be easier to **act** it?" Whatever works for Dustin Hoffman and whatever works for Laurence Olivier – do whatever works for **you**. When she acted a scene with her father, Jane Fonda needed to look him in the eyes as she acted – and he needed to act to an empty space. (See *Contrasting styles* in *Time codes* at the end of this chapter.)

John Malkovich talks about "truth" in screen acting in his interview in *Side by Side*: "Because film – it sees what it sees. It may not at all be what you intended, it may not at all be what you thought you were doing, or what you had in your heart, or what you could have sworn you were doing – it just sees what it sees." (See *The truth is not your friend* in *Time codes* at the end of this chapter.)

There are quite a few performers (and directors, and certainly those who train actors) who are quite wedded to the belief that the actor **must** feel and recreate the feelings of the character at any particular moment. I am very wary of **must**, since I know that **whatever works** incorporates a large collection of conflicting **musts**. To explore this idea further, we need to go back in time for a quick dash through the history of acting.

Acting through the ages

Way back in the days when players started to get at least pocket money from performing, when the pageant wagons hosted the medieval mystery plays, and audiences gathered in town squares to listen, join in, and shout at the actors, there was little that was "realistic" about what went on. Performances were in the open air, in natural light, showing images and metaphors of life, rather than trying to imitate life itself.

When theaters became more established in the Elizabethan era, when Shakespeare wrote about "to hold as 'twer the Mirrour up to Nature" (*Hamlet*), and the best actors were praised, as John Webster put it in *An Excellent Actor* (1615), "for what we see him personate, we thinke truely done before us," plays were still acted out in front of an audience who formed part of the production. The audience always watched the plays in the same light as that playing on the actors; everyone was in the same room, and to see an actor was no different from seeing someone else in the audience. There is strong evidence that the actors addressed the audience rather than each other, for there was no question of fooling the audience that this was in fact a slice of life. It was a representation of life, not a replication.

As theaters developed, and artificial light came into the theaters, there was still no absolute division between those on stage and those in the audience, who were still lit by candlelight, even though the actors had slightly more playing on them. Even at this stage, **the actors could see the audience**. This was an important factor in the relationship and the interaction between the actors and their audience.

Later theaters were built on a larger scale for the melodramas that followed the Industrial Revolution. These theaters accommodated a mass audience who wanted simple dramas reflecting the life they – or their parents – had left. (It was no coincidence that the villain in his black frock coat and top hat was dressed exactly the way the factory manager would be dressed, rather than in the simple country wear of the heroes and heroines.) The theaters were lit first by candlelight and then by gaslight; the actors were still presenting their performances "out front," so to speak. They were concerned with presenting the performance to the audience, **not** with experiencing it.

I have experimented with the sort of lighting that would have been used in this period, and, yes, you can see the audience through the footlights of candles and also through flaming gas jets. The new Sam Wanamaker Playhouse in London at Shakespeare's Globe only presents productions by candlelight, and the experience is truly magical, and influences how the actors act, and how the audience receive the play.

(A digression: Did you know that following a bad theater fire caused by an eager actor getting so close to the footlights that he set his trousers, and subsequently the theater, on fire, it was decreed that candles must be floated on a trough of water as a safety measure? Hence, in the UK, the terms "floats" and "the trough" were used for the footlights.)

It was only with the introduction of the electric light at the turn of the last century that the blaze of illumination became so great that it was impossible for the actor to peer through this "wall" of light to see the audience. It is no coincidence that the introduction of electric lighting to theaters exactly corresponds to the rise of the so-called "naturalistic" and "realistic" plays. Now viewers could watch a slice of life, and actors started to believe in a "fourth wall" as the audience in a darkened room watched actors in a box of light.

It was the fact of the actors being bathed in light, and the audience being in the dark, that led to the disappearance of the sensation of audience and actors being "in the same room," and observing each other. So the actors started, oh dear, to believe that in order to be "truthful," they had to gaze into each other's eyes. (See Chapter 11, "Directing actors for the screen," for further blasphemy on the results of eye-to-eye contact.)

When a new entertainment medium arose, that of the silent movie, different styles of acting were demanded. The camera (and the audience behind it) was acknowledged, often directly, as the brilliant comedies of Buster Keaton and Charlie Chaplin still illustrate. Strangely enough, when the movies added sound, a lot of the skills and artistry of the silent era disappeared, and actors started to carry on about "reality," as if that had been the basis of acting all along. As we can see, to "be truthful as in real life" had been the predominant acting style only from about 1908, when electric light was introduced, to the

1920s, when silent movies gained mass popularity. And even in our lifetimes, styles in acting have changed. (See *Different versions of the same scene* in *Time codes* at the end of this chapter.)

The Method

A brief word about Stanislavski. (Take a deep breath now, and hear me out.)

The theater that Stanislavski worked in was based on broad strokes, on a lot of "out front" acting and melodramatic presentational techniques. To these qualities the famous and revered director added his techniques, which are now known under the title of "the Method." It was a system that, **combined with** the existing ways of acting, led to the wonderful, legendary successes of the Moscow Art Theater.

Applying these same techniques, however, to those who do **not** have the same presentational background has led to some of the confusion about Method acting. (This also explains why such techniques work wonderfully well for contemporary plays, but are woefully inadequate to tackle classic plays of any period.)

Perhaps we should instigate classes to teach modern Method actors the other side of the coin – the side that Stanislavski was originally on. Just as he developed a process complementary to what he found then, we should develop the equivalent complementary acting now – by teaching our actors to share out front, to make sure that everything good is shared by the audience, and to always know for whom a play or production is done. (I would call it "The Entertainment Class" or "How to Act without Feeling a Thing!")

One of the best examples of this kind of performance on the television screen is that of the Muppets, who are not only believable, but also know exactly where their audience is, and play shamelessly to it by acting everything out front. If you want to play Restoration comedy, I recommend a careful study of Kermit and his friends! (See *Technique* in *Time codes* at the end of this chapter.)

Modern theater, with its roots in small modern theaters and halls, with modern lighting that has done away with the footlights (and so allowed the actors to be in contact with and see their audience again), has, I believe, led to the growth of the presentational play, and the decline of so-called "naturalism." The modern actor will often play knowing exactly where his friends or relations are sitting, and so his performance will be given in that light – and a successful one will use **whatever works**. **Whatever works** must also include within it what the **audience** expects and wants to see, and that varies according to the period in which they are watching the performance and the medium used to convey it. For plays written during the "fourth wall" period, then, of course, fourth-wall acting will work best, but for plays written outside that period (including a lot of scripts for the screen), other techniques should be looked to.

But what about all those classes on acting
based on variations of the Method?

There are so many really wonderful teachers and theories of acting in the US
– with its large population producing so many really wonderful actors offering
themselves up for parts – while in the UK there are far fewer of both. So I have
often wondered why, in the past few decades, actors from the UK have won a
disproportionate number of Oscars, Emmys, and Tonys.

I do **not** believe those in the UK are born better actors, that their background
and culture are better for acting, or that somehow English theater prepares actors
better than those from other societies. There must be something else.

Stand by for another personal theory.

In the UK, with very few exceptions, acting is taught to those who are
preparing to be professional actors, at establishments that are not universities
but drama schools.

In the US, on the other hand, acting is taught at universities where there is
a thing called *Acting 101*. Acting is a class that is taught to a whole range of students, from those who want to become professionals, to those who take it as an
interesting elective. The class must accommodate a broad range of experiences
and talents, and the class must be able to deal successfully with those who have
flair and talent, as well as those with only one of these, or those with neither!

Just as *French 101* is not the best preparation for negotiating a street market
in rural France, but is a very good way of "teaching French" to a range of
students, some of whom need the necessary credits and grades, so *Acting 101* is
good for "teaching Acting," without necessarily being connected to the world
of professional acting.

This is certainly not a criticism. It is, in fact, a praise and a wonder. The
teachers of acting at academic institutions have to devise a way of teaching
acting to students who sometimes have more ambition than ability. They have
to provide a course that can be graded, that can take its proper place alongside other disciplines, and that includes written essays and the reading of textbooks for the course. Once there is a need for textbooks, someone will write
them – and along come the theories and different "schools" of acting. The
teachings can lead to wonderful results, and to some unexpected consequences.
Eli Wallach, a veteran of the Actors Studio, at his afternoon acting class was given
a severe lecture on the need for an actor to put the actions they had discovered
and worked on into practice. He was so consumed with his teacher's instruction that he went on that night as the Messenger in *Antony and Cleopatra* and
immediately blurted out his news that Antony had married, to the grief of his
Cleopatra (Katharine Cornell), who had thirty-two of her favorite lines cut by
this "truthful" performance.

When it comes to screen acting, the authors like trying to prove that most
of American Hollywood acting is based on "the Method," and so there is a lot
of comment along the lines of how brilliant Dustin Hoffman was to take all

intelligence out of his eyes when acting in *Rain Man*. I am not denying the power of his wonderful performance, but giving all credit to the actor denies the presence both of the director and of the editor, who, I am sure, would only choose those takes where there **was** no intelligence in his eyes. If there were a glimmer of it, then that material would have been left on the cutting room floor.

How can you give a shy nonperformance student the confidence to go on stage and speak? How can you give someone with a great desire to act, but not very much instinctive ability, the solid background to be believable? Acting based on the Method in its various forms is a triumphant solution for these classroom situations, and it is what accounts for this particular approach to acting, which is brilliant for its needs – *Acting 101* – but not necessarily the pathway to great professional achievement.

Perhaps we should leave the last word on the Method to Stanislavski himself (as quoted in *The Player* by Lillian and Helen Ross). Speaking to Vladimir Sokoloff in the 1930s about his famous book *An Actor Prepares*, Stanislavski says, "Sokoloff, if you go with Max Reinhardt to America, if you want to help youngsters, forget all this theory. Don't apply this. Don't pay any attention to this. Everything is different in America. The education. The psychology. The health. The mentality. Even the food is different there. We needed this book to open actors up in Russia. In America, it is different. They don't need it there. If they try to use it, they will unnecessarily spy on themselves, asking 'Do I feel it or not?' Tell them 'In America the actor is free.'"

I hope you are still out there, because the story gets better from now on.

Good acting – and good screen acting

My best friend was an excellent actor who had trained with me in Boston. Back in England, after becoming a successful stage actor, he got a small role in a television series with Roger Moore. I was delighted, because I **knew** my friend to be a really wonderful actor, and I thought that I knew that Roger Moore was a really boring actor (he was the one who took over from George Lazenby, who only did the one James Bond film). (See *Bad acting* in *Time codes* at the end of this chapter.)

I eagerly watched the result, and that is when my journey that led to this book began: Roger Moore was much, much better than my friend. I was **so** confused because I thought: "My friend is a better actor than the ex-007, but Moore gave a much better performance on screen than my friend." It was time to think this out.

Roger Moore may not have been the most incandescent star on the screen (I think he would admit that), but he is a **superb** screen technician, and his craft at this is what registers, along with his good looks. If you feel I am concentrating too much on techniques rather than feelings, well, I think that is what screen acting is. There are many books dealing with the recreation of moments of emotion, but not so many dealing with the matters I am laying out here.

110

There are certainly moments in screen acting when it is absolutely essential for the actor to be completely immersed in the part – for the real tears to well up in the eyes, for the nose to redden and the veins fill with blood as the deep emotion floods into the face. Now, that cannot be faked and must be "real." Yet these moments also have to be within the framework of hitting the marks, the short scenes, the out-of-sequence shooting with any number of takes that is demanded by this work. Do we really believe that Russell Crowe understood all those mathematical formula in *A Beautiful Mind*? Of course not – his job was to convince **you** that he did, not that he himself **actually** did. (See *The truth is not your friend* in *Time codes* at the end of this chapter.)

There is sometimes a serious undercooking of moments that are meant to be a recreation of life. For example, let me tell you about my friends, Rod and Lynn. He has always been a great practical joker, and managed by some other pretext to get his wife to the steps of the luxury liner *QE2* before she knew they were traveling on it to New York. As he handed over the tickets, photos taken by a friend show the complete set of reactions that they both went through. Now, whenever I explain the complete story to a set of actors, and ask **them** to reenact the scene from handing the tickets over onwards, no one is able to give such huge, committed reactions to the moment as the two originals did.

What I am getting at is that this was a peak moment in the lives of Rod and Lynn, and yet actors recreating the moment instinctively play it "cool," play it offhand. Most moments in drama **are** peak moments, and too many actors, by approaching it through **what they think they would do in those circum-stances**, end up with a pallid, small and ultimately boring result. To do more, in fact, is to replicate what people do in real life when faced with enormous problems, enormous moments (which soap actors seem to do every episode). To reduce our reactions to "naturalism" can be **unnatural**, as every actor who has ever tried to act out either Rod or Lynn for me has proved.

And don't forget, although a screen actor **may** be acting so well as to tweak your emotions, there is also the swell of music under an emotional scene that contributes a lot to the final effect. Watching certain performances without the help of music makes you realize what a debt is owed to some film composers!

I was having supper with a dear friend, Val Avery (now alas lost to us), in New York, and he had just put the lamb chops on the grill. (He was a superb cook, and I was really looking forward to them.) At 6:50 P.M. the phone rang, Val was on the 9:45 P.M. flight to Los Angeles, and he appeared on set the next morning at 7:00 A.M. to shoot his first scene. Now – how much preparation, how much . . . but do I need to go on? He was employed because he is a wonderful screen actor, and **that** includes his techniques as well as his talents. This fast preparation is becoming all too familiar and more common, as budgets tighten and savings are made in – yes – the actors' rehearsal time. My partner was minding her own business when the phone rang, and twenty minutes later she was on her way to a film location to take over from another actress, and she found herself that night standing on a box, in the rain, holding a heavy brick, singing into the camera a song she had only just been taught (*The Harry Hill Movie*, if you must know). (See *Technique* in *Time codes* at the end of this chapter.)

Although films were made very fast in the old days, they still knew that they had to produce good expressions and good moments, and fulfil the audience's expectation of what to expect from a Humphrey Bogart, a Sidney Greenstreet, or a Peter Lorre:

Good expressions and reactions

Digital acting

The first thing to note is that digital cameras can run for a very long time; unlike film cameras, they are not restricted by the amount of film that can be loaded, and it does not cost you every time you expose some film. This means that directors can now be more gentle with shouting "cut" to halt proceedings, and may in fact keep the camera running as they give some notes or thoughts to the actors and then go again without everything having to grind to a halt. Digital also allows them to point the camera at the sky, go for lunch, and afterwards use the footage speeded up to indicate time passing as clouds rush across the sky (it also allows them to speed **you** up as you walk across the room if they feel you were a little languid). Actors can do all the moves and even facial gestures for a monster, with markers stuck all over their bodies, and the end result is filmed before digital editing changes the actor for the CGI image created in the computer, but the body language and even expressions are now seen on the monster. (See *Digital acting* in *Time codes* at the end of this chapter.)

They can now also reproduce human beings in digital form, this technique being used when the character needs to show some specific skill, and they film the artist and then superimpose the digital face of the lead actor. Some worry that this may mean that in the future they may indeed use digital images instead of actors – but here's the thing. They can make an avatar to resemble a particular human being, but how can they reproduce talent, excitement – the thrill of an unexpected movement. The only way for this to happen is for the controllers of the avatar, the programmers, to have the same artistic instincts that good actors have. Since they are not actors but very gifted technicians, it is usually beyond their ability to create those exciting unexpected moments that true acting talent can put onto the screen. (See *Surprising truth* in *Time codes* at the end of this chapter for moments that an actor – but no code writer – comes up with.)

Versatility

This is a much overused word, as if it were the elixir of acting. Many claim the wish to be versatile as the very reason they wanted to become actors. Yet I seem to be preaching the opposite, that you should only do the one thing.

Not really; I honestly do believe that all actors must be versatile:

We improvise for two weeks before you get the scripts	**now act.**
We block the play with its moves and business on the first day of rehearsal	**now act.**
You are given extraordinary choreography and strange moves	**now act.**
We do weeks of research, reading books, watching movies, hearing lectures	**now act.**
Tell us about your worst fears, tell us about your father's death	**now act.**
Hello, we haven't met before. Here are just your lines; you don't need the rest of the script; we shoot it tomorrow	**now act.**
Here are the re-writes. I know it changes your character, but we have to shoot it in ten minutes	**now act.**
Stand in front of this green screen for your fight with the aliens; we will tell you when to react and when to swish your sword	**now act.**
Have the ping pong balls stuck all over you, and do the moves and gestures your creature would do	**now act.**

The good actor's versatility is to be able to act under whatever circumstance of rehearsal and shoot he is given.

Advanced techniques

If one studies the great exponents of film acting, certain similarities crop up. The first is the observation that they often do something that is completely unexpected, but when they do it we totally accept that this is what their character would have done – I call this **surprising truth**. We delight in such moments, precisely because it was not where we anticipated the scene would go, so we have to watch carefully; we cannot predict what will happen next. (See *Surprising truth* in *Time codes* at the end of this chapter.)

When there is a repetition of a word or phrase, the great actors plan carefully to do each one differently, or to use the repetitions to great effect. They will also flash their eyes **up**, rather than the natural and usual looking down, which is what we do in real life, and which means that we are lowering our head and shading our eyes from the lights. By looking up, you open up your face to the camera. It will, of course, feel odd – but it will look great. (See *Technique* in *Time codes* at the end of this chapter.)

A good way to get a handle on all this is to watch the same scene acted by different actors, at different times. What at the time seems natural may, to a later audience, seem stilted or unreal. Watch the different versions I have collected for you. (See *Different versions of the same scene* in *Time codes* at the end of this chapter.)

Give yourself – and your character – time

As you can imagine, I have spent hours whizzing through DVDs of films, looking for examples for this book. I found that there were certain actors I always stopped at to see their scenes, and I realized that one of the reasons was that they always put their thoughts on their face, reacting before they spoke, so giving the audience a richer experience. Stars are given time – or they give themselves time – to really explore a moment and a thought. Lesser-known actors have a pressure on them (often self-imposed) to get on with it, and so often do not produce those interesting thought changes and electric screen moments.

If you are doing the right things, putting out good acting information with either reactions or words, then no one will want to cut it short. If, however, you only act with the words, then there will be a tendency to ask you to speed it up (or worse still, have the director make a mental note to leave this bit of the film on the other actor's face). Remember, screen events are not just words, but reactions and words.

An acting process

And how about this as a summary of the acting process?

An acting process

- What do I want my audience to know and feel?
- How can I convey this?
- **Now**, let's make this appear believable.

And to illustrate this, I shall describe my famous sneeze exercise.

I interrupt myself with a big sneeze; I blow my nose into my handkerchief (and take a quick peek at it before squidging the handkerchief away). The audience looks embarrassed.

The whole thing is, of course, a big fake. I wanted to convey to the audience that I was blowing a stuffy nose, but could not do it realistically because there was, to be brutally frank, no mucus up my nose. The way to do this is to blow a "raspberry" through the lips that **sounds** as if you are blowing your nose. Now, by surrounding this fake moment with the sneeze, and with the looking at the handkerchief, the audience believes in the whole moment. Yet at the heart of it – the truth of it – I was not blowing my nose but going "brrrrp" with my lips.

What do I want?

How can I achieve it?

Now, make it believable for the audience.

To repeat the words of John Wayne: "You've got to **act** natural – You can't **be** natural, that would stop the tempo. You've got to keep things going along, to push your personality through."

Television director Guy Hamilton says to the author in Peter Barkworth's book *About Acting* "Speak as quickly as you can, act as slowly as you can" and "Save up your reactions until just before you speak. I shall probably cut to you then."

So finally let me talk about a scene between a cop and a criminal having a showdown conversation sitting either side of a table. It was written, directed, and produced by Michael Mann, and the film, made for television, was called *L.A. Takedown*. The powers that be loved it so much they did not show it, but instead gave Michael Mann a whole lot more money to make it again – with stars. It became the film *Heat* starring Al Pacino and Robert De Niro. Studying how they do the scene compared with the first version (remember, it was the same writer/director/producer), let's see first hand what it is the stars **do**. Yes, they do indeed act better, but the interesting thing is what they **do differently** to the first cast. They talk softer in the close-ups than the actors in the first version, they always react before they speak, and they do not hold their eyelines – they constantly look away from each other, whereas the first pair of actors religiously kept their eye contact. Here is an analysis of a few of their exchanges, showing how long they took to answer, and what they did:

DE NIRO: *(6½ seconds: looks down; turns head; works lips.)*

Guy told me one time, don't let yourself get attached to anything you are not willing to walk out on in thirty seconds flat, if you feel the heat around the corner. Now, if you are around me, and you gotta move when I move, how do you expect to keep a marriage?

PACINO: *(2 seconds: turns head; looks right.)*

That's an interesting point. What are you, a monk?

DE NIRO: *(1½ seconds: nods; eyes look left.)*

I have a woman.

PACINO: *(1 second: makes small head movement.)*

What do you tell her?

DE NIRO: *(3 seconds: eyes look left; takes breath.)*

I tell her I'm a salesman.

PACINO: *(7 seconds: nods; eyes flicker right; looks back, then right again.)*

So if you spot me coming around that corner – you just gonna walk out on this woman? Not say goodbye?

DE NIRO: *(1½ seconds: nods.)*

That's the discipline.

These technical differences are as much the reason the scene is so much more effective as the fact that they just "acted better." Watch it carefully – and put the lessons you learn from it into your next performance. (See *Different version of the same scene* in *Time codes* at the end of this chapter.)

At last – the secrets of acting

- Use whatever works.
- Acting through the ages has always incorporated the audience.
- Method acting is a specific acting style for a specific purpose.
- Real life is often more interesting – and larger – in actuality than it is in our imagination.
- A good versatile actor is versatile in approach.
- It is enough to be truthful – but truthful actor/audience, not necessarily actor/actor.
- Give yourself time to do insightful reactions, putting your thoughts onto your face.

Working with directors

More so than theater directors, screen directors are hassled for time. The clock is the constant enemy, and they are not happy to be engaged in a long debate with an actor who probably is not aware of the complete situation. Do not get into a confrontational situation unless you are more powerful than the director. He will not want to lose and can often solve the problem by sacking you.

Instead, ask the director for help. We are **suckers** when asked for our help, because now when we give a suggestion, it can lead to solving the problem, and we can gain praise and thanks. In a confrontation all we can do is back down, which makes us feel terrible – but help? How can I help you?

If a director comes to you with a whole lot of notes, **write them down**. This has several useful functions: It prevents you from arguing back right away; it gives you a breathing space when you can read the notes after you have got over your rage at receiving them (and, who knows, some may be valid); and most important of all, writing down the notes acknowledges your relationship with the director. Sometimes he is quite happy that you have written down the notes and doesn't always notice if you don't carry them out. (Once I had a particularly difficult producer who came storming out at me, "You haven't put all my notes into practice." I looked in my notebook with astonishment and then with huge apologies. "You are right!" I said and wrote them down all over again. I still didn't use them, though, because I thought I was right, and he didn't storm at me again. No, no, this is dangerous advice: treat it with caution!)

You have a different problem if the director does not come to you with a whole sheaf of notes, but seems to ignore you. Do not assume it is because you are beyond help, but realize that the director has many, many different areas to put his concentration into, and may not get down to noticing the performance until after the first take at the earliest. After all, the rehearsal and setup of the shot is the first time the director gets to see what the set/location looks like; the props and costumes and makeup are also up for his attention and comment. And then there are all the extras – he has to check that they are all doing the right things. There are many calls on his time.

An exasperated actor went up to his director and complained, "You haven't given me any acting notes." The director looked puzzled: "I am only the director – you're the actor." You see, he considered that his job was to choose and direct the shots, and the actor's job was to act. (I got a big hug once from an actor in a soap drama. "What was that for?" I tentatively asked. "Because that is the first acting note I have received from a director in more than a year." Ah.)

Working with writers

Whether you are joining a regular series or just playing one small role, it can sometimes happen that the writer has written the part in a neutral way until he sees what the actor is going to do with it. Finding the variations in the script that allow for larger acting choices (or putting them in if they are not there) can encourage the writer to flesh out the script your way. Certainly, if you are a regular character, you can help your future development by "showing" the writing team what you are capable of. Really cheeky actors in a soap have been known to talk about events in their lives (true or not) in the hearing of the writers and then have shown great surprise when the same events turn up for them to play in their scripts.

But whatever you do, get skilled at showing suffering – remember John Barrymore! (He was the actor who always went for the part that had the most suffering.)

Bad acting

I shall end this chapter with a word about bad acting on screen, which is to talk not of bad technique, but of simply not being believable. We look at the screen and do not believe that that character would say those things in that way at this time. This book is not a substitute for good acting – you must still prepare your character, and create situations and characters that appear truthful, but you must also do it with proper technique for it to be effective. I am a great admirer of the work of the French director Luc Besson, who has done amazing work with cameras and with actors – so I shall let him carry the burden of being the example in *Time codes* for *Bad acting*.

Chapter 8: Time codes for acting

(Rounded up to the nearest 5 seconds)

Bad Acting

The Big Blue (receptionist: I shall keep him anonymous)	00:43:15
The Big Blue (eating spaghetti: and her)	00:47:30
On Her Majesty's Secret Service (George Lazenby with girls)	00:55:25

Contrasting styles

American Gangster (Denzel Washington and Russell Crowe boasted about the "truth" of the cup business – but did you enjoy or notice it?)	02:13:15; Extended: 02:28:40
Marathon Man (Laurence Olivier and Dustin Hoffman: relief or discomfort?)	01:12:15
Marathon Man (Olivier and Hoffman: swallowing diamonds)	01:52:15
Michael Clayton (George Clooney and Sidney Pollack: one does little, because he is drop-dead gorgeous; the other is not – and so does a lot)	01:14:55
The Missouri Breaks (Marlon Brando and Jack Nicholson)	01:25:20

On Golden Pond (two different approaches: Jane Fonda feeling it; Henry Fonda more technical)	01:31:55

Different versions of the same scene

The Importance of Being Earnest, 1952 (Gwendolyn and Cecily at tea: Joan Greenwood and Dorothy Tutin)	01:02:30
The Importance of Being Earnest, 1986 (Gwendolyn and Cecily at tea: Amanda Redman and Natalie Ogle)	01:13:50
The Importance of Being Earnest, 2002 (Gwendolyn and Cecily at tea: Frances O'Connor and Reese Witherspoon)	00:57:40
L.A. Takedown (confrontation across the table – and two actors, Scott Plank and Alex McArthur)	00:54:35
Heat (same script, director, and producer – and two stars, Al Pacino and Robert De Niro)	01:25:15
Hamlet and "To be, or not to be" (Laurence Olivier, 1948)	00:59:45
Hamlet (Innokenti Smoktunovsky, 1964)	00:46:40
Hamlet (Nicol Williamson, 1969)	00:30:40
Hamlet (Derek Jacobi, 1980)	01:25:20
Hamlet (Kevin Kline, 1990)	01:04:45
Hamlet (Mel Gibson, 1991)	00:49:25
Hamlet (Kenneth Branagh, 1996)	01:29:45
Hamlet (Ethan Hawke, 2000)	00:38:35
The Prince and the Showgirl (Marilyn Monroe sings)	01:35:30
My Week with Marilyn (same sequence with Michelle Williams as Marilyn)	01:19:10

Digital acting

Atonement (James McAvoy acting with extras and CGI extras)	01:02:35
Black Swan (Natalie Portman and ballet friend as the White Swan)	01:25:30
Black Swan (and both as the Black Swan)	01:32:10
Enter the Void (looking in mirror: the whole film is a POV of Nathaniel Brown)	00:12:40
The Lord of the Rings: The Two Towers (Andy Serkis as the Gollum tries to regain the Ring)	00:06:40
Side by Side (Disc 2: Walter Murch and Keanu Reeves talk about digital acting)	00:12:25

Surprising truth

The Fifth Element (who could predict the Mathieu Kassovitz performance?)	00:18:15
The Graduate (an amazing reaction from Elizabeth Wilson at the start)	01:09:20
Heat (Al Pacino's vocal levels cannot be guessed)	01:14:40
Heat (Al Pacino and Diane Venora)	01:02:00
A History of Violence (William Hurt is unpredictable)	01:55:55
Julie & Julia (Stanley Tucci tells Meryl Streep to go on TV)	01:41:40
Julie & Julia (Meryl gets her acceptance letter)	01:45:40
Love Actually (Emma Thompson asks Alan Rickman the difficult question)	01:50:20
A Prairie Home Companion (Meryl Streep acts and sings with Garrison Keillor)	00:28:55
Sense and Sensibility (Emma Thompson discovers that Hugh Grant is not married after all)	02:04:35
Sherlock (we first meet the unpredictable Andrew Scott as Moriarty), season 1, "The Great Game"	01:22:10
Sherlock (can you tell what Andrew Scott will do next?), season 2, "The Reichenbach Fall"	01:08:40
The Shining (can we predict when Jack will smile?)	US 00:05:10; UK 00:04:50

Technique

Closer (Julia Roberts shows Jude Law how it's done)	00:10:00
Donnie Brasco (Val Avery had minimum time to prepare)	01:01:05
The Harry Hill Movie (that morning Christine Ozanne had no idea she would be here doing this in the evening)	01:02:25
Marathon Man (Laurence Olivier repeats "Is it safe?")	01:09:10
Master and Commander (Paul Bettany learns from Russell Crowe)	00:16:10
The Muppet Show (any episode)	
Rain Man (Dustin Hoffman convinces as an autistic savant)	00:18:15
Sophie's Choice (Meryl Streep in the doorway shows how it's done)	00:08:00
Sophie's Choice (conversation with Peter MacNicol where she does a lot – and he doesn't)	00:41:25
Sexy Beast (Ben Kingsley repeats "Yes" to Ray Winstone)	00:43:45
Sexy Beast (Ben Kingsley repeats "No" to Ray Winstone)	00:51:40

The truth is not your friend

The Artist (Jean Dujardin cannot see what the camera is seeing)	01:23:00
A Beautiful Mind (Russell Crowe is no mathematical genius, even when manic)	00:16:25
A Beautiful Mind (or even when he is calm)	00:24:20
Bridget Jones's Diary (Hugh Grant and Colin Firth fight – so unlike the usual filmed fisticuffs)	01:06:15

Close Encounters of the Third Kind (Cary Guffey's look of wonder)

Theatrical release; Special edition; Director's cut 00:12:25

(Disc 2: Documentary: background to child's look of wonder)	00:40:45

Close Encounters of the Third Kind (Cary Guffey looks up)

  Theatrical version 00:45:25; Special edition 00:47:30; Director's cut 00:47:20

(Disc 2: Documentary: background to child's looking up)	00:39:40
Marathon Man (Dustin Hoffman running)	01:24:35
Side by Side (Disc 2: James Cameron: what's real)	00:20:10
The Sopranos (James Gandolfini and Michael Imperioli get far too close together for people having an argument), season 1, #1	00:55:55

The complete list of films, dates, and directors is in the *Index of films* at the end of the book.

All the time codes are taken from my DVD player in London, with the DVDs bought in the UK, so you can know how many minutes and seconds the clip is from the start of the movie. Where I can, I have noted the different versions of the films.

There may well be variations in the time for different machines and formats, but these should be consistent for your download, DVD player, or computer, and so once you note the differences, you will know where to find each of the above clips.

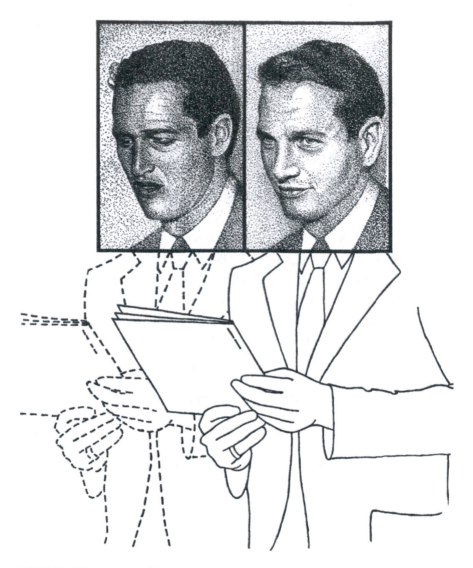

Which Paul Newman would you cast?

9

AUDITIONS

An audition is not just the moment when you meet a potential employer and perhaps read for her; it starts when the casting people see your photograph and ends when you get back home after the audition/meeting/reading.

Since every actor has a set of photographs and is only too eager to send these out to potential employers, you have already accepted the concept of typecasting, that is, that we can get an indication of your acting from your photograph. Or, more precisely, we can get an impression of the type of acting you do from your photograph – the main factor being the way you look.

This has been dealt with in detail in Chapter 7, "Typecasting."

You can never tell when you will meet the person/people who will be auditioning you, so it is a good plan to get into your presentation mode from the moment you get within one hundred yards of the place where the audition is to be held. (Someone may, you see, be coming back from a coffee break and bump into you.) There was the actor who told the person she was sitting next to in the waiting room how rotten the script was that she was preparing to read. Since this was the writer – who had popped out of the auditioning room for a breather – this actor was quickly shown the door.

At the audition, you will often be asked to fill out a form with the most comprehensive list of your measurements – including such specifics as shoe size, hat size, or glove size. Have these all written up (and kept up to date) on a separate card. (They do this so that, when they do cast someone, they don't have to go to the bother of contacting the actor for her measurements. Of course, **you** have had to go to the bother of filling out all those forms, 99 percent of which will get thrown away and have to be filled out all over again.)

You will often have the vast excitement of entering a room full of people waiting to be auditioned and finding it full of "you." You will be amazed just how many other actors there are who look just like you. Do not be disheartened – after all, you don't know just what aspect of "you" they are looking for. (It is even more worrying, however, to enter the room and find that no one there is of your type.)

Be prepared to make sudden and radical changes in your appearance. Your agent – or the booking agent or casting department – can often make mistakes, and you can turn up all ready to audition for a "jogger" and find they are looking for a "doctor." (That happened to a friend of mine; he tried to convince himself and them that this was a doctor out on a jog, but no, they could not think further than collar and tie, and maybe even a white coat and stethoscope.) Actors – male and female – should carry with them the basic minimum for changing – a tie, a sweat shirt, classy or junk jewelry, a silly hat, and so on.

Be particularly careful with your hair, since there are many styles that allow it to obscure your eyes. Do not forget, during an interview, reading, or improvisation, that you will be seen from the side, and hair hanging down to hide what little can be seen of your eyes does not help your cause.

Do not be tempted to change your approach judging by what you hear in the audition/waiting room. After all, your competitors don't have **your** interests at heart, and even if they did, they could be mistaken as to what the casting people are looking for.

My advice is not to tell them your real age. If they really insist, then simply say that all actors lie about their age don't they? And then lie. I once was looking for someone to play a sixteen-year-old and was having difficulty in finding someone who both looked right and had the talent and experience to do the rather tricky role. An actress arrived who looked and sounded simply wonderful, so I told her not to tell me her real age – so she didn't. When my producer asked for her age, I was able to pass on the lie. She did play the role, and acted it very well. After it was all over, I asked her her real age. She reluctantly told me she was really twenty-nine – but what was more revealing was that the same producer had turned her down a few years earlier as being too old to play a twenty-two-year-old! And you know, I think I might have been adversely affected if I had known just how old she really was, but I was happy with her lie – and very happy with her performance.

There are teenagers in their thirties – and certainly many middle-aged teenagers. Find out how you come across, and play – and admit – to **that**.

Auditioning for a part in a drama

If you are to read for the part at an audition, you should be given a script in advance. Yet all too often it is only at the audition that you are given a script (a good reason for always arriving early).

Don't spend ages looking at it, trying to imagine what it all means and what the difficult words are.

Find out where your **reactions** could be.

Work out some nice practical business to do.

Practice positive **listening** for the lines that will be read to you. Go back to Chapter 5, "Reactions and business," if you want to remind yourself of this aspect. Remember the use of unexpected elements. (See *Surprising truth* in *Time codes* at the end of this chapter.)

When you enter the room and meet the director, often with one or two casting directors present, your audition has already begun.

124

A ballet dancer already knows how to do a plié, but she practices them every day. A musician knows her scales but still does them. A champion tennis player knows how to hit the ball and serve, but she still does it every day in practice.

How long do actors practice in private? **And what?**

How many times do they practice walking across a room, shaking hands, and saying, "Hello"?

Silly? Hardly, when so many actors put possible employers off with a tepid, slimy, ill-considered handshake and a nervous greeting. It is part of their **job**, yet so many leave it to chance, leave it to the inspiration of the moment.

Try it now. Shake hands with everyone, say "Hello," and then discuss these questions. Were some handshakes better than others? (Yes, they will be.) Why were they better? Carry on shaking hands until people agree that your version is good. It could be that you have been going around for years with a handshake that secretly no one liked but no one was willing to tell you about.

Is your hand sweaty? Then have a convenient pouch with talcum powder in it. Do you have bad circulation and really cold hands? Then slip a hand warmer into your pocket. Do your fingers dig in another's hands when you are really trying to be firm and positive? Then practice different ways of grasping, because your handshake should also match your personality. A large handshake from a diminutive person, and vice versa, can be quite confusing, and the same goes for sensuality, toughness, and so on.

The auditioner will often start off by asking you a few questions.

Why?

Because they **really** want to know where you spent your last vacation, or what your favorite part was, or if you put your face or your back to the taps in the bath? I don't want a rational answer; I want the artist to get talking and emoting. We want to get to know how you are when you are not "acting," how your natural voice sounds, how you "come across." Give us a helping hand: initiate the conversation; tell an anecdote that shows off your strengths; **help** the auditioners get the information they need.

The moment has come for the reading. At this stage, they will often turn a camera on your performance, for if you are at all suitable, many others may have to view this clip. You don't know where this digital moment of yours is going to end up, so make sure it contains excellent screen acting.

They will often position a monitor to one side of you. This is so that when you are reading they can look at you on the screen. That means, you need to give a **screen reading**.

A reading consists of two parts, which are, I would claim, equally important:

1. How you deliver the lines.
2. How you listen to the lines given to you.

A good tip is to practice keeping your eyes up and listening to what the other person says, with full interest and sparkling eyes. Only when she finishes speaking do you drop your eyes to pick up your next line. (You can do this by keeping your thumb on your next speech, and moving it further down as you get to that particular speech.) Look again at the picture at the beginning of this chapter (page 122) – notice the difference between Paul Newman with his head down reading the script and the version with his head and eyes up.

The person reading opposite you may seem to give an inexperienced, flat, monotonous performance. This may be because she is not a performer or because she has been **asked** to give a "neutral" performance, so that what you do will stand or fall by your talents and not those of the other reader.

Oh, so **many** actors, when they have finished one speech, pay no attention to what is said to them. Instead they frantically scan their next speech to make sure that there are no words they are going to stumble over, no words with difficulties, and to remind themselves of what the interpretation "ought" to be.

Why do actors do this? Why should I, the auditioner, **care** if they get a word wrong? After all, **I, the director**, am only too glad to tell them how to say it. And interpretation? **I, the director**, will be telling them that. So all that hard work preparing the text to be analyzed and thought about – who cares? Concentrate on presenting a fascinating, screen-friendly person, who, if she needs **my direction**, is even more attractive. (Directors love giving direction, love being needed, love having their skills used. Why not flatter the director by involving her in the audition? Ask which of two interpretations she thinks is the better? Ask whether an alternative accent – **if you do it well** – would be a more appropriate choice.)

A word to the inexperienced (and moderately experienced) at being in front of a camera at auditions: Your résumé should tell me that you can act. I will read what you have done in the theater. I can see you have done little or no television or film, so my one fear is that you will be "too theatrical." **That** is why, in an audition, you should assume that the whole thing is being shot in a big close-up (BCU). After all, if you have done any theater, I **know** you can do the long shot style of acting, even the medium close-up style, but can you do the close-up or big close-up style of acting? Go to Chapter 1, "Screen versus stage," to remind yourself what this means.

I doubt if anyone has lost a job because she was too intimate and quiet. However, many have been left by the wayside because they were too loud, too intent on impressing those in the room, rather than coming across well on camera. They were too **theatrical**. They read the piece **too loudly** – and this is the most common fault for less experienced actors. My friend David H. Lawrence XVII (letter in the Introduction) solved this in a novel way. His first reading for *Heroes* was very quiet, and although they liked it, they asked him to speak a little louder, as the microphone was on top of the camera and too far away to pick up his words clearly. So he calmly picked up his chair, moved it over to be close to the camera (and microphone) and read his part again in the same soft tones. He was cast in the role. (See *Soft speaking* in *Time codes* at the end of this chapter, and also Chapter 6, "Sound and vocal levels.")

If they stay to ask you more questions after the reading, be happy and revel in the knowledge that they are investing some time with you. If they ask you to read some of it again, pay close attention to **precisely** what differences they are asking for. They do not have the imagination (or the ability to convince their producer unless they have checked) to guess if you can do it a more preferred way. You must **prove** it to them, there and then.

A different accent, a different attitude, something completely different? (That is my favorite to ask of an actor, if I feel that she has churned out something that has been carefully drummed into her, or if she has done an audition piece that I feel she has done all too often before. "Do it again, completely differently," I ask and see what **she** is about rather than her expensive acting coach or "helpful friend.") Be particularly careful, if given something different to do, that you don't get louder. My experience is that a wonderful close-up version of a reading suddenly goes into back-of-the-balcony acting style when the actor is asked for a different accent or attitude. (See *Auditions in a film* in *Time codes* at the end of this chapter.)

Whatever you do, do not fall into the trap of being more entertaining in the interview than you are in the reading. If you are vivacious, funny, and bubbly, and then give a cold, quiet, little reading, we will feel a little let down, a little cheated. Play to your strengths, so if you are a laughing happy type, play the part putting in some of your natural personality. After all, there must be a reason why the casting people chose you from a submitted photograph or why your agent put you up for the job. Too many actors start to play, say, gruff when they are naturally light-hearted performers, and vice versa.

The late and lamented Margot Stevenson looked just like the owner of Tweety Pie (the cartoon canary that Sylvester the Cat is always trying to munch). She had just returned from a commercial casting session where she was auditioning for a granny type of role. I asked her to do for me what she had done for the audition. She played a gruff, angry granny, but she was a most wonderful, cheerful, apple-cheeked, **happy** granny. When I made her do it again in her **own** manner and style, the reading took off and blossomed. "Why didn't I do that the first time?" she mused. But of course she was acting what she thought they wanted, an angry granny, rather than presenting her strengths and specialities.

So if this is one of those auditions where you seem to have been sent to the wrong place, where they are looking for a "student" type and you come across as a young parent, or a flashy blonde seems to be what everyone else in the room is, and you are a quiet brunette, do not try to compete with the other actors on their own terms. After all, they have had many years to practice this. Concentrate on **your** image and personality, and convince the auditioners that maybe **you** are what they are looking for. Don't attempt something that is not one of your positives. As I said in Chapter 7, "Typecasting," **always** play to your strengths.

Auditioning for a drama, be prepared to

- be the photograph they sent for
- change appearance
- give a good greeting
- lie about your age
- act reactions as much as the text
- speak very softly (as if in a BCU)
- exit gracefully

The auditioners usually have many people to see, so don't overstay your welcome. Sometimes – it's not your fault – they know from the moment you come in that you will not be right; perhaps you look too similar to one of the main characters, or you do not look as if you could be related to that other one. You should concentrate on making a snappy impact, and then get out quickly. This makes us like you, for it gives us time to go to the bathroom or have a cup of coffee.

Give yourself a good exit. Nothing is worse than making a good impression with your reading and then slinking off. **Do not** groan, moan, or utter cries of anguish in the corridor. It is very off-putting for us to hear (for we do) someone indicating that the occasion of meeting us was so very painful.

I once auditioned a young actor, and all went well. After he left, my secretary said, "There goes a happy actor." I looked out of the window, and there he was, leaping over the fences in the park and crazily making his way off. He had obviously enjoyed meeting me.

He got the job.

Auditioning for a commercial

At these auditions you will be surprised at how many people will be called in, or how long the audition has taken for a part that is, frankly, just a look and a smile.

The audition will most likely be with a casting person and a camera.

The producer/director could well be thousands of miles away, and will be sent a digital clip of the "best" results. This can mean that, if you get the job, they might expect to see the same type of clothes you wore to the audition. A colleague of mine got into trouble because, cast in a commercial, he smartened himself up by getting a haircut – and they had cast him **because** of the lock of hair that fell across his face. Another actor went for a casting session where there was no one else in the room – just an unmanned camera. The audition and filming were conducted and operated from afar, so be prepared for any such strangeness.

Actors need to be able to produce what is required remarkably quickly. In Europe, a lot of the commercials are cast and made using actors from the UK. It is not just because British actors are cheaper; it is because they are faster. They don't waste time asking about motivation or waiting until they "feel right" before going for a take. They just get on with it.

You can be asked to do something as small as, "Say your name and agent to the camera, and then eat a piece of chocolate and say, 'Wow!'"

It can be as long as doing a complicated improvisation with a fellow actor, where you act up a storm doing and saying wonderful things, and those auditioning you write down the best lines they hear. (They couldn't possibly do this, could they? That would be stealing your ideas!)

How often have you practiced saying your name and agent into a camera? You can guess the rest of my argument: If a ballet dancer practices at the bar every morning ... There is a serious point to this, though. Since the digital clip of your audition (and the hundred or so others they saw that day) could well be sent on to the producer or director elsewhere, if they do not like the way you introduce yourself, well, there is always the fast forward button. They might never even get to see your wonderful reading – your dull introduction would have put them off.

And yet, too many actors are really indifferent to this – the first impression you are going to give on a tape that will be watched by someone in different circumstances, thinking different thoughts. By using **this** moment to give us an impression of "you," your subsequent audition can be a chance to show a second variation on what you are about.

So many actors are quite timid and small on doing a "Wow," or in giving a **big** reaction to "seeing" something, but that is what is required in the split-second world of commercials. It always surprises me that actors who, along with the rest of the population, have seen **thousands** of commercials with these clear, positive reactions are so timid when reproducing them themselves. It is as if they had never truly sat down and watched what it is that they themselves would like to do at some time in their careers. (Financing a season of acting in the theater via a few good commercials is a very acceptable way of running a career.)

Here is an experienced "Wow!" followed by an inexperienced one. Which do you prefer? Can you be as committed as the experienced one?

They are not looking for someone who quite likes their product and thinks it is the best chocolate she has eaten this week. They are not looking for someone who, with her "Wow!" shows that this is the best chocolate she has eaten this year. They are looking for someone who will radiate that this is the very, **very** best chocolate she has ever, **ever** eaten. It is an extreme that they are looking for, and if you do not give it, there are many other people lined up outside the door who will want to give it **their** best shot.

Deeply committed emotions are not all that is required; timings need to be extreme as well. There was a very good commercial in the UK (for Carlsberg

An experienced "Wow!"

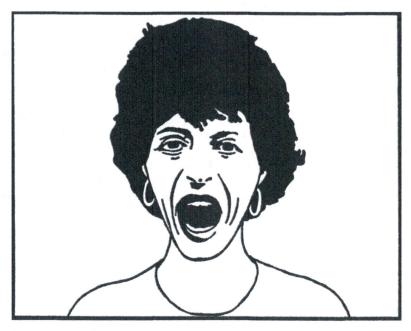

An inexperienced "Wow!"

lager) in which a customs official looks up with glee at the prospect of catching travelers returning from Denmark laden with that particular beer. In close-up, his face (and I timed it) did five distinct reactions in three and a half seconds. Now **that** is good screen acting and very difficult to do. Try it yourself – **now** – to see that this requires **technique**, like so much else.

Sometimes at an audition they investigate your talents by giving you an improvisation that is based on the circumstances in the commercial without performing it exactly. In such an improvised scene, remember where the camera is, and keep close to your partner, so that the shot can always be the tightest two-shot of both of you, and so that your faces will be correspondingly larger. Again, inexperienced actors position themselves as if on a mini-stage. They keep a horizontal distance between each other, necessitating a very **wide** shot, and resulting in a correspondingly very **small shot of their expressive faces. Remember, it is not what you feel**, but what the camera **sees** that counts.

Often, at these improvisations, they do not record the sound at all. They already have expensive, skilled copywriters and are interested in the actor's skill at transmitting emotions, not in inventing dialogue. So don't spend too much of your energy trying to be witty – treat it like a silent movie and put your skills and talent into visual moments.

Auditioning for a commercial, be prepared to

- do the same as for a drama audition
- please the casting director
- give fully committed reactions
- be willing to go along with what they want
- show results, not just potential
- keep from getting depressed at the constant rejections

Talent versus results

I suppose the biggest difference between auditions for the screen and for the stage is that for the stage they are often looking for talent, looking for potential. The stage audition is to find out those who – with rehearsal – can give excellent performances. For the screen, and particularly for commercials, they are not looking for talent or for potential: They are looking for results. It is as if the audition is the job itself, and they are looking for someone who, if she is chosen, will be expected to do exactly the same at the shoot as she did at the audition. Treat the audition, then, as the job itself. Although casting people and directors know that actors have potential and can improve with work, the advertising executives and all manner of people who actually decide who will be the face for the commercial can only judge by what they see.

My partner went for a commercial audition that included a photo session, and they asked her for several specific expressions. She gave them, and they took seven shots of her. She got the job, and when she turned up for the studio session, the photographer they had hired to take the pictures had on his storyboard (a rough drawing of what the advertisers wanted) **six** of the original seven shots he had taken at the audition. He and the actor were not supposed to create magic, to create some wonderful pictures that matched the copywriters' ideas: They were to **recreate what had happened in the audition**.

This happens so often because – although the casting director and director can imagine how an actor might be in different circumstances after a little direction and so on – the clients cannot. **They** think that what they see is all they are going to get, and so they choose actors for results, not for potential. Richard Dreyfus only had one line in *The Graduate*, but made it count; Kevin Spacey only had a short part in *Heartburn*, but did the same. Aurore Clément had lots of lines (and a nude scene) in *Apocalypse Now*, and was looking forward to a future in Hollywood, only to find her entire part had been cut from the movie (but you can see her in *Apocalypse Now Redux*). (See *Small and cut roles* in *Time codes* at the end of this chapter.)

So what happens if you commit yourself to a performance that does not fit into their preconceived idea? Well, if you do it well, with deep conviction, you might change their minds. It is possible (likely?) that you won't get the job, but if you have impressed the casting director, then you still have the future.

Not getting the job

Now, there are a lot of jobs you are not going to get. You should **hope** that there are a lot of jobs you are not going to get, because that means that you are going for a lot of auditions. Do not work yourself up into a lather of expectation about a particular audition, declaring "This is it!" and setting yourself up for a major trauma when the job does not come your way. There are many, many reasons why you may not get a job, one of which may be that there was no job in the first place; it had already been cast. Why should we audition if we know the part has already gone? Insurance, union necessity, because the room is booked, and it is cheaper to audition than let everyone know not to come – there are **lots** of good reasons.

Then again, your hair may be the wrong color. No, don't shout that you will dye it. It is quicker and easier to get someone with the right hair (which must not be exactly the same as the star's, otherwise the audience will get confused) than to risk a wig or dye job. Also, the bright lights needed for shooting sometimes make false colors look odd. (This is why hairpieces look so fake on our screens, as they look so different under studio lights than in real life.) Usually a wig is more expensive than an actor, and I would prefer using my budget for two actors rather than just you plus the cost of a wig.

It is possible you might not get the job because you would overshadow someone else in the cast. Putting a cast together is sometimes an instinctive process that does not bear logical study. However, we do feel sad for those not cast and would hate to say that you didn't get the part because, well, just because. So we add "reasons," hoping you will feel better, like: too old, too young, too tall, too short, too blonde, too dark. Anyone who has auditioned can add to this long list. These are not the **real** reasons, but the trouble is that actors seize upon these little snippets and put a religious certainty upon them, trying to solve what they **thought** was the reason for not being cast. Actors have made themselves ill by taking seriously a little comment that was only said to make them feel better.

You didn't get cast? Oh well, it would have been nice; now on to the next. The only strong advice I would remind you of again is: **Never be more interesting in the interview than in the reading**.

(There is a lot of good stuff about auditions in the book *Getting the Part* listed in the Bibliography.)

Casting directors

Sometimes these people seem to be an impenetrable barrier between you and a job, but you should instead look on them as part of the process, a part you need to get along with.

Many casting directors will not interview actors individually, but will add the odd unknown actor to a casting session to see how she does. Oh, they have no belief that you will actually get the job, but it gives them a chance to see how you act under these conditions and how you come across.

If you come across well, then it is good for their reputations to call you up, even if you are not quite right for the job. A friend of mine was sent to casting sessions for ten years by a particular casting director before she actually landed a job from one of them. Her auditions had always been good, but none of the commercials had come through because, well, because there are so many people auditioning and just so many parts. She met him at a party and jokingly apologized to him for never getting the job. "Don't worry," he replied, "the clients always **love** you." And that is why he kept sending for her, because she always gave a good account of herself and never let the casting director down.

Add to the process the clients themselves, the creative team, the account executives, and advertising managers, who **all** contribute to who they think should be the "face" that sells a particular product, and there are many fences to fall at. Don't forget, delivering a good performance at auditions throws credit onto the casting director, who you may well need later on in your career.

To be depressed about not getting a job for some while is understandable, but it is not necessarily a criticism of your ability. It is certainly **not** true that you will definitely make it if you are really talented. This is a myth circulated by those who **have** made it, to prove that they themselves must have talent.

I know a lot of really talented actors whose expertise has not been used to the full – and I am sure **you** know of people whose achievements are greater than their abilities.

The casting director may well cast both dramas and commercials, so be sure to make a very good impression – even if it is a commercial for a product that you either don't believe in or would rather not be asked to do due to political or environmental considerations. I myself have often contacted a casting director or agent and asked to see the most talented underused actors they have. They always want to know how I want the actor to look, but I reply that I am after talent, not looks. They need a lot of convincing that that is what I really want. Another time I was happy to cast a young actor for a theater part, as the previous year I had tried to cast him but he had not been available. During his rehearsals, which went very well, he shyly asked me why I had not cast him previously, so I told him I had, but my casting director had reported back that he could not do the role. This turned out to be how the casting department got their preferred candidate into the role. The next time I was told an actor was unavailable (this time it was for a television role), I was able to tell the casting people that by coincidence I had been talking to the actor's agent, and that they were in fact free to do the role, so I would have my first choice after all. Hmmm.

Another word about casting – and an answer to those stories you have heard where someone was cast by being seen serving behind the counter at a coffee bar. If you were to audition enough people, you would by accident alone find someone who could act one particular part. The casting of Macaulay Culkin, the star of *Home Alone*, was the result of many, many auditions. It was only after he was famous that he got chosen for a role before the script was written; up to then it was: Here is the script, now let's go out there and find someone. If you audition a whole room of inexperienced screen actors, then some, just by accident, will manage to "come across" on the screen better than others – and that is how I believe a whole lot of casting has happened in the past.

We no longer accept that theater actors "just happen," and we acknowledge that training is an important part of getting ready for performing on stage. I believe it is the same for the screen. If a magic wand were waved and we were plunged suddenly back into the silent movie era, **some** of our current stars would flourish using the "new" techniques – and some would not. I do not believe in accident, and prefer to think and analyze, and work out what is needed to work in any particular time and medium.

And an answer for all those who complain that things are now so rushed and mechanical compared with the "good old days":

My friend, the "laughing granny" Margot Stevenson, was asked to audition for *Gone with the Wind*'s Scarlett O'Hara in the great search for the right actor in 1937. At that time she was starring in a play on Broadway, but she still went to the trouble of hiring a period dress, rehearsing and practicing a wonderful piece, having a special hair-do and special makeup, and arriving in a hired limousine.

When she got to the studios where the tests were being made, she was asked to walk up to a mark and say her name, then look left to "see" Ashley, then look right to "see" Rhett, and – and that was it!

So when you next come back from an unsatisfactory experience, be thrilled that you are now part of the great tradition of auditions!

Chapter 9: Time codes for auditions

(Rounded up to the nearest 5 seconds)

Auditions in a film

Mulholland Drive (Naomi Watts rehearses her audition)	01:07:35
Mulholland Drive (but she does it very differently for the producers)	01:13:00

Small and cut roles

Apocalypse Now Redux (Aurore Clément's cut scenes)	01:58:50; 02:07:55; 02:11:00
The Graduate (Richard Dreyfus's first line in films)	01:19:15
Heartburn (Kevin Spacey's first film, but he looks like a veteran as he holds his own with Meryl Streep)	01:06:15

Soft speaking

Affliction (Nick Nolte and Sissy Spacek on the bed)	00:41:10
Blue Velvet (Kyle MacLachlan and Laura Dern in a diner)	01:02:00
Closer (Julia Roberts and Jude Law in a studio)	00:10:00
Dr. No (Sean Connery got it right from the start)	00:07:25
Last Night (Keira Knightley and Sam Worthington in the kitchen)	00:14:50
Last Night (Eva Mendes and Sam Worthington in the pool)	01:03:30
Layer Cake (Daniel Craig eats with Kenneth Cranham)	00:09:55
The Lord of the Rings: The Two Towers (Hugo Weaving and Liv Tyler are practically whispering)	01:35:15
Margin Call (Kevin Spacey and Jeremy Irons)	00:53:00
Master and Commander (Paul Bettany is treating Russell Crowe)	00:16:10
Six Days Seven Nights (Harrison Ford and Anne Heche want to kiss)	01:05:05

Surprising truth

The Fifth Element (Mathieu Kassovitz does a dance after holding up Bruce Willis)	00:18:15
A History of Violence (William Hurt's surprising truth compared with the predictable Viggo Mortensen)	01:55:55
Julie & Julia (Meryl Streep shares good news with Stanley Tucci)	01:45:40
Love Actually (Bill Nighy with all his twitches and snorts is interviewed by Marcus Brigstocke)	00:19:40
Sense and Sensibility (large reactions from Emma Thompson discovering that Hugh Grant is not married after all)	02:04:35
Sherlock (see how unpredictable Andrew Scott can be as Moriarty), season 1, "The Great Game"	01:22:10
Sherlock (even up to his death), season 2, "The Reichenbach Fall"	01:14:40

The complete list of films, dates, and directors is in the *Index of films* at the end of the book.

All the time codes are taken from my DVD player in London, with the DVDs bought in the UK, so you can know how many minutes and seconds the clip is from the start of the movie. Where I can, I have noted the different versions of the films.

There may well be variations in the time for different machines and formats, but these should be consistent for your download, DVD player, or computer, and so once you note the differences, you will know where to find each of the above clips.

136

Roseanne Arnold. . .

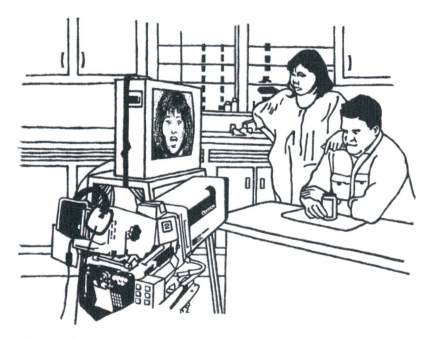

. . . checking the correct Roseanne is there

10

REHEARSALS AND TECHNICALS

An actor I know was once called up by a casting director and told that she was wanted to play the small part of a nun. Could she travel up to Scotland from London that night? Of course, she said yes, and a page of script with a few lines for "Nun" arrived just before she set out for the station. The train arrived in the north, where she went straight to a hotel. Early the next morning, she was dressed as the nun, driven across wild roads and windswept moors, and delivered to a field where there was a film crew. A man wandered up, vaguely greeted her and said that she was to stand on this mark, a car would drive up, and the dialogue would be delivered. As he wandered away she called after him (for he **was** the director), "You did want a Scottish accent, didn't you?" "Sure: Action!"

This is known as a short rehearsal period. Long rehearsals can take, well, much longer, involving months of research, living as your character would live and work – oh, all sorts of things. But the shorter rehearsal period is becoming more common, and it is therefore up to the actor – and his preparation – to give the best results on the screen.

If it is going to be your first ever piece of screen work, do **not** pretend you have been doing this all your life. After all, the crew will all know it is your first time, and all that energy and concentration would be better spent on learning about and observing your craft. Far better to be the known novice. It allows you to ask naive questions; it allows you to take lots of notes – and you should. How do you know which ones will be valuable? Only experience will tell. So take lots of notes until you know which are to be most valuable to you. Nothing is more irritating to a director than to block a scene or make a little comment about some business or mood and an hour later to find the actor in his excitement has forgotten it!

Film

Some movies assemble their actors for some form of get-together, read-through, and so forth. But the trouble is that with schedules and budgets being so tight, it is often a matter of the main actor flying in just for his scenes and flying off again as soon as possible. It is no exaggeration that, within half an hour of meeting someone for the first time, you can be in bed with him shooting an intimate scene.

Actors usually grab any opportunity they can to go over their lines with each other, and if you are cast with fellow performers who like this way of working, then quite a lot can be done during the inevitable delays on a shoot. But be warned that there are those who believe in spontaneity and will **not** rehearse or read with anyone until the take. Don't forget, you will have the technical stagger-through with the camera to try things out and do your own rehearsal if others won't join in. Do not let the technical demands of a particular shot take away from your performance – just as the camera operator, the boom swinger, and so on all need to do their job well under the most trying circumstances, so must the actor. (See *Technical demands* in *Time codes* at the end of this chapter.)

Christopher Guest has specialized in making films where the situations are set up, and he films the ensuing improvisations. (See *Semi-improvised scenes* in *Time codes* at the end of this chapter.) We have discussed the ideal versatile actor earlier; whichever way of working seems required, **you** should be able to do that!

And how do the modern masters of their craft rehearse? A colleague was desperate to find out how Steven Spielberg went about it, so he got himself onto the set as an extra, and was able to see his working process. Spielberg approached the three actors who were to be in the scene, but had not had it blocked or rehearsed yet, and said to them: "Well, fellers, let's see what you've got." You see, having cast the right actors in the roles, and polished the script to get it exactly right, he **expected** them to arrive on set with performances already prepared, to which he would then react. (See *Rehearsal and result* in *Time codes* at the end of this chapter.)

Single camera television

There have been many improvements in the quality of television: stereo sound, greater use of camera mounts and moves, the Steadicam, and using many more locations for shoots. In the bad old days a boom shadow could be got away with or a fluffed line obscured by putting a dog bark onto the sound track. Now that everyone has the ability to freeze frame, well, everything must be made to higher technical standards.

All this costs a lot, and that money has to come from somewhere. All around the world, advertisers are paying less for commercials, since there is now competition from satellite, cable, downloads, and DVDs, but the money to pay for all these technical advances must come from somewhere – and do we **really** need all that time to rehearse the show?

Rehearsal times for single camera shoots have been decreasing as well, as the demand for more product in less time has increased. (This is another reason why typecasting is only going to get worse, for it is quicker to get an actor to play their type than to rehearse them into something different.)

There can be a short rehearsal period, which has to be fitted around the current shoot (if it is a regular drama). A typical rehearsal would entail a quick read-through, a block of the moves, and a run-through so the script assistant can time it – yes, just twenty minutes to rehearse a two-minute scene. Since the actors would not have learned their lines (and those on the current shoot might not even have thought about them), there is not much scope for more than a broad approach to the scene. Details would come later in the actual shooting period, which is the only time the actors would have memorized their scripts (we hope).

Often now in single camera dramas there is not even time for a read-through; the actor is expected to be on the set knowing his lines and is immediately put into his first setup ready for the camera. Then there is a stagger-through of the moves planned by the director. This start-and-stop is purely for the camera and sound people to sort out their problems. An actor, asked to stop and then start again, should not "back up" his lines and begin from an earlier moment the way he would in theater, but should pick up exactly from where he left off. You see, the camera operator is memorizing the scene from picture to picture, and to go back in the scene would confuse him; after all, he looks upon this as **his** rehearsal.

In this modern age, it is by no means unusual for the director to meet the actor for the very first time when they walk onto the set, lines learned, ready to be told where to stand and when to move. This can happen when directing a regular drama, and a previous director has cast a new character. You could experience "Hello, I am your director today; stand there, and move there at the end of your line. Stand by – rehearsal – **action**!" It might be daunting, but it **is** realistic.

Having staggered through, we hope there will be time for a run-through. **This** is when you get a chance to try out some acting, although it is often only after the first take that the director is able to zero in on your performance and is able to think about acting and acting notes. You may be involved in long, long takes, so take the opportunity to be creative (that is why they employed you, isn't it?) and add interesting and informative little bits of business and moves. (See *Walk and talk* in *Time codes* at the end of this chapter.)

Actors deal with this situation in different ways. There are those who come in to the shoot with their scripts covered with notes. They have tried out everything and ask rather shyly if they can just possibly change the order of the words in this speech – they have **tried** to make it work, but it just does not flow.

Then there are those who come onto the floor of the shoot, ask what scene it is, grab a script, scan it quickly, agree that they think they have got it now, and then perform it with their hands in their pockets (to avoid any continuity problems). These are the actors who also make the most fuss about how the writers never invent anything interesting for their characters to perform.

141

Which actor do we love the best? Which actor will we do our utmost to accommodate? If the actor shows he has done his part of the work, then we are willing to adapt our work to match his opinions.

Multi-camera

Rehearsing a multi-camera television show can be quite different from rehearsing for a movie, although there are some common elements. In multi-camera shoots each and every move needs to be rehearsed and plotted throughout the scene, so the delicate ballet between actors, cameras, and sound can take place. With a single camera, on the other hand, you tend to rehearse each shot as it comes up. I hope you will not skip this next bit about multi-camera just because you are so certain you will only be doing single camera movies. After all, Tom Hooper, the director of *The King's Speech* and *Les Misérables*, started his directing career directing multi-camera dramas in the UK, and you would like to work with and impress such a future star director, wouldn't you?

The rehearsal starts with everyone sitting around a table for the read-through. This is the beginning of your opportunity to convince and persuade everyone that you are going to give a good **screen** performance. First rule – don't read too loudly; don't read to all the others as an audience; read it as if you are being shot in close-up. I have known actors who have had to study the faces opposite them to see when the lips stop moving as the only way to know when to come in with their next speech. Second rule – start to put into your performance indications or possibilities of business or reactions that you have planned to match the thoughts and emotions of the piece. Don't wait for rehearsals – it will be too late, with your fellow actors already far, far down the road. Most newcomers are amazed how **quickly** their fellow professionals are working and committing themselves to performances. But then, the professionals have been around for a while and are probably acting the reason they got their part – their type.

In all good acting (am I actually going to lay down what I think good acting is?) it should appear that the lines said are exactly what that character wanted to say at that moment. Does this sound too trite? Then I'll put it this way: The lines should fit you like a glove, and if they don't, **and you do not have the rehearsal time to get them to fit you like a glove**, ask to adjust the line. Most theater actors regard this as sacrilege, and take it upon themselves to say all their lines as written. In all screen work I have been involved with, the first thing that happens is the experienced actors come up with suggestions for line changes.

You see, the writer may have had one idea in mind when writing the piece and the director another when he cast it. The writer may have written it with the accent and rhythm of a certain region in mind, and you come from another. Sometimes one of the reasons you have been cast is indeed to bring to the script your knowledge and experience of the particular role you are playing. (In the same way, it is a very good idea to get an actor who used to be a real doctor or nurse to play a doctor or a nurse; he will know all the correct procedures, and if we are lucky we can get him to teach the rest of the cast for no extra fee . . .)

I was talking about this to a regular in the New York daily soap *As the World Turns*, and she reckoned that her best contribution to the show was not her performance, but the rewrites she made overnight to change the turgid script she had been given into something a little more bearable and believable.

Always check with the production assistant or script supervisor (script girl) if you want to suggest a line change, and since others will need to know if the script is going to be different, do it as far in advance as possible. In particular, sound people who are waiting for a certain word as the cue to fade a microphone up or down get very testy if an actor comes up with a different one unannounced.

The scenes will then be blocked, that is, all the moves decided and given out. Don't forget that blocking is a way of getting the camera to see your face – sometimes with another face at the same time. If there is a rather free air to the blocking, you might decide that your character is rearranging flowers, while the person you are speaking to is seen over your shoulder. This would help the camera see both of you (and would also mean that you were seen in a nice big close-up). Usually, though, the blocking is worked out meticulously in advance, so you must do exactly as you are told, but it is good to understand the reason behind blocking and also good to be helpful.

In the theater, blocking moves are often given to reveal character or change of mood, and the moves are often not finalized until the actor has experimented with all sorts of combinations. In the rehearsal room for a television production, if they have time for such a thing, the moves are planned not only to reveal faces, but also to set up pictures that tell stories. The rehearsal room often has the positions of the walls taped to the floor, with tall poles at each corner so the director can check whether he is "shooting off," that is, to make sure that a camera will only shoot the scenery and not peek off the edge of it. If they do not have time for all this, then the moves and cameras are given just before it is shot – known as rehearse/record.

Beware of soft-spoken directors.

No, not that they are not to be trusted; it is just that when a stage director wants you to be infected with his enthusiasm, he tends to give instructions in a nice loud voice, whereas the television director, wanting the intimate approach, will be soft and quiet in his instructions and commands. The trouble is, they don't always **sound** like instructions and commands, and you can fall into the trap of thinking these are only suggestions, rather than the more precise demands of the screen.

This rehearsal period may be completed all in a day, or may extend over a longer period. The actor's job is to discover all the usual wonderful, exciting emotions and so on **within** the tight framework laid down. So watch the director, see where he stands, and start to spot the sort of shots he is planning. (Perhaps he is checking to see whether his pre-planning is actually working.) Start to **adjust your performance to the choices of shot**. If you are unsure, always assume that you are being shot in tight close-up: It is so easy to bring a voice up a bit – so hard to reduce a theatrical shout to a filmic murmur.

Next might come a technical run-through. Here the technical people in charge of cameras, lights, and sound get to see the show to work out solutions to the problems they will encounter in the shoot. The problem for inexperienced actors is that here, for the first time in the rehearsals, they have an audience, and there is a danger that they will **act**. What a mistake! All that energy, all that passion and commitment, for an audience looking at camera angles and lighting possibilities, discussing how to avoid boom shadows and having no eyes for any of the performances – just the actors' positions.

The experienced performer knows what technicals are all about and uses the rehearsal to check where a shot may change and what size it may be. Since there will always be a boom shadow somewhere, the technicians must work out where to put the lights in relation to the boom so the camera does not see it. The director will usually stand wherever that shot will be taken from (to let his technicians know), and the observant actor can start to learn the shooting script and figure out the camera plan.

Roseanne Arnold has the reputation of being very demanding, but then it is her performance and her talents that the audience wants to see. She is being professional when she wants to have input into the script, the style, even the shots of her show. See her at the beginning of this chapter (page 138) making sure that a sequence worked the way she wanted it to work. She uses the rehearsal period to make certain that the show is as good as she can make it – she does not sit back and hope that others will sort it all out.

Shooting script, plans, and cards

The system for operating a multi-camera studio to record a drama is a little like the orchestration of a piece of music. Only the conductor has the complete score; all the others have just their own bits, which if played correctly at the right time will lead to a successful performance of the whole symphony.

The individual camera operator does not have a script of the drama or anything like it. He has camera cards that list numbered descriptions of shots. When he hears on his headphones that one of his shots is coming up, he gets ready for it, he shoots it, and then he looks at his camera card for a description of his next shot. If the camera has to move, it will say so on the camera card, and the camera operator can consult the camera plan to see exactly where his camera is due to go next.

In the control room (or gallery), a switcher (or vision mixer) switches between cameras according to the shooting script. This is the script as studied by the actors but marked up to show where there is a cut from one camera to the next. It has descriptions of each shot, including size and content, alongside each line of text. This shooting script can also contain information about where music or sound effects start and stop; where bits of scenery fly in or out; where certain flats (swingers or flippers) are brought around to stop the camera seeing off the end of a set; where furniture or fireplaces must be moved to allow a camera to get farther into a room: all these sorts of things.

This shooting script is the lifeblood of the show; it is the complete score. It was prepared, of course, by the director. (**This** was what he was doing in rehearsal so frantically – not worrying about your performance, but wondering if camera number two had time after shooting through the window to rush around to get you coming through the door.) It is usually prepared before the director meets the actors, which can explain his extreme reluctance in rehearsals to change a move, for it might mean having to change a lot of camera positions and descriptions, which would mean changing the camera cards . . .

This Bible of information tells the individual cameras what to do: the switcher when to change shot, the scenic crew when and what to move, or the sound department when the shot changes from a tight one to a wide one so they can get the boom out in time before it is seen on the wide shot. It is so useful and is not, of course, given to the actors.

Well, they might want to know the size of shot or something, and we know actors only want to know about their close-ups so we had better keep this away from them and just tell them to act. (In most studios there is a pile of these camera scripts around somewhere, and it is usually possible to snatch a look to check whether your big moment is in long shot, medium, or close-up. At the very least, you can casually wander behind a camera and read the camera card to see whether it says "CU: You" or "2-s You & Him" so you can prepare yourself.)

If you are really lucky, you may be in a show that has a dress rehearsal (or dry run) after the technical and before the shoot. It is more likely you will be in a show that does rehearse/record – which is exactly as it sounds.

The reduced rehearsal time in all of the industry applies to soap operas too, and it is now possible to find yourself in a multi-camera shoot where there is no rehearsal at all – you arrive on set with your lines learned, the scene is blocked, and then it is shot. The read-through is disappearing, and the results need to be more instant – but a well-prepared actor is still able (and expected and needed) to contribute all the extras.

Nudity

This is increasingly used in main line shows, such as *Game of Thrones*, and as performers you need to be careful how to handle it. You should never be asked to disrobe unless it has been discussed and agreed at the audition and contract stage. If you are unexpectedly asked, then do not refuse, but say that your agent

145

has insisted that you contact them before any such event (and then tell your agent to order you not to do such a thing?). It is shoot etiquette that if you are to be shot in the nude, then you can ask for the set to be closed, as it is strange just how many people feel they have a nearby job to do when there is nudity involved. (See *Nudity* in *Time codes* at the end of this chapter.)

Being late

It is really bad to be late. It holds everyone up and makes for a negative atmosphere on the set. So don't ever be late. And if you **are** ever late, don't compound the error by coming up with a boring excuse. At the very least come up with a plausible explanation that makes us feel better – "I had to help an old lady who was knocked down at a crossing and whose wig came off" – rather than an explanation that makes us feel worse – "I overslept."

Think about it. It can be better to be interesting than to be truthful – a familiar refrain?

Secrets from the rehearsal room

- Do not pretend it is not your first time when it is.
- Come in with a committed performance already planned.
- Do not read too loudly.
- Check from the blocking where cheating will be necessary.
- Learn the shot sizes, and adjust your performance accordingly.
- Take careful notes.
- DON'T BE LATE!

Chapter 10: Time codes for rehearsals and technicals

(Rounded up to the nearest 5 seconds)

Nudity

Before the Devil Knows You're Dead (straight sex between Philip Seymour Hoffman and Marisa Tomei – were they embarrassed?)	00:00:25
Game of Thrones (Emilia Clarke: Don't forget that bikini line), season 1, #1	00:54:25

The Last Combat (Le Dernier Combat) (Pierre Jolivet and acceptable sex)	00:01:30
Mesrine, Part 1: Killer Instinct (L'instinct de mort) (Vincent Cassel and clever male full frontal)	01:13:05

Rehearsal and result

Day for Night (La nuit américaine) (cat rehearsal)	00:51:20
Day for Night (La nuit américaine) (cat performance)	00:53:25
Magnolia (Disc 2: Magnolia diary: rehearsing a Steadicam shot)	00:45:45
Magnolia (Disc 2: Magnolia diary: boy in car on set)	00:16:20
Magnolia (boy in car in film)	02:18:50

Semi-improvised scenes

Apocalypse Now Redux (Martin Sheen's improvisation)	00:06:20
Side by Side (Disc 2: Walter Murch on Martin Sheen's improvisation)	00:14:30
Best in Show (Eugene Levy and Catherine O'Hara checking in)	00:33:00
Best in Show (Parker Posey searching for Busy Bee)	00:50:05
Heartburn (pizza interlude with Meryl Streep and Jack Nicholson; they needed more footage as for legal reasons they had to cut lots of the original script)	00:25:05
Roman Holiday (Audrey Hepburn did not know what Gregory Peck was up to)	01:15:15
Waiting for Guffman (auditions that were a surprise for everyone)	00:13:20
Waiting for Guffman (Chinese meal for Eugene Levy, Linda Kash, Fred Willard, and Catherine O'Hara, with improvised dialogue)	00:29:10

Technical demands

GoodFellas (introductions and precise moves)	00:16:00
Hanna (Eric Bana gets out of a bus, walks, and then fights – all in one shot)	01:01:45
Marnie (Bonus Material: Documentary: technical kiss by Tippi Hedren)	00:22:10
Panic in the Streets (Richard Widmark and Barbara Bel Geddes in a complicated scene all in one shot with lots of moves and business)	00:11:05
Sexy Beast (Ian McShane ringing doorbell, with Ray Winstone in background)	01:13:10
Unbreakable (mirror or not for all the actors)	00:00:30

Walk and talk

Serenity (Nathan Fillion walks everywhere inside his spaceship)	00:09:55
The Town (Jon Hamm walks and talks, and the camera swoops around him)	00:30:05
The West Wing (the first of their famous walk/talk sequences), season 1, #1	00:06:00
The West Wing (Emmy-winning episode's walk/talk), season 1, #10	00:00:40

The complete list of films, dates, and directors is in the *Index of films* at the end of the book.

All the time codes are taken from my DVD player in London, with the DVDs bought in the UK, so you can know how many minutes and seconds the clip is from the start of the movie. Where I can, I have noted the different versions of the films.

There may well be variations in the time for different machines and formats, but these should be consistent for your download, DVD player, or computer, and so once you note the differences, you will know where to find each of the above clips.

Spencer Tracy and Katharine Hepburn

Eye-to-eye contact

11

DIRECTING ACTORS
FOR THE SCREEN

You might wonder what a chapter addressed to directors is doing here in a book for you actors.

Well, it should interest you to see what directors ought to be thinking of, and it would be nice for you to know what they are trying to achieve, so that you can help them get there more easily – **and** help yourself to be more effective.

So here we go.

Script

When studying a scene, note which moments are confrontational and which are cooperative. As a very general rule of thumb, cross-cut between shots or cameras on confrontational moments, and try to keep a contained shot for cooperative ones.

To "bat-and-ball" (cut from one person to another on each line of alternating dialogue) in a scene where there is no conflict **creates** conflict between the intent of the scene and its style.

Note where there are changes in thought or mood in the scene, and mark these with moves or pieces of business. An actor who, in the middle of a scene, gets up and moves away or takes off her glasses is helping the audience to understand that here is a change of tack, a change of thought.

By so marking these moments, you also help the actor to remember where she is emotionally and so guide the interpretation of the scene. It is very important that all the major turning points in a drama – whether the whole thing or just a scene – are marked carefully, with either a change in the shot or a change in the acting, or both. (See *Turning points* in *Time codes* at the end of this chapter.) In particular, note that in the film *Quartet* neither the actor nor the director marked the major turning point in the character's attitude to his ex-wife – and at least one of them should have done that.

Acting

Beware of eye-to-eye contact.

This may seem radical, since an alarming number of actors do not feel comfortable unless they are actually looking the other person in the eye. In many cases, this very eye contact **stops** them from performing well. (See *Curse of eye-to-eye contact* in *Time codes* at the end of this chapter.)

Let me explain.

When we are talking to someone, we put onto our faces and into our demeanor the "social" message that we wish to convey: our niceness, our desire to be liked, our wish to gain influence, and so on. None of these would be possible if we put onto our faces exactly what we **really** felt and thought about the person we were talking to. That sickly smile as we talk to the traffic officer, wondering if we are going to get a ticket, is a good example. The honest, helpful look as we gently remove a loaded gun from the hand of a five-year-old is another. We do not radiate what we really feel; we show what we believe to be appropriate at that moment. When actors maintain eye contact, this is what they are doing – reflecting what might be deemed appropriate in a social context.

If we want to know how they **really** feel (the **subtext**), then we must look into their minds, or stage the scene in such a way that the one person **cannot see** the other's face, and so **both** actors can share with the audience how they really feel, while saying the "polite" thing.

This explains why we in screen work so often place one actor behind another, both looking the same way, something we **never** do in real life. On screen it allows us to get at the subtext of a scene. Look at the beginning of the chapter (page 150), where Katharine Hepburn is sternly addressing the back of Spencer Tracy. In a real-life situation she would never stand there, but for the screen, it worked just fine, as we the audience can see both the intensity on her face and the resignation on his listening one. (See *Talking to the back of the head* in *Time codes* at the end of this chapter.)

Get an actor to come **towards** the camera (to get something from a foreground table or to gaze out of an invisible window, for example), and both the actor **and** the other actor(s) in the scene will present to the camera both the text **and** the subtext. The wife washing the dishes as she asks her husband over her shoulder for a divorce is shot in a manner that allows both characters to share with the audience how they feel about each other, and about the current situation.

Gazing into each other's eyes would have destroyed all that. If the actors get too bothered, tell them that it **is** OK for them to have eye-to-eye contact, as long as they imagine that their partner has a transparent skull – so they can "see" the eyes through the back of their head – and the camera can then see both their faces, and the audience at home will really think they can see each other. Look again at Katharine Hepburn at the head of this chapter – can you see how she is keeping eye-to-eye contact with Spencer Tracy by looking **through his head**?

There are, of course, many moments when the characters **will** be looking straight at each other as you cut from one to the other. Ironically, this cross-cutting can sometimes work better when they are acting with no one rather than with their partners. The following exercise might help to demonstrate this idea. I have done it often, but don't believe me – try it yourself.

Fake eyes exercise

I set out to shoot a whole series of two-handed scenes (scenes with two people in them), shooting two matching over-the-shoulder shots. I tell the actors that later on I shall shoot the scenes again after they have seen the rushes and noted how they did. I then play the results back to the participants.

When I do in fact repeat the exercise, I pretend that the other "actor" is unavailable, so every scene has to be recorded as two matching close-ups. The floor manager reads the other person's lines in a monotone, and an assistant holds a piece of paper on which is roughly drawn a pair of eyes (to give the actor the correct eyeline). It is **this** that each participant has to act with. The two actors in the scene, then, are not allowed to act with each other as in the first time they performed it, but have to do their parts of the scene separately with the floor manager reading in the lines.

Every time I do this, every actor gives a **better** performance the second time. In other words, when there is no other actor to relate to (or be distracted by?), there is a better actual performance. Now that there is no one glaring her in the eye, the actor no longer has to do the "polite," social, "true-to-life" thing, but can allow her face to show her inner thoughts – the very thing good screen acting is all about.

So an actor works better without relating to anyone else? Without getting any eye contact? Yes – it is a bit worrying, isn't it? (But there is a famous international actor who is very nearsighted and refuses to wear contact lenses on stage or set. This way, she says, she can react to how she thinks the other actors ought to be reacting, rather than be limited by what they actually do.)

Jane Fonda had never had an easy time with her father off-screen, and the making of *On Golden Pond* was in part as real a meeting of the two generations as it was in the script. In the great coming-together scene, for her close-up she asked that a light be shone on her father's face (life imitating art?), so that she could **really** act to her father's face as her character asked for understanding and forgiveness. The shot completed, the camera was turned around to shoot Henry Fonda's close-up. "Do you want me to stand in your eyeline?" she asked, anxious to give to him what she had needed for herself. "No," he replied, "I am not that kind of actor," and he proceeded to do all **his** reactions and speeches to an invisible partner.

By the way, I believe that neither was right or wrong. Each was using **whatever worked** to get the best results. (I am not so sure it did that much for father-daughter relationships, though.) (See *Different styles of acting* in *Time codes* at the end of this chapter.)

The frame

Every picture tells a story, and when you are shooting pictures, stories are being told whether you like it or not. Actors' instincts are very good about relationships and character moves, but only the very experienced understand how this relates to the actual images presented on the screen. Sometimes actors have to be where they are because the picture demands it, and your job (and their job) is to make it appear that is what their **characters** wanted to do – but they must be in the correct place.

Here in the West our eyes scan a picture from left to right. We have done this millions of times as we read from left to right, and it carries over onto the screen. This means that our attention to the screen is not balanced, that a person on screen right will get a little bit more attention than one on screen left. You can use this to strengthen a weaker than hoped for performance (put the actor screen right) or to hide a less than effective performance (put her screen left). Movement from left to right as you look at the screen gives a smoother feeling than movement from right to left – it is not accidental that in the early Westerns it was common for the good guys to gallop from left to right, and the bad guys from right to left. (In English pantomime, a centuries-old tradition, the Fairy always appears on the left as you look at the stage, the Devil on the right.) Directors like the picture itself to be part of the story, and that might mean asking actors to do something that does not feel good to them, but produces a picture that makes the director (and eventual audience) feel very good indeed. (See *Picture tells the story* in *Time codes* at the end of this chapter.)

The shoot

Actors love to "act" (of course), but they sometimes deliver better reactions when they are relaxed and at ease than when they are "acting." I have already talked earlier in Chapter 8, "Acting," about how non-real actions can convey an apparent reality (remember the sneeze?). Once for a two-character scene, Robert De Niro wanted to feel very bad to get the correct expression in his eyes, so he hit the other actor – whom he liked. This resulted in excellent acting for the screen: Robert De Niro has tears in his eyes. (What was in the eyes of the other actor, I wonder?) When Steven Spielberg wanted a look of wonderment in the little boy's eyes in *Close Encounters of the Third Kind* he had one prop man dress up as a clown and the other as a gorilla for the boy to see in different parts of the room to get the reactions he wanted. Was this moment "truthful"? Have I ruined it for you now you know that the little boy was **not** looking at aliens? Would it work with adult actors? For directing as for acting: whatever works. (See *Different styles of acting* in *Time codes* at the end of this chapter.)

I was once shooting a large crowd scene, and by accident the camera was recording the moments leading up to the start of the scene. During editing, this is what I saw: actors milling about, moving, looking really at ease and realistic;

the first assistant shouts, "Stand by!" and the actors all settle down; the first assistant cries, "Action!" – and everyone freezes in unnatural poses. Makes you think, doesn't it: "Action!" equals freeze?

A way around this is to have a quiet word with your camera operator that she should start recording the events from just before "Action!" is called to **just after** "Cut!" is called. You will be delighted at some of the natural and imaginative reactions that you can use later in the editing sessions, sometimes for moments far removed from the time they were taken. Sometimes, they are put into entirely different scenes – but whatever works!

Single versus multi-camera

We all love to shoot with a single camera, for then we can be filmic and try out all sorts of things. If we are to work in a studio with many cameras, we can still do good work, but one of the biggest dangers in shooting with more than one camera is using too many of them. Try to stick to two for a scene whenever you can.

To explain: When two actors are talking to each other, and you are cross-shooting them with two cameras, you can light and compose shots well, because the key light for one actor becomes the back light for the other, and vice versa. The results very nearly match those you get with one camera. The moment a third camera is used for anything more than a close-up of a prop, a twitching hand, or a tapping foot, the lighting for that third camera comes straight at the actors, ruining the lighting for the other two, and you get that "generalized" look so common with multi-camera dramas. For a fast-paced soap, of course, there is no alternative, but it is surprising how often you don't really **need** all those cameras. By rationing them and using them cunningly you can get a much higher level of achievement in your shots.

Actually, with the increasing pressure on productions to get the maximum out of a shooting day, quite a few of the single camera productions do, in fact, use two cameras when shooting static two-handed shots to speed up the process and so buy time for the more complicated pieces of shooting (that is the theory, anyway). As long as the actors' movements are not too extravagant, there need not be too great a compromise in camera positions and lighting, but there **is** a compromise in not getting onto the eyeline.

I was called up to direct some episodes of *Brookside*, and was told that as they had to shoot more minutes per day than before, the producer had decreed that all two-handed scenes had to be shot with two cameras to save time. I ignored this, and showed that it is actually quicker to shoot with one camera rather than two cameras, as there are no lighting or camera compromises needed, the cameras do not have the problem of seeing each other, the actors are not so restricted as to where and how they move, and there is no need for two crews and equipment to cram into the restricted shooting space. The producer abandoned making his two-camera directive compulsory for future shoots.

Directors' secret thoughts

- Why won't actors cheat in a contained, cooperative scene when I ask them to?
- Why do actors always want eye-to-eye contact when it is often better without?
- Why do actors act better when they are acting with a blank space rather than with their fellow actors?
- Why do some actors freeze when I shout "Action!"
- Why don't actors give me more when I ask for it?

Even in the grand world of major moviemaking, there is an increasing use of more than one camera. Here it is common for one camera to shoot a two-shot and a second camera by its side to shoot a medium close-up, or tight close-up. Why not, if it saves time and gives more alternatives in the editing? (But it will not help the actors if they are working to a particular shot size.)

Digital editing

The universal use of computers to edit has also changed the way directors shoot – and, yes, how actors act. The ability of the editing program to try out endless permutations of a scene without it costing anything in materials, and with it costing not so much in time, means that the directors and actors can more easily experiment and try things out, knowing that it will not be a major task to fit little snippets into the eventual edited version. See more of this in Chapter 14, "The editor and editing."

Casting

There are so many stories of a wonderful production being cast by accident, of the wrong person being offered a part that turned out just right, that it almost seems a mistake to be too logical about casting. I would recommend going by instinct – cast who you feel is right, not who you think is right. If by chance you are wrong, well, next time your instincts will be even better. If you cast by logic, it is much harder to get better at it, as logic and acting are not always the best of bedfellows.

I hope some of the things in this book will push you gently toward one actor rather than another. But ultimately it is you who will be working with her, and you know what the pressures and opportunities will be. Just remember that there are those actors who are wonderful in the audition room – and are never as good again.

156

Beware of holding a casting session just to make people happy. Do **not** call in someone when you know the part is gone but you think it will cheer her up. (Yes, directors have been known to do this.) Actors are so keen to work, so anxious not to miss an opportunity, that they will cancel work (and lose money) for the day, go for an expensive hair-do, hire a cab – in other words spend precious time and money to turn up for what you were considering a favor to them. If they ever find out, they will not thank you.

Some while back I was asked to do a block shoot for *Brookside*, where I had to shoot thirty scenes from fourteen different episodes for the next four months in just three shooting days. (It all had to do with clearing an actor from the series, and with getting full value from an expensive set.) Jokingly, I told them that they only hired me to do it because I was very quick. "No," was the disconcerting reply; "It is because you are nice – and quick!" Nice and quick – the modern criteria. What an epitaph.

Chapter 11: Time codes for directing actors for the screen

(Rounded up to the nearest 5 seconds)

Curse of eye-to-eye contact

Carousel (we long to see them all properly to understand what they are thinking)	00:49:15
Carousel (as we watch three different exits we just see the back of their heads – so no expressions)	01:55:25; 01:58:30; 01:59:15
Words and Music (we never see Janet Leigh's left eye; we see Mickey Rooney's right eye ten times)	01:20:00

Different styles of acting

Close Encounters of the Third Kind (Disc 2: Documentary: child looks around)	00:40:45
Close Encounters of the Third Kind (Disc 2: Documentary: child looks up)	00:39:40
On Golden Pond (two different approaches from Jane and Henry Fonda)	01:31:55
Side by Side (Disc 2: John Malkovich on reality)	00:08:45
Sophie's Choice (What did Alan J. Pakula do to get the little girl to do this?)	02:09:30

Picture tells the story

A.I. Artificial Intelligence (photos: Haley Joel Osment wants to   00:12:00
be part of the family)

A.I. Artificial Intelligence (meal: he is isolated from his   00:17:45
new parents, Frances O'Connor and Sam Robards)

Close Encounters of the Third Kind (we compare the mountain
on the TV with the one in the room, and wonder if
Richard Dreyfus will ever get to see it)

   Theatrical release 01:09:50; Special edition 01:05:40; Director's cut 01:13:35

Lawrence of Arabia (just legs behind Peter O'Toole: the army is   02:06:10
behind him)

Léon (brow of the hill: has Jean Reno left   00:40:10; Extended 00:41:50
Natalie Portman? No.)

Léon (the difference in leg length showing the   01:16:15; Extended 01:36:45
impossibility of their relationship)

A Simple Plan (hall and doorway: Bridget Fonda is constant;   01:25:50
Bill Paxton is coming and going)

Talking to the back of the head

The Blind Side (what can Tim McGraw see of Sandra Bullock?)   01:44:20

Cat on a Hot Tin Roof (wouldn't Elizabeth Taylor need to   00:19:00
see Paul Newman's face, and his reaction to her advances?)

Heat (would you talk to the back of the boss's head if   00:39:35
you wanted a job?)

Men in Black 3 (would you talk to someone in an elevator like this?)   00:24:45

Panic in the Streets (the moves of Richard Widmark and   00:11:05
Barbara Bel Geddes are all for the camera's benefit)

The Wizard of Oz (what does the Good Witch see of Dorothy?)   01:34:35

Turning points

The Apartment (Jack Lemmon realizes that Shirley MacLaine   00:50:40
was his boss's companion at his apartment last night)

Casablanca (everyone important is seen in close-up)   01:09:10

The Matrix (the extreme shot and reflections in   00:27:40
Laurence Fishburne's glasses mark the main turning point for the film)

Quartet (Tom Courtney will never forgive Maggie Smith)   00:40:05

Quartet (she asks him on a walk: we don't see his decision)   00:43:15

Quartet (he agrees to help without us seeing him decide first)   00:49:30

The complete list of films, dates, and directors is in the *Index of films* at the end of the book.

All the time codes are taken from my DVD player in London, with the DVDs bought in the UK, so you can know how many minutes and seconds the clip is from the start of the movie. Where I can, I have noted the different versions of the films.

There may well be variations in the time for different machines and formats, but these should be consistent for your download, DVD player, or computer, and so once you note the differences, you will know where to find each of the above clips.

Oprah Winfrey's favorite snapshot

Oprah on screen

12

ANNOUNCERS (AND THE ART OF BEING INTERVIEWED)

The techniques and ideas dealt with up to now also work extremely well for announcers, as well as lecturers, newscasters, weather people, interviewees – even people stopped in the street by a news crew and asked for their opinions.

The same liturgy comes up:

- React before you speak.
- Project to the microphone only.
- Give extra animation when speaking at low levels.
- Happily present **yourself**.

The first three elements are easy to grasp and to practice – but happily present yourself? Here's how.

I was working with some businessmen on how to present themselves better for the in-house films their company send out. First I had them bring in their official "company" photo along with their favorite snapshot.

Then I had them give a short speech in the manner of their official photo. We repeated the exercise using the "favorite" snapshot, getting them to match their manner to **that**. All of them came across better during the second exercise. See Oprah, on the opposite page, showing her bubbly personality both in a snapshot and of course in the magic way she comes across on screen.

Once I was working one-on-one with a managing director who had come dressed in a rather tight double-breasted suit. Newly appointed, he wanted to make a film clip to be shown to all his employees to introduce himself, but when he made his presentation to the camera, he was stilted and stiff, not the image he wanted to project to his workforce.

I could see immediately what the problem was: He was ashamed of his waistline and was trying to hide it. Shock tactics sometimes work best. "Now do the speech again," I told him, "but this time with your jacket off. All I want you to concentrate on is showing to the audience what a wonderful, big, fat gut you've got." (Yes, I put it just like that!)

Well, he did – and the result was a wonderful, warm, witty, and effective speech. Having been forced to face up to his greatest fear, he wasn't spending any time fighting it, and this allowed his natural charm and intelligence to come through.

Do you think you have the nerve to present to the world your greatest secret fear? By doing so, you can release all that negative energy and channel it positively into presenting a nice talk, lecture, or interview. It also works really well for all Facebook and Skype performances.

Try the store window test.

Imagine you are walking down the street, and you look into a store window, but you are not actually looking at anything in the window; you are looking at your own reflection. Quick: **Which bit of you are you looking at?** You will find that it is usually the bit you wish was not the way it is (the big rear end, the balding head, the straggly hair, the stooped shoulders). This demonstrates what you need to face up to and boldly flaunt, rather than hide from.

I tried this test out with a group of professional actors in New York, and one admitted that she always looked at what she thought was her large rear (although the rest of her is quite, quite beautiful). Discussing this, she suddenly announced that all the mirrors in her home were half-length, only showing her from the waist up. My advice was to get a full-length one and to get to know **and love** the way she was. I even got her to act a piece while "showing off the rear." It did not show, of course, but her **performance** was so much more relaxed, convincing, and powerful. (See *Playing the way you look* in *Time codes* at the end of this chapter.)

Present yourself and your personality, and if in doubt, make sure that the relaxed and happy you we meet off-camera is the same person we meet on camera. So, actors and announcers alike, do not fall into the trap of being more interesting in the canteen than on the screen. Concentrate on that Audience of One (the camera), and give it those conspiratorial glances and asides, just the way you do at business meetings, planning meetings, and the like.

Technical points of view

The more you understand about the work and the problems of others, the better your contribution will be to the program.

Another personal anecdote: I was taking part in a documentary on aspects of television and was in a group of four having an unscripted conversation, supposedly over lunch. I could see that the director was going to have great trouble cutting the show together, because there were no linking shots. At the end of the group shot, he took some quick cutaways of each of our faces, so in mine I did a great deal of "eating" as I looked left, looked right, quickly flashed my eyes left again, and so on.

When the program was shown, my friends laughed because it seemed to be mostly about me eating salad. Whenever the director wanted to cut from one face to another, he would cut to my face to get him there, and this led to a lot of my face on the screen.

No, I was not smugly trying to be seen more; I **was** giving the director what I knew would be needed in the editing suite. (But it **did** get me more screen time.) Giving a television interview on one of my trips to Korea, I was asked to speak up – I agreed to do this, but in fact did not. Because I was speaking softly, they had to bring the microphone close to me; it got into the picture, and so I got a tighter shot, all the more to show my subtle expressions! This is dangerous advice, I fear.

The bit about "provide a motivation for all camera moves" from Chapter 4, "The camera," also applies to interviews and presentations, and particularly to the teleprompter or autocue. The audience at home must believe that the one thing you **want** to do is read those words at precisely that angle, at that height, and in that manner. When it goes wrong, it must be **exactly** the moment that you **wanted** to look down at the script on the table and read it from there.

This "make us think you want to" or "motivation" is not so easy at first, but as long as you know that it is your long-term goal, then you can start moving toward it from your very first screen appearance. (See *Interview examples* in *Time codes* at the end of this chapter.)

Announcers especially suffer from the "frozen butterfly" look, when as a result of the camera being turned on you, you seem to be riveted to the back of the chair, head clamped upright and generally stiffened up.

Just because you are sitting in a chair does not mean that you cannot move. Oh, I know that you should not move much from left to right, otherwise you might fall out of the frame. But you **can** move backward and forward. In fact you can see newscasters doing this often: " . . . and the baby elephant was happily reunited with its mother" – leaning forward as a serious expression comes over the face – "In the Middle East today . . . " (We know it is going to be bad news.) Again, watch the experienced ones, noting exactly what they do, not what you thought they did.

Interviews

In an interview situation, try to put yourself in the director's seat, and ask yourself, "What does he want to see?" The short answer is "good television," and **that** is more often a funny look, reaction, or grimace than a witty phrase or statement. Read Chapter 9, "Auditions," for confirmation that when you are being interviewed, you should work just as hard at listening as when you are speaking.

It is so embarrassing (and ineffective for your contribution) if, when you are introduced to the audience, you sit there like an embarrassed prune. **Do** something – be discovered looking down, look up after your name is mentioned, smile shyly into the camera as if to say, "There you are" to a well-loved friend (the audience behind the lens). Then look toward the introducer, smile at any witticism he makes, shake your head in wonderment at the nice things being said about you (or shake your head in sorrow at the lies they are telling about you). In other words, **actively** start being effective.

When you are asked questions, reply not to the questioner, but to where the questioner **would** be sitting if they were as close as your microphone. Since you are most likely to be rigged up with a radio mike, that is very close indeed. Be careful not to become dreamy and slow as you excitedly and enthusiastically go through your routine **with low vocal levels**. Well, it **is** a routine, isn't it?

If you are trying to get a particular point across, and you suspect that the questioner is speaking to a different agenda, use the John Wayne technique. He had a habit of having a rising inflection at the end of a thought. On one of those talk shows he was asked why he did this. "Easy," he replied. "If I had a downward inflection, then the camera can cut away from my face. But if I have a rising inflection, then I haven't finished yet, and the camera cannot cut away, and I get a longer shot of my face." He was a very skilled screen actor indeed.

Try it now. See how long you can go on speaking without ever dropping your voice.

What? You are starting to sound like a television evangelist? Well, why do you think **they** do it? It keeps the attention and becomes mesmerizing. Go on, do a speech again **in the manner of a television evangelist**. Effective, isn't it?

Public announcers (and smartphone users)

You are at the airport, the railway station, the bus station; you are in a department store, a bus, or a train – and an announcement comes up on the loud-speakers, only you cannot understand what they are saying. That is because the announcer is speaking as if the person they are addressing is a long way away, their voice is far too loud, and the result is a distorted speech that is hard to follow. The trick for the announcers is the same as for actors – **speak as if the person you are talking to is as far away from you as the microphone**. The same also applies to those who shout into their mobile or smartphone. How far away is the microphone? Three inches? Then you should speak as if the ear of the person you are talking to is only three inches away from your mouth – **now** how should you speak? (And it will stop the rest of us hearing, or being annoyed by, your loud voice too.) And whilst you are at it, notice how many gestures a person makes when they are speaking on a smartphone with no possibility of the person listening seeing what they are doing. Lots of lovely gestures, and facial expressions – so put some of these too into your interview.

Chapter 12: Time codes for announcers
(and the art of being interviewed)

(Rounded up to the nearest 5 seconds)

Interview examples

Close Encounters of the Third Kind (Disc 2: Documentary: background to child and stepladder)	00:39:40
Close Encounters of the Third Kind (Disc 2: Documentary: big or small boat)	01:36:30
Close Encounters of the Third Kind (Disc 2: Documentary: glass window)	00:57:45
Side by Side (Disc 2: Danny Boyle, James Cameron, John Malkovich, Martin Scorsese, Steven Soderbergh)	all

Playing the way you look

Accident (Michael York as usual)	00:10:35
Bonnie and Clyde (Gene Wilder's looks were perfect for being an undertaker)	01:04:30
Cat on a Hot Tin Roof (Paul Newman gets these parts, Burl Ives the other)	00:47:25
Donnie Brasco (Val Avery always gets the same sort of part)	01:01:05
Dr. No (Bernard Lee was perfect for the first "M")	00:10:10
The Guns of Navarone (George Mikell's looks meant he always got to play Nasty Nazis, or assassins)	01:25:50
The Long Good Friday (Bob Hoskins was always the crafty cockney)	01:45:20

The complete list of films, dates, and directors is in the Index of films at the end of the book.

All the time codes are taken from my DVD player in London, with the DVDs bought in the UK, so you can know how many minutes and seconds the clip is from the start of the movie. Where I can, I have noted the different versions of the films.

There may well be variations in the time for different machines and formats, but these should be consistent for your download, DVD player, or computer, and so once you note the differences, you will know where to find each of the above clips.

Goldie Hawn being simple and sincere. . .

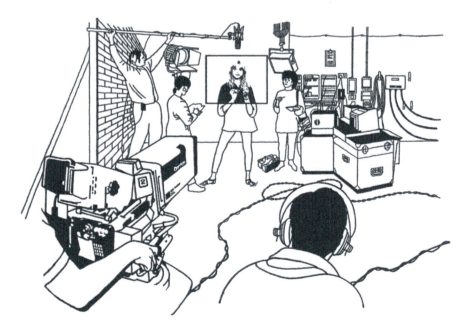

. . . in the chaos of a set

13

THE SHOOT

This is it: the moment of truth. This is when the preparation and work of all contributors is finally put to the test. Unlike in theater, you cannot hope to get it right tomorrow if today is not up to scratch. You have to be perfect – **now**.

There are many pitfalls that can prevent you from being at your best, the first being the fact of the shoot itself. There is no gradual build-up. You suddenly find yourself in the middle of bright lights, bustling people, and menacing equipment, and you are expected to be tender, vulnerable, emotional, and sincere. No wonder so many inexperienced actors find the pressure so intense that they retreat into safety, into the sort of acting which they have done before and which has brought them this far – theater acting.

It is so difficult to learn from your more experienced acting partners or from the experts you may encounter, because you just can't see what they are up to. (Remember Laurence Olivier and Marilyn Monroe? If **he** couldn't see what she was doing, what chance have you?) Look at Goldie Hawn on the opposite page. **Now** can you appreciate what sort of skills and talents are needed to come across as simple and sincere in the middle of all that chaos? (See *Working on set* in *Time codes* at the end of this chapter.)

The shoot can bring out the worst in actors: Their voices can get louder (but where is the microphone?), their gestures more expansive (but what size shot is it?), and their movements more flowing (but what mark must they hit?). Don't forget – in the theater we rehearse, and then we perform. For the screen we rehearse (if we are lucky), and then we **repeat**.

Single camera shoots

It is worth repeating: In the theater, we rehearse and then we perform.

On the screen, we rehearse and then we repeat.

On a shoot, your relationship to the work is very different from that of the other workers. For a start, they have all been working together on this shoot, usually in advance of any meeting with you, and so the camaraderie that theater engenders has already been created – between the director and the technicians.

Your scene is very important to you (of course), but you don't have a complete picture of all that is going on and cannot judge just how it fits in – whether it really is a scene that must have time spent on it, or whether it is one of those "bread and butter" moments that, frankly, are to be got through as efficiently and speedily as possible.

Your call has probably meant that you have been waiting around for quite some time before you are used. The director and crew will have been hard at it from dawn. You don't know what excitements they may have been through. Maybe they have been kept waiting by equipment breaking down, or the weather playing dirty tricks on them, or even an actor not delivering either lines or a performance. So to complain about being kept waiting is, to put it very mildly, not a sensible thing to do. The context, you see, is totally different for the crew than for the cast.

As you know (from all the other books on screen acting you have read?), things are not shot in any order that makes sense to you. **Learn** what that sense is, and try to understand why we work the way we do. This will enable you to contribute to the shoot better, rather than getting indignant and upset by imagined slurs or supposed incompetence.

It is so costly to shoot that the producers more or less try to keep the camera and all the associated equipment working all the time. This means that not only do they try to shoot all the scenes together that occur in one set or location, but they try to shoot **everything** in the same direction as well. After all, it can take a long time to move all the lights around from looking in one direction to looking in the opposite direction, and time spent moving lights is time not spent working with cameras and microphones and actors to get good results on to the screen. (Did you notice that actors were not put at the head of that list?)

Single camera shoot secrets

- Remember your Audience of One.
- Rehearse – then **repeat**.
- Remember you are part of a complex team, and learn to cooperate.
- Keep your eyelines during line up.
- Plan and rehearse your continuity.

If you have a costume or makeup change, that will take time too, so the shoot schedule is arranged so that, where possible, all changes take place at a time when the crew can keep working. The eventual shoot schedule, hopefully carefully worked out, may seem lunatic to you, but it would look quite good to a production manager who has to keep the director and the crew working in such a way as to get the job done on time, on budget.

Time (literally seconds) secrets

I have sometimes noticed an actor, on the way over to the location or set where we are waiting for her, stop for a brief word with someone. Oh, maybe it is only ten seconds wasted.

At the end of the shoot day, when your production manager tells you that you **have** to stop shooting in one minute, and you have this **two**-minute shot that you just **long** to do again, you think back and add up all those lost ten seconds when actors (or electricians, or makeup, or cameras) took an unnecessary extra few seconds all through the day, and you think dark thoughts about them all.

So – don't **you** be a second-eater-upper!

Practicalities

As each shot is set up individually, the actor is able to see and sense exactly what is required for each shot. Each time the camera is moved to a different position, or is shooting a section of a scene in a different size shot, it is called a setup. You can expect to go through anything from fifteen to forty setups in a day, depending on the complexity of the shot, whether it is outdoors or in a studio, and so on.

Sometimes the actors are taken through the scene first – they can even initiate moves in certain circumstances – then the lighting and camera people descend to work out where to put the camera and how to light the actors in the positions they are now in. For other shoots the whole sequence is carefully prepared, so that the actors are only called when the cameras and lights are ready, and then they go into a rehearsal. During the rehearsal a lot of activity can still be taking place, as the lighting crew adjusts the lights, the design crew finishes dressing the set, the prop crew sets all the action properties, and the sound crew works out how to get the microphones in the right place at the right time to get good clean sound.

If this is a shoot with stars, then their stand-ins will be doing the job of standing in the right place for the lighting crew while they line up the shot. The reason for this is simple. A shoot can be a very exhausting time, and we all want the stars to be at their best for the actual moment of shooting and not to waste their energies during the line up period. Of course, if you are not a star, then you will be required to stand around, but don't let this distract you from your ultimate job of being excellent for the camera when the shot is taken.

They then have a technical rehearsal, a stagger-through of the details for a particular shot. Keep your eyelines during this (that is, look in the directions you will be looking). One of the things they are checking is that you are correctly lit, and in particular that your eyes are properly lit – and you want that, don't you? Remember this technical rehearsal is as much for the crew as it is for you. Each department must be confident that their part of the job is ready at the magical moment of a take. It may just be a simple head-and-shoulders of one character talking to another; it may be much, much more than that.

When Alfred Hitchcock was making *Stage Fright*, he had a sequence that was all one continuous shot, running for two minutes and forty seconds. It took him two and a half days to rehearse and shoot it. Why did it take him so long? If you ever get a chance to see it, you will understand why. (See *Complex sequences* in *Time codes* at the end of this chapter.) In this shot, all in one room, Richard Todd and Marlene Dietrich move from place to place: She has to hit eight different marks; he has to hit eleven different marks; the camera moves to eleven different marks; and there are at least seventeen different points of focus that the camera has to find. During this sequence, furniture had to be put in then taken out again, and lights had to fly in and be fired up, then dimmed and flown out again before the camera could swing around to see them. A complicated ballet of all the technical elements of film had to take place to get this shot looking just right. There was even one moment in the middle of the sequence when Todd walked over to Dietrich and shadowed her face; immediately, he leaned back and took his shadow off her face. In the middle of all that complexity, of saying all those lines and hitting all those marks, the actor was aware enough of the technical elements to avoid making everyone go through the whole thing yet again.

You might ask why Hitchcock did it this way – why not break up the scene into little bits the way other directors do and film all those? He was creating huge problems for all the technicians and actors, but it **was** for a good reason. This sequence is part of the famous "lying" flashback that some criticized Hitchcock for: As Richard Todd's character is telling his girlfriend what had just happened, there is a flashback of his explanation, but by the end of the film, we discover that it was all a lie – the flashback is **not** what really happened. I think that the genius of Hitchcock is that he shot this sequence in this complicated, almost ostentatiously difficult way as a subtle way of saying to the audience that it was, in fact, a lie. We can debate the decision, but the result meant that the actors had to perform in a certain way to achieve the results – screen acting of the highest level.

After the technical, there is a complete run-through (sometimes called a dry run or dress rehearsal) for which the stars replace their stand-ins, and are told of any particular things to look out for in the sequence. They then start shooting. Any particular setup may be repeated a number of times, and each is called a different **take**. Some actors give their best performances on the first take, some on a much later take; some directors do not like going for more than a handful of takes, and some go on and on. There is no regular pattern. Sometimes the actor is given different acting notes for each take; sometimes no notes are given at all. The actor will however be expected to repeat the same moves and bits of business, and this opens up the world of continuity.

It always surprises technicians that an actor can pick up a spoon with one hand, and a few moments later when repeating the scene, pick it up with the other. Film books (and IMDb details) are full of examples of continuity mistakes: It is easy to criticize from the sidelines, but much harder to cope with in reality. Sometimes an actor will do exactly what she is told, even matching the screen shot that was taken of a previous moment, and the continuity will **still** be wrong. It is not always the actor's fault. Try to protect yourself against mistakes, and try to prevent that most dreaded of all things – a continuity supervisor (or continuity girl) giving you a long list of continuity notes. The way to avoid this is to arrive on the set with all your continuity already worked out and part of you; it should be as much a part of your performance as your lines, so that whatever thought is thrown at you on a set, you can devote your talent to playing the part, instead of trying to remember continuity details. (See *Continuity problems* in *Time codes* at the end of this chapter.)

Hugh Grant tells of how he works: He does the first three or four takes exactly as the director asks, and then does another three or four takes where he tries all sorts of things, experimenting with moves, words, and looks, and putting in all his "Hugh Grant-isms." This means that he is doing what is required of him – both by being obedient and then by supplying all those extras that we expect from a Hugh Grant performance: What a good screen acting approach. (See *Complex sequences* in *Time codes* at the end of this chapter.)

Problems on set

We often hear of problem actors, and the mayhem they may cause. We hear that Marilyn Monroe, when making *Bus Stop* and being unable to remember her script, had to have all her lines fed to her by an assistant. When you watch the scene, you realize that this was not quite true – since it was mostly a held two-shot, there is no way all her lines could have been so supplied. (See *Trouble on set* in *Time codes* at the end of this chapter.) The whole celebrity industry needs feeding, and so any piece of gossip or rumor quickly becomes fact – and that allows the public to enjoy the discomfort of those they have elevated to the heights. (I read that with his facial expressions David Hyde Pierce had upstaged Mark Rylance during his huge opening speech in the play *La Bête* – I saw the production and, no, he absolutely did not.)

They made a movie about the making of the Marilyn Monroe and Laurence Olivier film *The Prince and the Showgirl*, called *My Week with Marilyn*. They wanted Judi Dench to play the part of Sybil Thorndike, but she was unavailable on the shoot dates. So they built the sets, and got her in just to do her shots (not her whole scenes, just for when the camera was looking at her) three weeks before principal photography was due to start, and then matched everyone else to what she had done when they actually made the film some weeks later. (See *Unreality* in *Time codes* at the end of this chapter.)

Shooting tricks

- When you are given some instructions, repeat them back to the giver. Don't say "Eh?" or "Can you repeat that?" It is even worse if you don't understand an instruction but don't say anything – and then get it wrong in the shoot. When you repeat an instruction, it provides the note giver with an opportunity to confirm that you have understood, and it gives you the confidence that these rather odd instructions are **really** what you need to do.

- It is so important to hit your marks that you must develop a sense of where they are without looking down. Practice so you know how many steps it is to the mark, or work out your position in relation to the furniture, or line up two distant objects (a lamp, an exit sign) so that when they are in line you are on your mark. By standing on it, and then walking backwards, you can judge how many paces it will take you to be exactly on your mark.

- Cheat your face around to the camera by placing any property in the **camera**-side hand. This means that when you look at the book, drink the drink, examine the rings, or lift the pencil, all these actions will bring your face more around to the camera than it was.

- In the same way, when talking to another actor, talk to her **camera-side** eye, or even her ear, with your **off-camera**-side eye – in order to bring your own face around more to the camera.

- If you are positioned slightly behind the person you are talking to, do not move your head to really see their eyes – remember, if you gaze **through** obstacles of hair, even of their head itself, the camera will make it seem that you have good eye-to-eye contact with them.

- When you need to turn your head, let your eyes move first, **then** let your head move. The camera will hold on you for longer, since the cut will come in the middle of the head turn after you have moved your eyes.

- Always have some expression on your face at the end of a shot. **Always** think through some extra business or line that your character would do **just after the word "Cut" is shouted**. This will keep your face alive and alert right until the end (and can sometimes lead to **your** face getting the last shot of a sequence, since some of the others' faces will have turned off). One trick I have learned is to ask an actor to end a scene by vigorously exhaling. It doesn't actually mean anything, but it keeps your face alive while they are cross-fading to another scene.

- Always ease yourself into the correct shot by putting weight on one leg or the other, and be ready to change weight immediately if you are not correctly positioned for the camera. Take a manic joy in being in the right place even if you have had to move, because all the other actors have missed their marks, but you **still** got into a good three-shot.

- If you are much taller than your acting partner, and it is inconvenient for her to stand on a box for a nice two-shot, make yourself shorter by

172

standing with your legs spread far apart (surprise – this usually applies more to men than to women).

- When moving, talk fast but move slow. When walking along with the camera tracking you, lift your knees to give you the animation of walking while you are actually moving through space rather slowly. Do not let slow movements slow down your speech.

- If you need a cue to speak (because the other actor is so far away or speaking so intimately that you cannot hear her), be bold and ask for one. The crew would much rather give you a cue than not have you speak at the proper time.

- In a similar way, if you are really having problems with your lines, ask for a few of them to be placed in appropriate places, or even have them written up on boards for you to know they are there. You will have the confidence to act without having to spend too much energy trying to remember the lines. Oh, I know that it is your job to remember your lines (and because a shoot can be so complicated, you need to know your lines **really well** to cope with whatever instructions you are given just before you are about to act), but we would rather put up idiot cards for you than have endless takes ruined by you forgetting your lines.

- Assume that no note means you are doing fine. Just as I do not shout out "Good boom" after a take when the microphone was not seen, I do not necessarily give approval to any other member of the team who got everything right, and that of course includes the actors. To assume that silence means that everyone hates you leads to a life of paranoia.

- I have read in a book on film acting, "Don't blink." This has led to a lot of watery-eyed actors all over the world. It is right – and it is wrong. **If you have fair eyelashes**, when you blink it looks a little odd. So if you have fair eyelashes then, yes, don't blink. If on the other hand you have nice, thick, dark lashes that can flutter away to tremendous effect, then do just that. This is all part of the idea that you should do **whatever your face does best**. If you have very small eyes, then maybe you should use them a lot; very large eyes should be used with care, and so on. Develop your own personal vocabulary of what works for you. (More of this in Chapter 17, "The editor and editing.")

I do not recommend the following tricks, but I have seen them used, and they do give an indication of the sort of things that can happen on a shoot.

There was an actor being filmed in a long shot. He thought it should be a much closer shot, but the director wanted the long shot, so that was what was done. The only thing was, the actor could never remembered his lines properly in the long shot – they only came to him perfectly when he was being filmed in close-up. Funny thing, memory.

Another time, I heard an actor mention that he thought the two-shot he was in would be better as a single on him. The director thought otherwise, so they set up the two-shot. Only the actor spoke so softly, even when asked to speak up, that the only way to get proper sound was to bring the microphone really close to him. Since this meant that the camera could see it, the only way to get rid of the microphone was to tighten the shot. The actor ended up with his single shot after all. (Remember my interview in Korea?) What a strange series of events.

Multi-camera shoots

A multi-camera shoot is a continuation of the process already described. (See Chapter 10, "Rehearsals and technicals.") Things happen very quickly, with instructions usually channeled (and sometimes re-translated) through the first assistant/floor manager. If the cameras cannot see you according to the pre-planned camera script, then it is likely that **you** will be moved rather than a camera. (Moving you is easy; moving a camera may affect many other people.)

When a scene is shot, the director has just a few seconds to decide if: (a) it is all acceptable and she can move on to the next scene; (b) it was not acceptable and she must repeat the scene just done; or (c) one or two shots of the scene need to be repeated, and just those will be done. It is always a good idea for you to quietly tell the assistant director if you feel you could do it all better. The director may feel you were just fine, or she may add your concern to her own and decide to do the whole thing all over.

In the middle of a scene, do not stop – unless you are about to be seriously injured. Don't stop – even when everything seems to have gone wrong.

Let me tell you a story. I was shooting a multi-camera drama and got to my last three-minute scene with twenty minutes to spare. (Here I should add that I was working at the BBC, and when your time is up, that is it – they pull the plugs out!) I relaxed a little as we got ready for the last scene, which was set in a pub. I did not worry when first a light fell over, then a camera went on the blink, and then . . . And **then** it was five minutes to the end of recording time, and I realized that we would have to get the scene the first time, since there was no time to do it twice.

The scene was going nicely, the actors were acting, the smoke machine adding that haze that looks so nice in a pub setting, and the main character went off to get cigarettes and returned to his friends. We reached the last page of dialogue, cutting between nice close-ups on screen, when one of the friends (actually, a friend of mine – correction, a **former** friend of mine) stopped acting. "Sorry Patrick, we have to stop; his cigarette is on fire." And yes, it was indeed burning the way a cigarette shouldn't, but the point is, **it was not visible on screen!** By the time we had sorted it out, the deadline had been reached, the machines turned off. My producer had to negotiate with the unions for extra time, which was reluctantly granted; my show therefore cost several thousand pounds more than it should. If my "friend" had just kept on acting, all would have been fine. As it was, that producer has never re-employed me, and, no, I have not re-employed my friend. You see, **his** perception of what was going on was not the same as ours in the control room. Never stop acting – please!

Another one:

For the final image of an episode, I very much wanted a rising crane shot of the nurse-heroine walking down her hospital ward. My producer told me I could not afford the crane, so I had to abandon the idea. In the middle of the shoot, the technical director told me that they could rig a camera up onto a lighting hoist and get the shot that way. So we rushed and rushed, finished the show with five minutes to spare, got the camera rigged, rolled tape, and asked the heroine to walk. As she did, we started the lighting hoist – and she stopped walking. She stopped because she did not expect a noise (it was the noise of the hoist), and she thought something had gone wrong. By the time it was explained to her, time had run out, the cameras had been switched off, and she and I had lost her shot – because she had stopped acting before hearing the magical word "Cut."

In the shoot, the operative camera is the camera with a little red light on it. Although you should not wait for the light to come on before you act, it is certainly information that you can put to good use in a shoot. Imagine, for example, that you are facing another character, and you know that there are three cameras on the scene: one over her shoulder looking at you, one over your shoulder looking at her, and one out to the side getting a two-shot of the both of you. Well, if you can see the red light **ahead** on the camera, you know it is a tight shot of you (so you can do some good facial reactions). If you glimpse the red light out of the corner of your eye, you know it is the camera to the side with a wide two-shot (and so you can put in some good character revealing gestures). If you can't see a red light at all then that means that the shot must be coming over your shoulder to your fellow actor, so you know not to waggle your head into her shot.

The simple geometry used in shooting can teach you where the cameras will be, and how to guess what the shot is. When you act, part of your brain deals with the acting side and another part of your brain must function as your own private technical director, keeping tabs on where the cameras and microphones are, and noting and remembering which marks have to be hit.

Speaking of marks, the most useful actors are those who can hit their marks and find the camera. Although this applies to both single and multi-camera shoots, I am putting it here, since finding the camera is much more necessary in a fast-moving multi-camera shoot.

On page 177 is a picture of a bad three-shot, along with what the actor involved would see. This is followed on page 178 by a picture of a good three-shot, with the point of view of the same actor.

As I have mentioned before, one of the problems with working on a shoot is that, unlike in the theater, practically no one on the technical end has actually acted in front of a camera. So what is perfectly obvious to them can be all too obscure to you. As an example, looking at the first example of a bad three-shot, it is so crystal clear to all the co-workers – the director, the switcher, the camera people, the sound people – exactly **where** the actor should be standing that they can't understand that it is not at all clear to the actor. If you make sure that you see the **camera lens** exactly in the middle of the gap between your two fellow actors, then you will be correctly placed in the three-shot. (It is the same point of view as properly cheating yourself around, as in Chapter 4, "The camera.")

To act brilliantly, but to miss your mark and so put your face partially behind someone else, means that we cannot use the material at all. To act in a so-so manner, but to be in the correct place at all times, means that we can use the material. In other words, it is often more important to be in the right place than to act well, for your best acting moment can be rejected if you are one inch off your mark.

This upsets some actors, who know that a change of a move or gesture means a change of thought, but you must remember that a director can say to the camera operator, "Move the camera left," and it moves; to the boom operator, "Raise the boom," and it moves. When she says to the actor, "Move a little right," she does not want to hear, "What's my motivation?" I am afraid that there will be a tendency to treat you like all the other elements on the set, something to be moved and adjusted minutely and at will to suit the framed picture. As long as you understand this, you can contribute to the shoot as a co-worker, and not play actor-as-victim.

Be aware that as a scene progresses and the tension rises, it is more than likely that the shots will get closer; so your vocal level should be adjusted down. It is a very strange experience, building a speech emotionally, but getting quieter as you do it. Remind yourself of this from Chapter 6, "Sound and vocal levels."

Multi-camera shoots – film

These shoots are most particular to some Hollywood situation comedies, where the cameras waltz around the studio to meet actors who have rehearsed moving around a rehearsal room. Instead of video cameras all connected up to a control room, however, there are four film cameras all shooting simultaneously. (This means that everything is recorded all the time, not just the stuff seen by the camera with the red light.) It used to be all on film stock, but is now shot mostly on high definition digital cameras.

The director stands on the floor looking at a monitor with the four camera outputs on it. The advantage of this is that if anything goes wrong, it can be put right immediately. The disadvantage is that no one can be **sure** which shot is going to be used and so cannot be sure what size of shot to act for. (See *Complex sequences* in *Time codes* at the end of this chapter.)

What a bad three-shot looks like on screen . . .

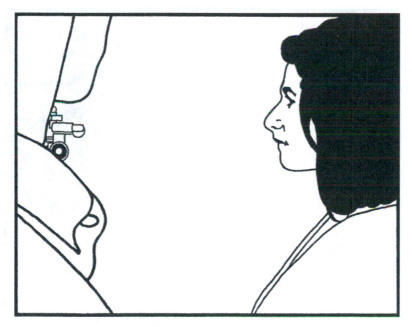

. . . and what the actor sees of the camera

What a good three-shot looks like on screen . . .

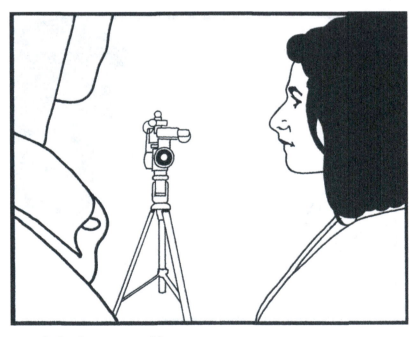

. . . and what the actor sees of the camera

Multi-camera shoot secrets

- Don't stop.
- Be aware of the red light on the front of a camera.
- Hit your marks – and hit the deep three-shots.
- Build your emotions as you decrease the volume.
- Particularly with a studio audience, don't speak louder than the star.

I was watching the making of one such comedy in Los Angeles. The director was a courteous gentleman ("Action, please!"), and the actors were superb. There was a large office in the set's background, full of bit part actors doing wonderfully directed detailed business. When the director called out for a line to be repeated (because the actor had just spoken through a laugh by the audience), all the background artists quietly backtracked two or three steps, ready to be in the correct position for the repeated line.

Good, good screen acting. Perhaps I should talk here again of what to do with audience reactions. The main thing is, do **not** pitch your performance to them – and there will be a tremendous temptation for you to do so. That whole, lovely audience is sitting out there just waiting to receive your finely honed performance, but you must never forget: **It is only an Audience of One**. Look closely at the people in the audience, and you will see that they do not watch the actors on the floor. They watch the nearest television monitor and listen to the sound as it comes over the loudspeakers. So you perform for the cameras, as usual, and use the audience reactions to give you **timing** for the laughs.

And because the energy level for a comedy is higher than for, say, a heavy drama, you can use the simplest of my rules: **Never speak louder than the star**. After all, the regulars in the show will have evolved a style and format that fits the show; and the audience, both in the studio and at home, will assume that whatever the stars do is correct. Base your performance on **that** level.

Conclusions

I think it takes a lot of talent to come across as ordinary.

If you come across very well, with good, believable acting full of emotion and passion, and you hit all your marks and always project to where the microphone is, well, I think that takes extraordinary talent.

We sometimes disparage good actors, precisely because of their skill at making a difficult, technical sequence appear easy and ordinary. "Well, I could have done as well as that," we confidently claim, not understanding quite how difficult it is. You, having read this far, will now know that you cannot just walk into a shoot straight off the street and achieve instant overnight success.

It takes work, hard work, and this book is showing you just what sort of work you need to do. For some good examples of this, of wonderful performances – both artistic and technical – watch *Nine Lives*, a series of nine ten-minute scenes all shot in one take. (See *Long takes* in *Time codes* at the end of this chapter.)

Then, take a look again at the beginning of this chapter (page 166), and the seemingly calm Goldie Hawn surrounded by all that chaos and elements of a shoot. Never forget when you see a nice quiet moment like this on the screen that just outside the frame is a different world of people and equipment – and appreciate the talent and skill needed to act serenely in these circumstances. Remind yourself that the rule is **whatever works** – what feels right may not look or come over as right. (See *Unreality* in *Time codes* at the end of this chapter.)

Things that I hate that actors do on a shoot

- Actors who stop acting before the assistant director or the director shouts "Cut!"
- Actors who don't remember what they did when the camera is moved to shoot the "reverses."
- Actors who want to be "real," and so will not properly cheat their faces around to the camera.
- Actors who (unannounced) change things "because it feels wrong."
- Actors who just do not understand (or have never taken the trouble to understand) the craft of the job they are undertaking – acting on screen.

Things that I love that actors do on a shoot

- Actors who come to the shoot with all their business planned and rehearsed and who know their lines very well.
- Actors who add extra ideas and business to the shoot, understanding what is possible and what is not.
- Actors who do the same business on the same syllable of a speech in every take.
- Actors who automatically ease themselves into the right position so that they fill the screen, their two-shot is maintained, or they come to a perfect deep three-shot.
- Actors who understand the craft of screen acting and make additions and suggestions within the framework of what is possible both technically **and** in the time available.

Chapter 13: Time codes for the shoot

(Rounded up to the nearest 5 seconds)

Complex sequences

Barton Fink (leaving John Turturro and Judy Davis, we go down the plug hole)	01:04:40
The Blind Side (lots of mirrors for Sandra Bullock and Tim McGraw)	00:53:40
Bridget Jones's Diary (two cameras simultaneously shooting Renée Zellweger singing with different sized shots)	00:05:35
The Dead (mirrors and moves for Donal McCann and Anjelica Huston)	01:05:25
The Ghost (how long to rehearse and get the note passing to be correct?)	01:56:05
Heartburn (jeweler's shop with reflections for Meryl Streep and Sidney Armus)	01:32:45
Munich (inside the car: cleverness of camera and Steven Spielberg's staging)	00:56:10
The Shawshank Redemption (long shot and close-up all put together)	01:57:35
Stage Fright (two and a half days for Marlene Dietrich and Richard Todd)	00:00:55

Continuity problems

GoodFellas (toy bricks all over the place for Ray Liotta and Lorraine Bracco)	01:21:00
Match Point (Jonathan Rhys Meyers's hand is down or up on the bench)	01:11:05
The Usual Suspects (an airplane with a changing number of engines?)	00:30:00

Long takes

Atonement (very complicated walk for James McAvoy and friends)	01:02:35
Barton Fink (a long take to start the film)	00:01:35
Bonfire of the Vanities (an opening "clever" shot)	00:01:25

Carlito's Way (a complicated escalator sequence with Al Pacino)	02:04:55
Children of Men (a car chase full of "how did they do that?" moments; see "Camera Movement Children of Men" YouTube 2011)	00:25:05
Children of Men (baby rescue, with guns and explosions and – everything)	01:20:20
GoodFellas (back entrance to club: the underbelly and the surface sheen)	00:30:10
Hanna (Eric Bana gets out of a bus, does a long walk, and then has a long fight)	01:01:45
Henry V (very long walk for Kenneth Branagh, with lots of soldiers)	01:50:05
A History of Violence (a slow opening shot with terrible consequences)	00:00:15
Love Actually (following the Prime Minister from his car to deep inside Number 10, where he talks to his staff with his Hugh Grant-isms)	00:07:05
Nine Lives (all nine little films are one continuous shot – but look particularly at the Robin Wright and Glenn Close scenes)	
The Player (a very long opening shot, competing with all others)	00:00:10
The Protector (Warrior King) (Tom Yum Goong) (the longest single developing shot Steadicam fight)	00:59:15
Touch of Evil (Orson Welles's long complicated opening shot, which started the trend)	00:00:55

Trouble on set

Bus Stop (lines fed from above to Marilyn Monroe? – not if this is the edited version)	00:56:00
Day for Night (La nuit américaine) (the cat won't do what is wanted)	00:51:20
Day for Night (La nuit américaine) (finally a cat performance that works)	00:53:25
Lady in the Lake (what Robert Montgomery has to do when the camera "is" him)	00:03:55
The Prince and the Showgirl (we are told that it was Marilyn's fault it needed twenty-five takes to get this shot right – and now see that it is a very complicated track and crane sequence, needing many takes to get it right)	00:14:40
Roman Holiday (William Wyler told Audrey Hepburn she would be sacked if she did not improve)	01:34:00
Sirens (fast circular track round the table of seven people arguing)	00:35:45

Unreality

Children of Men (Disc 2: delivering a baby)	00:00:00
Contact (Special Features: Alien Encounters: The Special Effects: Bill Clinton)	00:04:20
Day for Night (La nuit américaine) (a false window for Jacqueline Bisset)	01:20:25
My Week with Marilyn (Judi Dench at the read-through – but she was not there)	00:15:05
Side by Side (Disc 2: James Cameron on what's real)	00:20:10
Side by Side (Disc 2: John Malkovich: camera truth)	00:08:45
Sin City (opening sequence)	00:00:20

Working on set

Day for Night (La nuit américaine) (opening shot of what it is really like)	00:01:50
Magnolia (Disc 2: Magnolia diary: first shot)	00:10:55
Magnolia (Disc 2: Magnolia diary: tracking on set)	00:46:15
Magnolia (what the tracking shot looked like in the film)	02:51:25
Marnie (Bonus Material: Documentary: technical kiss)	00:22:10
Marnie (Bonus Material: Documentary: Hitchcock moves her face)	00:31:05

The complete list of films, dates, and directors is in the *Index of films* at the end of the book.

All the time codes are taken from my DVD player in London, with the DVDs bought in the UK, so you can know how many minutes and seconds the clip is from the start of the movie. Where I can, I have noted the different versions of the films.

There may well be variations in the time for different machines and formats, but these should be consistent for your download, DVD player, or computer, and so once you note the differences, you will know where to find each of the above clips.

Bette Davis

A bit of Bette we don't use

14

THE EDITOR AND EDITING

General

The most common experience a director has in the editing stage is staring at the screen and wondering why he did not **insist** that the actors do more. There it is again – more, rather than less.

It does not matter what the writer intended or the director planned; in the editing, the editor is only dealing with what is **there**. The raw material he uses is no more and no less than what the camera recorded – and what the actors put into the lens. (See *Acting* in *Time codes* at the end of this chapter.)

Reactions

I know I have gone on about reactions before in Chapter 5, "Reactions and business." Now, here is another way of looking at them.

When two people are talking to each other, it is often filmed by putting the camera on one of them and recording all that he says as well as the moments in between when he listens. The camera is then pointed at the other actor, and the process is repeated. In the editing, the editor does **not** just put the person who is talking on the screen; it is **not** talking heads that we are after.

The editor will often start off on one person, and then look at the shot of the other person listening, to see if there is anything of interest going on. (See *Listening reactions* in *Time codes* at the end of this chapter.) Frequently – especially with inexperienced actors – not a lot is, in fact, happening. I have watched in horror as a three-minute take went by in the editing room all on one actor's face, and he did not do **anything** except say his one line.

We must start again with what **is** real and what **appears** to be real. In real life, if you are listening to another person speaking, you tend to put on a "polite" expression; you certainly do **not** allow your face to reflect everything you are thinking as that person is speaking. You do **not** let large expressions flow across your face, for that is a social "signal" that you wish to speak, that you wish to interrupt the conversation with some comment of your own.

On stage, if you were to react clearly and largely during another person's speech, then you would be rightly accused of "upstaging" and would be given a bad time in the dressing room afterward.

In other words, it is "unreal" to react while another person is speaking; it is "real" for your face to react only a little. But it is also boring and unusable if you put **that** onto the screen.

When an editor/director is cutting from someone speaking to the person listening, he often only wants to take a second or so of the listening shot to liven up the talking shot.

As I described before, one can scan **reams** of listening before finding something that is usable. (Yes! **There** is something. Oh, he was only blinking.) Now, if the actor did three different reactions in a row, it would **feel** most peculiar. If it were shown to an audience, it would also **look** very peculiar. But the editor is **not** going to use **all** the reactions: He is just looking for a snippet, a "nice slice of a reaction," and if you present several, it makes you a more useful actor, doesn't it? You will **feel** peculiar doing it, but you will be presenting the editor with choices and allowing the artistic process of editing, shaping performances in the editing room, to progress with plenty of good raw material.

I was once shooting a scene between a husband and wife, where the wife had all the talking – the husband listened throughout and had just one line. By the time I got to the scene I was running late, so I shot the close-up of her first, getting all her lines down. I then turned the camera on the husband and shot what was mostly him listening. It was really boring, so seeing that I had just a minute and a half before the compulsory wrap, I asked (actually, I probably shrieked) for the camera to keep turning, rushed up to the actor and begged and implored him to let all sorts of emotions and feelings cascade across his face. I promised faithfully that I would not use anything that appeared unnatural or untrue. We then shot his reaction shots for one last time before the end of the shoot.

His face **still** showed practically nothing, so, walking away from the shoot and finding myself alongside the actor, I gently asked him why he had not done what I had asked him to do. "Well, Patrick, I **wanted** to," he replied anxiously, "but it felt like I was just pulling faces."

Yes? There was no reply I could give him, and in the editing we played the whole scene on the wife's face, for there was nothing I could cut to that added to or advanced the story. (You see, directors are not as powerful as some actors would make us out to be.) If only he had "pulled" just one face, maybe that would have been all the editor needed to cut to his face briefly and so help the audience understand what his character was feeling as his screen wife went on and on.

Secret thoughts

When the screen is showing only you, the audience have this belief that only **they** can see what you are going through. If your face expresses how you really feel, the audience will believe that they are being "told" a secret, a secret that the other character cannot see.

I was directing a scene where a wife had to indicate to her husband that she did **not** want to be invited next door for a cup of tea. I suggested that she give a little "no" shake of her head toward her husband. "I could not do that – the next door neighbor would see it," she anxiously told me. But for this moment she was being filmed in close-up, and I reassured her that although **in real life** the neighbor could see her negative reaction, when it was on the screen, the audience would believe that only her husband would be let in on her "true" feelings.

She did it – very reluctantly – and when cut together it worked very well. It showed again how unwise it is to trust your feelings until you are experienced enough to know what "true" feelings are as defined by the camera. Anamaria Marinca did not want her fiancé's family to know she was not happy, Jean Hagen did not want her audience to see how angry she was – but both were able to show the screen audience what was going on in their minds. (See *Secrets* in *Time codes* at the end of this chapter.)

Eye-flashes

When you are in a scene with anybody else (but particularly three or more), the editor likes to cut from face to face with motivating moments, and one of the easiest of these is when one character flashes a glance at another.

By doing these flashes, you help the editor (and, incidentally, get your face onto the screen more often as the editor uses your face to "bounce" from one face to another). No, it is not just a selfish thing, but a practical one; I worked with an actor who had the habit of looking **away** from the other person he was speaking to, especially at the beginning of a speech. This meant that when the shots were edited together, you often forgot where the person he was speaking to was, and it all got very confusing.

Continuity

It is, of course, in editing that the effects of good and bad continuity become apparent.

It is a truism to say that your moves, and in particular your bits of business (drinking from a glass, turning the page of a book), should be at the same **precise** point in a speech when it is shot from different angles.

It always astounds screen people (but not stage people!) that an actor can act a speech one way and then a few minutes later do the same speech with the pieces of business in different places. (Part of this is that an actor always wants to improve things and so regards the shooting as a continuous process. This naturally works well on the stage but can be a drawback in screen work.)

Now, there are many people who should (and do) remind the actor of his continuity – the continuity supervisor/girl (or script supervisor/girl), the production assistant if there is one, the camera operator, the director. It is,

187

however, no consolation to you that it is someone else's fault if you have such differing continuity that the editor cannot cut to your best moments.

We all want the best, and the editor wants to put on screen the best moments that he sees in the rushes. It is always sad when we cannot use them, because, in the two matching shots, the moves (or angle of head or angle of shoulders) are such that we cannot cut to and from each shot where we **want** but only when we **can**. (See *Continuity problems* in *Time codes* at the end of this chapter.)

Once two actors were filmed walking across a field. The camera tracked alongside them shooting two different setups: One was a two-shot looking one way (one character nearer the camera) and then the other way (positions reversed). One of the actors was smoking, and the director and editor were astounded to see that he took the same puff on the same syllable of the speech all through the long scene. This meant that they could **always** cut from one shot to the other, and they could cut to the best moments, not just cut when they could.

How much better it is to be this sort of actor. It is protection for you to go into a shoot with your bits of business already mapped out and rehearsed.

It can be a great distraction to you and your interpretation if you are acting in a meal scene, the camera pointed over your shoulder toward the other actor, and then the camera turns around; and just before you are about to launch into your close-up speech, the continuity supervisor hands you a whole **sheaf** of notes about **when** you should lift the glass, take a mouthful, lean forward, and so on. I have seen performances suffer from too many continuity notes being handed over – but they **have** to be given.

Some actors decide that getting all those continuity notes is too boring, so their solution is to keep their hands in their pockets all the time, eat nothing at a meal time, and never smoke. It does, of course, make their lives **easier** on the shoot, but does it make their performances **better**? It is far preferable to work out business in advance, bring it into the shoot, and allow excellent continuity to add to the performance (and add to the number of times the editor can cut to you). Expert film actors as different as Michael Caine and Peter O'Toole admit to extensive preparation – rearranging the furniture in their hotel rooms or laying out a table – and going over and over the moves or business until they are completely at ease with it all. On the shoot they can devote their time and talent to the important things, like sharing their best moments with the camera, rather than struggling to remember which hand picked up which spoon when.

If an actor already knows and appreciates the importance of the continuity, then he can turn it to his advantage.

For example, an editor likes to cut from one picture to another with a large piece of business. It helps to motivate the cut and disguises some of the inevitable mismatches in continuity, for unless you are working on a project that can take infinite pains, it is almost impossible to cut from three people at one angle to the same people from a different angle, and find a moment when all the heads, shoulders, arms, hands, and so on are perfectly matching for a good continuous cut.

So the editor looks for that piece of business, and the experienced actor finds that his character just happens to want to do a nice big movement or gesture just before a moment he thinks would be good to be featured in. And he has helped the editor decide by giving him some cut-motivating business.

Wise actor.

Visitors to America are often surprised at how big the skies appear in Cowboy Country. This is because in the films they have seen at home filmed in these locations, the sky has been left out. And why? The changing patterns of clouds make it a nightmare to match one shot with another when the sky keeps changing, so the directors and DOPs have got used to having as little sky as possible, to avoid cloud continuity problems (See *Continuity problems* in *Time codes* at the end of this chapter.)

Digital editing

Now that all editing is done on a computer, this changes the way the editor works. For a start, it is much easier to experiment, to try things out – often in the absence of the director, who is not as continuously welcome in the edit room as he once was. I have found that when I make a suggestion or ask for a change, the editor has already tried it out in my absence (and in many cases can immediately show it to me) and found that the change did not work. (See *Acting* in *Time codes* at the end of this chapter.)

This even applies to multi-camera shoots, where the cameras are in effect edited together at the time of recording. With digital editing, cuts are tightened, actors' pauses are taken out – all the tricks of a single camera edit session are applied in part to the multi-camera shoot.

Editors tell me they now spend a lot of their creative time correcting directorial errors in "crossing the line," "breaking the 180 degree rule" – or in layman's terms getting their film grammar wrong. As an actor you can help by being aware that if in **this** shot you are looking or moving in a certain direction, then you should be doing the same in the shot that would come next – and the actor you are having a conversation with should be looking in the **opposite** direction (but put your concerns through the first assistant – not the director, for obvious reasons). (See *Crossing the line – the 180° rule* in *Time codes* at the end of this chapter.)

Michael Caine's famous (if flawed) advice to actors not to blink no longer applies, as editors can easily – and do – remove any blinks they do not like. (It is flawed because it only applied to those actors – like Michael – who have fair eyelashes and refuse to wear mascara.) In his last film, *The Score*, Marlon Brando refused to smile for director Frank Oz – so after the shoot was over they edited one in with a digital effect. In the film *Black Swan*, Natalie Portman's face was (on occasion) superimposed on the ballet dancer who was doing all the tricky stuff for her. These digital tricks are being done now – so they can only increase in the future. (See *Digital effects* in *Time codes* at the end of this chapter.)

Put yourself in the editor's shoes to think "What would they like to see in the edit suite?" – and then provide it. Guy Ducker has written a very good article on this, "Acting for the Edit," which is well worth tracking down.

Watching an editing session

If you ever get the chance to sit in on an editing session, **take the opportunity**. By watching what is kept (and what is not), what is effective (and what is not), you will quickly see what is required to be a good performer on the screen, and you will be able to put these ideas into practice the next time you are in front of the camera. A fractional difference, such as the slight change in Bette Davis's eyes at the beginning of this chapter (see page 184), can make a huge difference to what the shot means to us, the viewers. Don't, whatever you do, say anything in the edit session, however much you may be tempted. Bite your tongue, for any comments you may make will usually be about getting more of you onto the screen and will annoy the editor, as well as feed the belief that actors are only interested in their close-ups.

I know that there are actors who insist that they "never watch their performances" or "never watch the rushes/dailies." That is like a stage actor paying no attention at all to any audience reaction or giving his best performance after the audience has gone home. (Alright, I know there are **some** who do that.) Be proud of your craft: Learn all you can about it, and enjoy practicing it.

Editing secrets

- More reactions can give the editor more choices (to cut to you).
- Give plenty of eye-flashes to the editor.
- Good continuity gives more chances to the editor to cut to your best bits.
- Put in a nice bit of business before a moment you want on screen.
- Don't think about reality; think about creating the appearance of reality.

Chapter 14: Time codes for the editor and editing

(Rounded up to the nearest 5 seconds)

Acting

Side by Side (Disc 2: Walter Murch on digital acting)   00:12:25

Continuity problems

GoodFellas (toy bricks come and go for Lorraine Bracco and Ray Liotta)	01:21:00
Jubal (vast skies with very different cloud covers)	01:28:05
Match Point (hand on or off bench for Jonathan Rhys Meyers)	01:11:05
No Country for Old Men (overcast skies with a sudden burst of blue)	00:29:40
The Usual Suspects (how many engines does the airplane have?)	00:30:00

Crossing the line – the 180° rule

Hamlet 1996 (Reece Dinsdale as Guildenstern barely gets a look in)	01:09:05
Hanna (who is looking at who in bed? Which shoulder for Saoirse Ronan? Or for Jessica Barden?)	00:58:10
Journey to the Center of the Earth (two in doorway looking the same way)	00:04:10
Journey to the Center of the Earth (three in doorway all looking the same way)	00:14:20
The Shining (Kubrick deliberately chose this confusion for Jack Nicholson and Philip Stone)	US 01:27:05; UK 01:08:25

Digital effects

Atonement (James McAvoy acting with many invisible background extras)	01:02:35
Black Swan (Natalie Portman and friend as the White Swan)	01:25:30
Black Swan (and both as the Black Swan)	01:32:10
The Lord of the Rings: The Two Towers (Andy Serkis as the Gollum)	00:06:40
The Score (Marlon Brando is made to smile)	01:52:40
Side by Side (Disc 2: Anne Coates on tears in Keanu Reeves's eyes)	00:16:25

Editing tricks

The Day of the Jackal (edited to hide the mistake of Edward Fox and the policeman looking the same way)	01:41:40
The Fifth Element (cut where you can between Gary Oldman and Tricky)	00:44:45
Rain Man (making sure there is no intelligence in Dustin Hoffman's eyes)	00:42:20

Listening reactions

Before the Devil Knows You're Dead (Marisa Tomei has good reactions in car)	01:17:45
Bonnie and Clyde (everyone reacts well in the car)	01:03:15
Last Night (Keira Knightley, the wife, and Eva Mendes, the rival, react differently)	00:05:20
Love in a Cold Climate (no one speaks for twenty-two seconds)	01:12:20
Prime Suspect (Prime Suspect 1: A Price to Pay) (two acting giants, Zoe Wanamaker and Helen Mirren, battling with reactions)	03:00:10
Six Days Seven Nights (sugar coated between Harrison Ford and Anne Heche)	00:28:25

Secrets

4 Months, 3 Weeks and 2 Days (4 luni, 3 saptamâni si 2 zile) (family meal, with Anamaria Marinca showing us what she is feeling)	01:14:00
Bridget Jones's Diary (Renée Zellweger's secret thought)	00:52:10
Bridget Jones's Diary (and now her MCUs)	00:52:40
Hugo (Ben Kingsley's thoughts on seeing the drawings)	00:05:35
Last Night (Keira Knightley's secret thoughts seeing her husband with another)	00:04:55
Magnolia (Tom Cruise trying not to answer questions)	01:24:25
The Prince and the Showgirl (big close-up of Marilyn Monroe giving a toast)	00:24:40
Singin' in the Rain (Jean Hagen would not really let her beloved audience see how upset she was – unless only the film audience was seeing it)	00:11:45

The complete list of films, dates, and directors is in the *Index of films* at the end of the book.

All the time codes are taken from my DVD player in London, with the DVDs bought in the UK, so you can know how many minutes and seconds the clip is from the start of the movie. Where I can, I have noted the different versions of the films.

There may well be variations in the time for different machines and formats, but these should be consistent for your download, DVD player, or computer, and so once you note the differences, you will know where to find each of the above clips.

EPILOGUE

A good workman has a good box of tools and knows how to use every one. An expert workman also knows **which** tool to use **when**. Everything in the toolbox is not used on every job at every moment.

In this book I have tried to teach you the whys and wherefores of different techniques for the screen. Not all of them will be of use to all of you all the time, but they should give you a better range of choices to make when faced with differing problems of acting in front of the camera.

A great deal of professional acting nowadays means working on the screen, yet those connected with training are mostly past and current stage performers. Even those who have screen experience often have only had it in front of the camera, but they do not always know what goes on behind the scenes that influences what goes onto the screen itself.

It is wonderful to have a strong belief about styles of acting. It becomes wrong, however, when it is religious in its intensity, and the belief grows that there is only one true faith. Just as many find different ways to worship, so there are different ways to act.

When you started to drive a car, you wondered how on earth it was possible to talk and drive at the same time. It all seemed very difficult, and yet soon you were chatting away, weaving in and out of traffic. Maneuvering the car has become so automatic you barely notice or think about it.

That is how screen acting can be when you are experienced. It **will** feel a little odd at the start. Just as you did not give up driving because it felt strange at first, so feeling strange while screen acting should not put you off, but should lead to more study, practice – and wild enjoyment!

You may well find that for a long period of time you will not be bothered with these techniques, that your natural acting is fine and just what the screen likes and needs. Then one day you will be asked to do something technical – "Raise that book right up into frame" – and if you are not ready for it, the demands of the screen can ruin your concentration and acting. It is for these moments that you need these secrets!

THE FAMOUS SCREEN ACTING CHECKLIST

You could copy these pages, put them into your pocket and reread them when waiting around on a set, or at an interview. Try not to show them to others – after all, you had to buy this book for its secrets – and so should they!

A. Etiquette

1: Keep going until the director shouts "Cut!" Then keep on acting for a bit. Do not stop a take for **any** reason (except injury or death).
2: If you mess up a line, still keep going, so it is the director who calls a halt to the proceedings – you do not know what they can get up to in post-production to fix things.
3: Never look directly into the camera lens unless you are specifically asked to do so.
4: Do not ask the director what size of shot it is. (Ask the camera operator where the cut-off point is.)
5: Hit your marks! Being in the right place is often more important than saying the right line – or even acting well.
6: Keep your concentration and eyelines all through the tedium of line up and rehearsal; it helps both your fellow actors **and** the crew.
7: An actor only has status between "Action!" and "Cut!" (but a star has it at all times between "Good morning darling!" and "That's a wrap for today – will we see you tomorrow?").
8: Never say "No"; say "Maybe," or "My schedule says I have a possible conflict; what is your project?" Never say you do not want to play a particular role; say (or have your agent or manager say – that is what they are for) that you have a scheduling conflict. People **hate** being rejected. (As an actor, you know that only too well.)

B. The camera

1: Let the lens be a magnet that draws your face toward it wherever it is, and always **motivate** this cheated eyeline.

© Patrick Tucker, 2015.

2: If both your eyes cannot "see" the camera lens, then your face will appear to be obscured when viewed on the screen.

3: Keep on the imaginary "red carpet" that stretches out from the front of the camera. Remember, shots are composed in depth.

4: In a deep three-shot, stand where you can see the camera lens in the middle of the gap between the other two people (so that on the screen you will appear to be in the middle of the gap).

5: Cheating your **shoulders** around to the camera (having your back to the person you are speaking to) makes it much easier to cheat. You will then look over your shoulder to speak to the other character, and your **face** will naturally come back round to the front.

6: Use that combination (your **off**-camera eye to the other person's **on**-camera eye) that shows more of your face to Mr. Camera when you are talking to another character.

C. The picture

1: Cheat business and hands up into the "hot" area.

2: The size of shot predicts the style of acting within the frame:

Long shot (LS) = large theater acting – big gestures.

Medium shot (MS) = small theater acting – theatrical truth and reality.

Medium close-up (MCU) = studio or classroom acting – the real thing.

Big close-up (BCU) = intimate acting – just think it, and put your energy **and** concentration into putting your thoughts onto your face.

3: Be prepared to stand embarrassingly close when acting and speaking with other characters.

4: There is no reality outside the frame; time and/or distance outside it may be expanded or contracted. The truth is what we see on the screen, not what we feel is true for ourselves.

D. Voice

1: Never speak louder than the star (or a regular in a series). They set the style for the program, so **match** their vocal levels.

2: Do not let the microphone hear your lines. It should **just** be able to eavesdrop on you, wherever it is. In a close-up, this will often mean **not** projecting to the person you are speaking to.

3: For greater intensity, **speed up** rather than **speak up** – listen to the way stars speak in their movies.

4: If you are told to tone it all down, try reducing **only** your volume but keep the scale of your gestures. The over-the-top bit (OTT) was probably just your voice.

5: When speaking at low levels, do **not** lose your sparkly energy or adopt a very slow pace. Every now and again have a loud moment, so the audience knows that your quiet delivery is an acting **choice**.

6: When using a strong accent that is not your own, you will tend to speak louder than usual. Speak **softer** than usual when using an accent.

7: As the scene builds, you would expect the voices to rise. But since the shots are liable to get tighter, you have to square the circle by getting more intense – and quieter – at the same time.

8: At low levels of speaking, all other sounds seem too loud, so be careful with all footsteps, clattering cups, newspaper rustling – sometimes even your breathing.

9: Do not whisper unless it is **meant** to be secret.

10: Do **not** overlap dialogue. The only exception is if you are in a contained shot, so gently inquire if they are going to cross-cut with reverses, or if it is all going to be shot in one setup.

E. Acting

1: Your main acting note is that **you** were given the part, so work your looks, personality, and background into your performance.

2: Remember – screen acting is **more real than real**, for you are removing your public mask and showing your private thoughts.

3: You often have no rehearsal at all, and only meet the director when you walk onto the set – so **bring in your acting decisions** to the shoot (actually, you ought to bring them in to the **audition**).

4: The shots the director chooses are in themselves acting notes, so obey their implicit instructions:

Long shot = let your **body** do the acting.

Reaction shot = **do** a reaction.

Two-shot = **react** as you listen to the other actor.

Close-up = put your thoughts onto your **face**.

Cutaway = put your acting **into** the extreme close-up on screen (your twitching hand, the property you are holding, etc.).

5: When the shoot starts there will be a lot of new things to learn (such as where to stand, when to move), and you might then forget your lines if you have not **learned them very well**. You may be required to change lines and business at the very last moment, so be flexible, in a **very** cooperative way!

6: Use surprising truth (be unpredictable); but when you do, the audience must believe that this – and any move or gesture you make – is what your character wanted or needed to do.

© Patrick Tucker, 2015.

7: Do **all** your acting for an **Audience of One** – the camera.

8: Create good acting reasons for all your pieces of business (especially camera-motivating ones).

9: The lines should fit you like a glove. If they do not, and you are not given the rehearsal time to create the character who **would** say those lines, then ask to adjust the dialogue to suit you (but ask for permission to say these altered lines, and make sure the production assistant or script supervisor knows).

10: Act a negative thought ("I am not going to speak") in a positive way (open your mouth as if to speak, then close it again).

11: Give yourself something to do **after** a shot ends. This will keep your face alive right to the end of the take.

12: Let your inner voice give you those continuous instructions that silent movie actors got from their directors' megaphones.

13: Let an acting impulse that would lead to a move on stage lead to a gesture or look on the screen.

14: When the camera is on you in a single shot, it is as if you were alone on a stage and all the other performers were in the wings: **Now** how do you act?

15: As you continue shooting, you will naturally enrich your performance as take succeeds take; make sure you still have good continuity – or that the director is consulted on any change you have discovered and want to include.

F. Reactions and business

1: React before you speak, and to the upcoming thought (this can be done on your intake of breath before a line). Sometimes you can do two or three reactions before speaking.

2: React **while** others are speaking – on screen we watch the listening person, and in a single shot on the other character it gives the director and editor an opportunity to cut to **you**.

3: The best moments are nonverbal ones – so give yourself **time** (just like the stars do).

4: Pace is a series of continuous events, **not** continuous speaking. Let your face show the continually changing thoughts in your head: "like a candle in the wind."

5: Remember the camera cannot follow fast movements, so lift that cup slowly; gently rise up out of that chair.

6: In a multi-camera studio a red light shows which camera is on, so keep a reaction on your face until it has been sampled by that camera, and the red light goes out.

7: Eyes can be very effective. Try looking up as well as down, especially when "listening" to another character. (Some try looking from one eye to the other, or from the eyes to the mouth.)

© Patrick Tucker, 2015.

G. Auditions and interviews

1: "The moment he/she came in the door, I knew I had found my actor," says the director, so enter the audition with that belief - doing **through-the-door casting**.

2: Get good at saying hello, shaking hands, and saying your name – give a good impression the moment you enter the room.

3: In auditions, they are not looking for potential, they are looking for **results**, so give a committed interpretation during a reading.

4: At an interview, plan at least one major reaction in **your** own lines and one in the **other person's** lines. **Positively** listen (react) during the "feed" lines, and keep your eyes **up**.

5: Don't be too loud; better to be asked to speak up than to be judged "too theatrical."

6: Proudly play your type – and then surprise them with your acting choices (like the British actor Bill Nighy).

H. The editor

1: The better your continuity, the easier it is for the editor to cut to you for your best moments. Excellent continuity is not your complete responsibility, but you **should** make it your ambition.

2: Editors like to cut on movement, so put some in before one of your important bits of acting that you would like to be featured.

3: Mark changes of thought with such pieces of business.

4: During a speech, look to the other characters. The editor needs your "eye-flashes" to motivate cuts.

5: Reactions do not have to be logical or consistent. The editor is only looking for a slice of a good reaction, and several different ones give him a better choice (to cut to you!). But is this just pulling faces? Yes, and it is gold dust for a director and editor.

6: Unless you are drop dead gorgeous (so we just want the time to enjoy your features), beware of **NOF** – "nothing on face."

7: Only **you** really care about how your character comes over – so fight for your character's moments in the sun; make sure they will want to cut to **you**.

I. Final thoughts

1: To come across as truthful on screen needs both talent **and** technique.

2: Less is **not** more; it is much less (because mostly you do not have your whole body to act with). Effective screen acting demands **more** reactions from you (but with **less** volume).

3: For television the crew will tend to work until the shot has no technical errors; for movies they will happily work until the performances are also there (so for television work you had better be right first time).

4: Preparing for a performance in the theatre you rehearse **publicly** with others; for the screen, you prepare **privately** by yourself.

5: Remember, in the theater you push **out** to the audience, but on screen you pull the audience **in**.

6: Do not panic over any problem. There never has been a trouble-free shoot, and anyway tomorrow's problem is already in the mail.

7: Do not do today's job as an audition for tomorrow's. Do it because **this** is what you wanted to do today. (Well it is, isn't it?) And when you are out of work, you will regret not concentrating absolutely on today's acting.

8: All rules are made to be broken – so **know which rules you are breaking**! (And have a very good reason for doing so.)

9: Screen acting is going to be a very important part of your acting career, so find out how to **enjoy** and relish it all. If you allow it, it can (and **should**) be a lot of fun.

ACTING EXERCISES

The relevant exercises and practical examples I have developed over the years are scattered throughout this book, and for those of you who are interested in teaching these, or in practically developing your own talents, I thought it would be nice to put them all here together.

Be careful that you don't just do an exercise without understanding the reason behind it.

The equipment needed is not so elaborate. As a basic minimum you need a camera and a monitor to show the results. But you **do** need to have a separate microphone (and those of you who have read from the beginning will know exactly why).

Do **not** use the microphone attached on top of the camera, for this will give you the wrong sound for the picture. Get a separate microphone, or remove the camera mike and use that with an extension lead, and attach it (ideally) to a fishpole to become your boom (a long pole with a cushioned mount at the end to accept the microphone). A fishpole can be bought for a reasonable sum if you get an aluminum one and somewhat more if you get the useful collapsible carbon fiber one.

If you do not have access to a fishpole, then a microphone can be attached to something as simple as a broom handle; the problem is that the microphone will pick up any and all vibrations, and you should try to find a way of cushioning the microphone from the pole. Manufacture something out of foam rubber or elastic bands.

Get everyone in the group to experience the different jobs needed to record screen work, and learn to appreciate the work each department does. Discover the teamwork necessary for anything good to be put onto the screen.

Camera operator   Operates the camera, pointing it in the right direction, and getting the correct size of shot by adjusting the zoom lens. Often, it will not be appropriate to leave the camera on autofocus (where it focuses on the nearest object), and as it is tricky for an inexperienced operator to point, zoom, **and** focus, an **assistant camera operator** can be used, whose job is to look at the monitor and keep the camera focused on whatever should be in focus at that time (maybe the actor farthest away, with the nearer actors out of focus).

Boom operator

Holds the boom, and thus the microphone, at the correct distance from the actor so that good sound is obtained and the boom is not in shot. During the technical rehearsal, the microphone should be dipped in and out of shot so the boom operator can gauge where the edge of frame is. The operator should always boom the picture that she sees; for example, if there are two people talking, one closer to the camera than the other, it is the **nearer** person who should be boomed, since the viewer would expect the person standing farther off to sound more distant than the one standing much nearer. A very common fault is to record a scene and discover there was no sound. (I speak from bitter experience.) A good way around this is for the boom operator to wear headphones that tell her what sound is being picked up. (These can also indicate if there is a lot of "rustle" from the boom and microphone itself, drowning out the actors' voices.)

Assistant director

Or floor manager: runs the floor; puts marks down where the director or actor wants; prompts during rehearsals where necessary; hands properties to the actors (sometimes lying on the floor and handing up a prepared cup of tea, sheaf of papers, etc.); and calls out the number of the shot and take.

Technician (not needed with digital cameras)

Operates the recorder, if a separate one is being used. Is responsible for seeing that the tape is actually moving and that sound is coming in from the microphone, as shown by the meter, if you have one.

Director

Plans, organizes, starts, and stops each take.

Actors

If it is not a fully professional setup, it is possible that the actors can actually **see** the monitor as they present their performances to the screen. They must **not get into the habit of looking at the monitor**, since, professionally, they will **not** be able to see a picture of their scene while they are acting it.

It is a good idea if the group gets used to using a regular procedure and vocabulary for starting each shot, such as:

Director:	"Roll tape." Technician/camera operator turns on machine.
Technician:	(or camera operator) "Running," when she sees numbers changing, sees the machine actually working.
Boom operator:	(or technician, if there are no headphones) "Sound," when she can hear sound coming through from the set.
Assistant director:	"Shot one, take one" (and next time, "Shot one, take two," etc.). This is the "slate" at the head of each shot, and in the movies it is that famous clapper board so beloved of Hollywood.
Director:	"Action!" It is such fun to say this for the first time. Actually, I still enjoy saying it.
Actors:	Act.
Director:	"Cut!" Actors stop acting; everyone looks to the director to see if the whole thing is to be repeated, or whether we all move on to the next shot.

The other piece of equipment that I find invaluable for classwork is a frame. This should be the size of a television screen and should allow everyone to see what happens when a frame is put around a person, two people, three people, and so on. I have made a collapsible one out of wood, but once when I was without it, I found I could make a very acceptable frame that illustrated all the points I needed by making four long rolls from newspapers, joining them together to make the right sized screen and then flattening the whole thing. Of course, when I started my screen acting classes in the 1980s the ratio for the screen was the traditional 4:3, but I now make it 16:9 to reflect the universal use of the wide screen (16 units wide, 9 units high).

A word of warning: Class members can often ruin a take by talking, even laughing out loud at what someone does (and so get their voices onto the sound track). It is easy to forget that when the camera is recording, this is not a rehearsal – this is the real thing, a performance.

The exercises are grouped under their chapter headings.

Chapter 1: Screen versus stage

1. Get the class to write down what they would do differently, if anything, in acting for the screen as opposed to acting for the stage. Store the results for reading back when the rest of the exercises have been done.
2. Hold up a frame, and have someone watch it from about eight feet away. Make actors stand as far away from it as is necessary for the observer to see them in the frame as long shot, medium shot, medium close-up, close-up,

and big close-up. If possible, sit in a theater with the frame, to see what seat corresponds to what size shot.

3. Try to convey different emotions at different distances, to see what techniques are needed. Get couples to stand at different distances to act "I hate you!" or "I love you!" and to see what changing the distance does.

4. Play a scene "as if in real life"; play the same scene "as if on stage"; play the same scene with the frame, and see what happens to the screen version.

Chapter 2: Different screens – different effects

5. Shoot a very emotional speech in close-up, and then play it back on the largest screen available – and then the smallest (a smartphone?). Get the class to observe what works well for both sizes – and what does not.

6. Do the same with a full-length sequence of movement or dance. Again, show and observe on the largest/smallest screens.

7. Shoot a scene and without stopping the camera give the actors notes that they have to put into practice immediately. Repeat the exercise with the actors having to say slightly different lines in the middle of a take.

Chapter 3: The frame

8. Put a frame around ordinary activities: writing a letter, drinking a cup of tea, knitting a sweater, repairing a radio. Then "cheat" the activity until all the important bits are in the frame – and see what the actor has to do to achieve this.

9. Take famous stills from movies or television programs, and get the actors to reproduce each moment **exactly**. Use blocks, cushions, or whatever to achieve the correct result, and compare the "look" of the result with the "feelings" of the actors composing the picture.

10. Do ordinary, everyday scenes such as, "Can you tell me the way to the station?" but stage them so that both faces can be seen in the frame that is held up to them. Insist that they get right into the frame, regardless of embarrassment, and then make sure they act not what they actually feel, but what they are supposed to be feeling.

11. Get the students to pick a moment from a movie or TV show, and get them to write down and learn the dialogue. Ask them to reproduce the relationships and moments **exactly** as in the original, then film the scene as they have prepared it. Get the class to compare it with the original (I find that the usual result is that the student always speaks louder than the original actor, but does less business).

12. Shoot each member of the group in close-up. Play back the results to see what is missing when only the head and shoulders can be seen, as opposed to seeing them full-length in real life.

Chapter 4: The camera

13.   Record twenty seconds of the actors doing anything previously learned. Play back the results: Note the vocal levels, the degree of stiffness, the **effect** that being on camera has on them, and see if it tends to drown their best moments.

14.   Play back the twenty seconds recorded from the previous exercise. Use a small masking device (I use an ordinary kitchen spatula) to block out the eyes and mouth, and see what the effect is when this area (a small fraction of the total area of the screen) is missing from the playback. Did any of the actors use the rest of the screen to communicate with their audience?

15.   Practice doing little moves of the eyes, head, or hands to **motivate** the camera to move off to another person. Practice moving slowly across the room to **motivate** the camera to zoom in or out on a figure in the center of the screen.

16.   Have actors walk past the camera as it pans with them, varying the rates of walking and of talking. Have them act very angry or very sad, and **see** what is needed from the actors to make the camera record the appropriate effect. Practice talking fast and walking slow.

17.   Record a group of three or four actors, rearranging them until they look good on camera, then compare the look on the floor with the look on the screen. Experiment with different staging, so the actors start to feel what is "good" screen staging and what is not. Try acting "on the red carpet" to see how different it is from theater staging.

Chapter 5: Reactions and business

18.   Shoot everyone doing just twenty seconds for the camera. See how few gestures and reactions they put in. Repeat with many reactions and gestures. See how **few** words an actor can say, while still being entertaining and interesting.

19.   Record each actor doing a series of unemotional bits of business: swallowing, clenching the back teeth so the muscles bulge in the cheek, brushing the hair off the forehead, sneering. Play back the results, but this time add dialogue that makes the gestures seem like a response to the lines just given.

20.   Shoot everyone saying a short speech, but insist that they all react **before** speaking. Compare how this comes across without such reactions.

21.   Shoot each person just listening to another talking. Shoot again, asking the listener to do too much, and find out how much **is** "too much."

22.   Shoot a scene to see how many different things the actor can do with a pencil, a telephone, a chair. See how different bits of business suit different actors.

23. Shoot the silent movie exercise. Choose an actor to be shot playing a hugely melodramatic moment. Repeat the exercise, but this time shout out instructions (using a megaphone?) for her to obey, keeping the instructions one on top of another in a continuous stream. Play back and compare the results.

24. Record some examples of television commercials that have many changing expressions by the performers. Get the class to reproduce them – exactly. Both in scale and in frequency, get them to feel what it is like to act the way that professional actors do on the screen.

25. Do the Alone on Stage exercise. Two people act in front of the group, with one listening while the other does all the speaking. Ask them to repeat it, but this time the speaker must be offstage, out of sight of the audience. Observe what happens to the listener when she knows that the audience can only see her and her reactions. Shoot her doing the same reactions in a single shot, and play back. Make sure that the reactions were as clear and large as when she was alone on stage, with the same increase in the scale and variety of the reactions (as well as reacting all through the speaker's lines).

Chapter 6: Sound and vocal levels

26. Play scenes with a high emotional content, using very little voice but a lot of everything else. If necessary, the director should put her face within six inches of the actor, and then get her to "perform" in a passionate way. Find out what it is like to have to work this way.

27. Watch some famous film or television scenes, and then reenact them using all the emotions **and vocal levels** that were in the original. Shoot the results. Be precise about the vocal levels, as it is usual for those doing this exercise to speak louder than the originals.

28. Have an actor play a scene that starts calm and ends up with a raging emotion. Shoot it starting in long shot, then zoom in during the speech to end with a close-up. See what adjustments are necessary to make the whole speech effective.

29. Set up the actors in couples to have private conversations seated some three feet apart. Repeat the exercise, keeping the seats three feet apart, but now the actors must project to the other person **as if** she were only six inches away. They must **not** slow down the rate of their delivery. (They will probably also laugh, it seems so peculiar.)

30. Shoot couples talking to each other in different circumstances, but only using "modern" whisper/speaking acting. See where it does (and does not) work. Then keep the very low levels of talking but increase the diction, using the consonants a great deal. Did this help?

Chapter 7: Typecasting

31. Get each actor in turn to read out the one-line description they think would be written about them after a short interview. Have a vigorous discussion and truth-telling session. (If these one-liners are put onto camera, it often happens that because the actors are concentrating on something new, most of what has been taught already goes out the window. The moral – something new tends to drive them back to what they know: stage acting.)

32. Get everyone to come before the camera, and record them saying, "I'd vote for her." Play back the results, and everyone shout out who the "she" is that each character would be voting for. See how the look (coupled with the way they are dressed) affects how they come across, and note that there is not necessarily a connection with how the actors themselves would actually vote.

33. Shoot everyone in profile, and tell them that when there is a click of the fingers, they must turn toward the camera with no thoughts whatsoever in their heads. Play back the results to see just how much information is in the change from profile to full face.

34. A nice variation of the previous exercise when playing it back is to speak some made-up dialogue just before they turn their heads, to see again how much is conveyed just by the changing looks.

35. Film everyone in close-up as they goggle their eyes, lick their lips, clench their teeth, flare their nostrils, blink and flutter their eyes, swallow, and so on. Play back the results, and work out which facial gesture suits which actors best.

36. Put a theatrical photograph of someone in front of the camera, so everyone can see the result on the screen. Get the actor whose picture it is to perform anything **in the manner of the photograph**. The audience critiques until a performance is obtained that matches the look. Sometimes this can be helped by adjusting how much of the photo is to be seen. The conclusion is often that the actor does not like the performance that matches the photo. In that case, she should get another photo.

Chapter 8: Acting

37. Recreate original theater conditions, and present a medieval mystery on a tabletop, a Shakespeare snippet in daylight, a Restoration piece to a room lit with candlelight, and a melodramatic moment lit by one candle with the audience at least thirty feet away. Sample and see what styles of acting are needed for the different audience/actor relationships and for what can or cannot be seen. Extend this practice to silent screen acting – what is the relationship and what can be seen? – and then extend it into spoken screen acting.

38. Get everyone to practice a sneeze done with the lips, a laugh done with vibrating the diaphragm, a cry done the same way, tears produced by some eye-watering vapor (onions?). Record the results and practice until the moves come across as convincing.

Chapter 9: Auditions

39. Have each actor practice coming in, shaking hands, and saying, "Hello!" Grade each one. Get the class to grade each other. Get practiced at this basic of any audition.
40. Record each person coming to a mark and announcing her name and agent (this can be a fictitious name) into the lens. Again, grade each person about how well she announces her name. (Actors hate being graded, but it will happen to them in auditions, so it is useful to get used to the concept that yes, people are going to sit and give them marks as to their effectiveness.)
41. Record some little two- or three-handed improvisations, seeing how at first most will go into "theatric" staging. Re-do the exercise until they can all do "filmic" staging as they improvise, staying on the red carpet.
42. Repeat the previous exercise, but this time record no sound. Play back the results, and repeat so that all the information that was in the improvised dialogue is now in their bodies and gestures.
43. Ask each actor to come to a mark, say her name and agent into the camera, then bite into an imaginary piece of chocolate and say, "Wow!" Play back the results, and cruelly decide who was "best." Repeat as often as necessary.
44. Find current commercials on television that demand similar deeply committed performances, and play the originals to the class. Then get **them** to do it.
45. Record each actor doing five distinct reactions in five seconds. If necessary, call out the changes to the actor, silent movie style. Then try doing five reactions in three seconds.
46. Practice a cold reading with a camera on the face, and see how much can be done in the "listening" phase of the audition. If the same reading is given to each actor, have them do the interview and reading without anyone else present, then play back the results so all can see (and judge) the relative effectiveness of each actor.

Chapter 10: Rehearsals and technicals

47. Have a read-through of a scene with everyone sitting around a table **giving a close-up vocal level performance**. Experience and practice how to do this, and notice the differences in the expressions on the faces when they are speaking at low levels.

48. Rehearse small scenes, with many marks to hit and moves to make. Get used to the extreme technicality that can be demanded from such a shoot.
49. If the equipment is available, do some longer scenes with two cameras cutting between them during the scene, so the actors get used to longer takes and to the multi-camera experience.

Chapter 11: Directing actors for the screen

50. Play a little scene with two actors facing each other. Get them to repeat the scene, but this time with one speaking over the other's shoulder. Repeat with different ways of not looking at each other.
51. Shoot an over-the-shoulder two-shot of a short, intimate scene. Shoot it again as a close-up, but with only one actor there playing to an invisible partner. (It can be a piece of paper with eyes drawn on it.) Play back and compare the results.

Chapter 12: Announcers (and the art of being interviewed)

52. Ask each actor to bring in an official photograph and a "favorite" snap-shot. Put each official photograph in front of a camera lens, and get the performer to do a speech in the manner of the photograph. Get the "favorite" snapshot from the participant, and (using the macro lens on the camcorder if necessary), blow it up to be seen on screen. Now have the announcer give a speech, but this time in the manner of the snapshot. It will usually be better, more relaxed, more **them**.
53. Dangerous exercise: Get the participants (helped by the audience if necessary) to identify those aspects of themselves they are least happy with, least proud of. Then get them to do a speech or interview presenting these negative aspects positively.
54. Get the participants to take part in an interview situation, concentrating not just on their replies, but on "active listening."
55. Get each member of the class to do a long speech, and see in each case how long she can go on without putting in a full stop. Pauses are possible, but the voice must never come to a downward inflection.

Chapter 13: The shoot

56. Shoot a little scene with many technical problems. Play back the results – and immediately shoot the scene again. This allows the actor to put into practice what she has just learned. (All too often in the professional realm, it is so long after a shoot that an actor gets to see what she has done that when viewing the result, she has forgotten what it was that led her to do it like that in the first place.)

57. Shoot little moments of actors coming into two- and three-shots, with them having to find their mark and making it look as if that is what the character wanted to do. Shoot the actors **motivating** a look downward to check a mark, an edge sideways to get into shot, holding a cup up high into shot and keeping it there, and setting their opening position by walking backwards from the mark.

Chapter 14: The editor and editing

58. Shoot a two-handed scene with munching of sandwiches. Shoot it again from the other side, and check how good the continuity was. Practice until members of the class can do complicated business and **repeat it exactly**.

59. Shoot one actor doing lots of differing reactions to a speech by another. Play it back, and only show, say, the middle reaction out of a sequence. See how reactions can stand on their own when only used as a quick cutaway.

Epilogue

60. Read back what the class **thought** screen acting was, and get their new thoughts on the matter.

GLOSSARY

Here are a lot of the words and phrases that you may hear on a shoot, or see on the credits, and have always wondered about. I have added those new terms that have come in with the advent of digital, high definition, and wide screen.

180 DEGREE RULE: (see **CROSSING THE LINE**).

A/B: as before – particularly when a **SHOT** is to be the same as the previous one.

ACTION: what the **DIRECTOR** or **FIRST ASSISTANT** says to start off a **TAKE**. You should start your acting just before it is spoken.

ACTION PROPS: objects used or handled by actors, as opposed to ordinary props used for dressing (making it look good).

ADDITIONAL CAMERA: used to give extra coverage to a once-only effect, such as an explosion or car crash. Some **DIRECTORS** think they can save time by using two cameras shooting simultaneously to record a two-handed scene; these are often labeled "Camera A" and "Camera B" in the credits. The use of an additional camera allows shooting in real time, but also restricts the movements of the actors, and increases the problems with lighting for two cameras.

AFM: Assistant floor manager.

ALAN SMITHEE: When one of the main team no longer wants their name associated with the film they are (or were) working on, in America they often use this name, as a signal to the profession of their attitude to the situation. Actors often use the name **WALTER PLINGE** for the same reason.

ANALOG: recording an event (sound or pictures) sequentially, either as a series of sound waves or as a series of pictures. If you record a recording and then record that, the quality will noticeably get worse as the errors and distortions increase. **DIGITAL** records everything as a 1 or a 0, and as a computer can police them and know which they ought to be, a recording of a recording of a recording should be the same as the original.

ANAMORPHIC LENS: a lens that squashes the picture horizontally, allowing a wide picture to be recorded on a standard size – either for film or for video. The squashed picture is shown through another **ANAMORPHIC LENS**, recreating the original wide frame size (see also **WIDE SCREEN**).

ANGLE: (see **CAMERA ANGLE**).

ANIME: Japanese animation, often of exotic or even erotic subjects, where everyone seems to have very large eyes. (Advertising something as an *Anime Love Scene* comes over so much better than as a *Cartoon Love Scene*.)

APERTURE: (see **F-STOP**).

ASPECT RATIO (also **FORMAT**): the width-to-height ratio of a screen. Academy Aperture, the original format for film, was 4:3 or 1.33:1, and it used to be the mainstay ratio of television, but now that is changing (see also **WIDE SCREEN**). Standard European **WIDE SCREEN** is 1.66:1; standard American **WIDE SCREEN** is 1.85:1; and very wide formats such as Panavision is 2.35:1.

ASSISTANT DIRECTOR (or **AD**, also **FIRST ASSISTANT**): the film **DIRECTOR**'s main link and help (and bully boy).

ATMOSPHERE (also known as **ATMOS**): (see **BUZZ TRACK**).

AUTEUR: The collaborative nature of the movie business was changed when the French critics came up with this word to describe the work of star **DIRECTORS**. When they are indeed involved in every aspect of the movie, then fair enough, but "A film by" implies that the star name did everything creative, which gets many a raised eyebrow from the co-workers on the film.

AUTOCUE: (see **TELEPROMPTER**).

BACK LIGHT: lights the back of the actor as seen by the camera (to make you stand out from the background).

BACKGROUND ACTION: what all the walk ons and extras (or supporting artists) do at the back of the **SHOT** in order to add to the bustle of a crowd (and to get themselves noticed).

BACKING TRACK: pre-recorded music to play when actors or musicians have to mime as they pretend to be actually playing.

BACK-STEPPING: If you have to hit a **MARK** whilst speaking dialogue, this is a good trick – stand on your **MARK** and walk backwards speaking your lines, so you will know where to start off from to **HIT THE MARK** without looking down.

BANANA: walking on a curved line, usually to allow the camera to see you earlier, or to prevent you **MASKING** a fellow actor.

BARN DOOR: metal flaps attached to a light to stop its light from spreading everywhere.

BCU: big close-up, full head from chin to hairline (see **SHOT ABBREVIA-TIONS**).

BEAT: a small pause; also the unit of action much loved by Methodologists.

BEST BOY: chief assistant to the **GAFFER** (the chief electrician). Now, there are two titles you always wondered about in film credits.

BG: background.

BIG CLOSE-UP: (see **BCU**).

BIOPIC: a biographical film, which tries to tell the life of a famous person whilst making money and avoiding law suits. The result is often a film with a glossy view of people's lives, but sparks off huge arguments on the internet as to which famous actor should play the **BIOPIC**'s famous subject.

BLOCKING THE SCENE: giving the moves for a scene (can apply to both actors and cameras); this is usually the first rehearsal.

BLUE SCREEN: (see **GREEN SCREEN**).

BOOM: telescopic arm that holds the microphone above the action. It can also refer to a movable arm that attaches the camera to a **DOLLY**.

BOOM UP/DOWN: moving the microphone and its pole up and down – or the camera up/down.

BREAK: stop work for a while.

BREAKING UP: (see **CORPSE**).

BUG EYE LENS: (see **FISH EYE LENS**).

BUSINESS: actions for an actor, usually involving a prop (sometimes, just **BIZ**).

BUZZ TRACK (also **ATMOSPHERE**): background sound recorded to smooth over possible unevenness in previously recorded background sounds from different **SHOTS**. Everyone must be very quiet while the **MIXER** records this.

CALL SHEET: the shooting schedule for that day, including the times people are needed in makeup, and when on set. We are not bothered if you have to wait hours before being used, but fall into a rage if you are ever late for your call time.

CAMERA ANGLE (also **ANGLE**): how high, how low, and in which direction the camera is to point.

CAMERA CARDS: cards attached to a camera in a **MULTI-CAMERA** studio telling the **CAMERA OPERATOR** what sort of **SHOT** (e.g. **MCU**) they should do at what time (e.g. shot number 114).

CAMERA LEFT/RIGHT: the left/right of the **CAMERA OPERATOR**, and so will also be screen left/right (and very different to the theater's stage left/right).

CAMERA OPERATOR: the person who actually operates the camera, although the **DOP** or **DIRECTOR** sometimes does so on the quiet.

CAMERA TRAP: a hole in the scenery that can open up, so a camera can pop through to get the **SHOT** required and then disappear, with the scenery closing up so that no other camera will see where it was. This explains some of those "How on earth did they get that **SHOT**?" moments.

CANS: headphones.

CANTING: (see **DUTCH ANGLE**).

CGI: computer generated image – so all those wonderful visions can be achieved using actors fighting shadows in front of a **GREEN SCREEN**, whilst they wait for the computer ideas, backgrounds, and alien creatures to be added later.

CHEATING: the art and craft of doing something that is untrue, but appears true to the camera – as in "**CHEAT** your eyes towards camera; **CHEAT** your height by standing on this box."

CINEMATOGRAPHER: (see **DOP**).

CLAPPER BOARD: (see **CLAPSTICK BOARD**).

CLAPSTICK BOARD (also **CLAPPER BOARD**; **SLATE**): used for **SHOT**, scene, and **TAKE** numbers; it has a hinged bit that gives the satisfying clap at the start of a film sequence that helps them synchronize sound and picture in the editing. (What a pity that for **DIGITAL** there is no such excitement, although some crews will use one so that they can pretend they are making a movie.)

CLOSE-UP: (see **CU**).

CLOSED SET: where only the cast and crew are allowed to be present on the set, especially when filming particularly intimate scenes, or scenes that are meant to be secret, or when the usual audience of hangers on and **PRODUCERS** has become especially irritating.

COLOR TEMPERATURE: the color a particular temperature is, especially in relation to lights used in filming; blue is much hotter than red.

CONTINUITY (also **SCRIPT GIRL** – since they were once always women – or **SCRIPT SUPERVISOR**): the person who takes copious continuity notes (with **DIGITAL** cameras replacing the ubiquitous Polaroids) so that the same business is done at the same time on all **SHOTS** covering the same sequence. Also refers to the way each gesture, head angle, costume, and property should be the same when we **CUT** from one **SHOT** to another (see also **HEAD TO HEAD CONTINUITY**).

CONTRAST RATIO: the difference between the brightest and darkest part of the picture. The human eye can cope with a **CONTRAST RATIO** of about 100:1; film less than that; video had the worst ratio of all – leading to difficulties in shooting with video against a sunny window (the actors' faces will appear black). Happily, **DIGITAL** and **HIGH DEFINITION** in this respect are improving all the time.

CORPSE (also **BREAKING UP**): when an actor comes out of character and laughs as himself instead of acting his character (called this because his character has just died).

COVERAGE: the number of **SHOTS** taken to cover a whole scene; "Is there enough **COVERAGE** for this sequence?" the **PRODUCER** may ask anxiously.

CRAB: moving the camera sideways.

CRANE: a device that can raise the camera; small ones take it to six feet up; giant ones take it up to look down on roofs. (These are very, very expensive, and **PRODUCERS** are very reluctant to pay for them.)

CRANE UP/DOWN: moving the camera up and down.

CRASH ZOOM: a very rapid lens change from a wide shot to a very close-up one indeed; used by trendy directors (not me this time) to give the audience a shock (see also **ZOOM**).

CRAWL: very slow movement of the camera.

CROSS-CUTTING: to cut back and forth, especially between two unrelated scenes when things are happening simultaneously (as in cutting between the maiden tied to the railway tracks and the hero riding to rescue her).

CROSSING THE LINE (also **180 DEGREE RULE**): the crime of getting the geography wrong, and confusing the audience as to where everyone is. If two **SHOTS** are taken of two actors talking to each other, then both camera positions should be on the same side of an invisible line drawn between the two actors. If the cameras are on opposite sides of the line, then the two actors on screen will appear to be looking in the same direction, and so will not seem to be talking to each other at all. The same happens at a televised football game if the cameras are on opposite sides of the field – to **CUT** from one camera following a player on one side of the pitch to one on the other side also following the same player will make the image on screen appear to change direction, and totally confuse the viewing public.

CU: close-up, neck to top of head (see **SHOT ABBREVIATIONS**).

CUE (also **Q**): the signal to start; often given by a frantic wave from one of the production team.

CUE CARDS: (see **IDIOT CARDS**).

CUT: the point where one **SHOT** is changed for another, either by editing ("I want to **CUT** as you get up out of the chair") or in the **MULTI-CAMERA** studio ("I will **CUT** from the close-up on Camera 1 to the wide shot on Camera 3 as the door opens"). Also shouted to end a **TAKE**, and to stop everything; the opposite of **ACTION** (and done very angrily when things have gone wrong!).

CUTAWAY: usually a **TIGHT SHOT** of an object or bit of a person, used to give a close-up view of an important property or face; also used to edit two bits together that do not match too well; often used in documentaries.

CUTTER: (see **EDITOR**).

CUTTING DOWN THE LINE: means that the camera is taking another **SHOT** from exactly the same position, but with a much tighter **SHOT**, so the effect on the audience is of jumping in, since the angle is the same, but they see a much closer **SHOT**.

CYCLORAMA: curved backcloth, sometimes painted to create the illusion that a scene set inside a stuffy studio is on the wide open spaces of a beach.

DAILIES (also **RUSHES**): When shooting on film, these are yesterday's **SHOTS** rushed back to the shoot and shown to all interested people in case anything needs to be re-shot. (Actors usually do not get to see them.) With **DIGITAL** shooting it is now possible to watch a **SHOT** the moment it is completed, so yesterday's **DAILIES** are becoming today's.

DAY-FOR-NIGHT: filming in daylight, and then adjusting the film so everyone thinks it is in fact at night. (Filmed with clear skies, underexposed, with a deep blue filter put on it.) Often ruined by having daytime birds happily flying across the "night" sky.

DEEP FOCUS: the system of wide lenses and small apertures that allow objects close and far away from the camera to be in focus. (Used to tremendous effect in Orson Welles's *Citizen Kane*.)

DEEPER: further away. A **SHOT** of two people close to camera, with a third way off in the distance between them is known as a **DEEP THREE**.

DEPTH OF FIELD: the area that is in focus. On a bright day it can be very large, covering people at different distances from the camera; on a dull day or in a dimly lit scene it can mean the focus is very precise, and the actors have to hit their **MARKS** within an inch or less, or they will be out of focus.

DEVELOPING SHOT: a style of directing where the actors and camera are choreographed in a long sequence all in one **SHOT**. This is very well liked by all show-off **DIRECTORS** (I particularly like doing them myself). **MISE-EN-SCÈNE** (French, meaning "putting into the scene") incorporates just such **SHOTS**.

DIGITAL: we are all going **DIGITAL**, which means that instead of recording or transmitting things in waves (**ANALOG**), they are recorded or transmitted as numbers. The advantage is that our computers can manipulate numbers and make corrections more accurately, so a recording of a recording of a recording still comes up looking fresh. The disadvantage is that there is a tendency to compress the information, with the result that definition is sometimes lost in certain circumstances. All **DOP**s wish to use film when they shoot (which has a high snob appeal), but if **HIGH DEFINITION DIGITAL** is good enough for George Lucas's *Star Wars* blockbusters, it is good enough for the rest of us, and for you to make budget **DIGITAL** films.

DIGITAL EDITING: editing using a computer, into which all shots have been imported. The **EDITOR** can call on any of them at any time; it's called nonlinear editing. This means that the **DIRECTOR** can really annoy the **EDITOR** by constantly fiddling with each cut, each scene. It speeds things up, because the **EDITOR** can experiment quickly without ruining any material, but purists complain that it removes the physical contact between him and his material. Popular versions of **DIGITAL EDITING** systems are Avid and Final Cut Pro.

DIRECTOR: the person in charge, who decides the **SHOT**, the moves, the acting, the set and costume designs, the makeup, and so on (but whom everyone else on the crew thinks could not possibly manage without their own particular input).

DIRECTOR OF PHOTOGRAPHY: (see **DOP**).

DIRECTOR'S CUT: After all the arguments in the cutting room between the **PRODUCER** and **DIRECTOR** as to what goes into the film and what stays out, it is a way of getting the film to be what the **DIRECTOR** really wanted when it is re-issued later in a longer version, or more likely issued as a **DVD**. If you are Ridley Scott, you may well issue the film in any number of versions, keeping film historians really happy.

DISSOLVE: cross-fading from one picture to another; it now has the symbolism of telling the audience that time has passed.

DOLLY: the truck on wheels that allows the camera to go charging about a studio, or off down some **TRACKS.**

DOLLY ZOOM: (see **VERTIGO EFFECT**).

DOLLYING (also **TRACKING** or **TRUCKING**): the act of the camera doing such moving; "**DOLLY** in to the actors" means the camera will now come satisfyingly close to you. **DIRECTORS** love these moves almost as much as they love a mirror **SHOT**. (This fixation probably started at an early age with the young **DIRECTOR**'s first train set.)

DOLPHIN ARM: (see **JIB ARM**).

DOP (also **DIRECTOR OF PHOTOGRAPHY, LIGHTING CAMERAMAN**, or **CINEMATOGRAPHER**): This is the person who decides the lighting, the camera lenses, the way a **SHOT** is to be done – and so is responsible for the look of it. The **DOP** gives instructions to the **GAFFER** and the **CAMERA OPERATOR**, and argues with the **DIRECTOR** as to the best way of achieving the best results.

DOUBLE: (see **TWO-SHOT**). Also another word for the **STAND-IN**.

DOWNSTAGE: stolen from the stage world, meaning closer to the camera.

DRY: forgetting lines.

DRY RUN (also **DRESS REHEARSAL**): rehearsing a scene without shooting it, finding out the problems before a **TAKE**.

DUBBING: transferring all the sound effects, music, replaced voices, and so on onto the finished product. It also describes the process in which your lovely voice is substituted by a completely different one when your performance is shown in foreign parts speaking the local language.

DUTCH ANGLE (also **CANTING**): putting the camera at an angle to the vertical, so that the whole picture looks aslant. Used to tremendous effect in Carol Reed's *The Third Man*, and with less effect by pale imitators. (Yes, I used it in my first feature.)

DVD: the disc which we put into a player to see films in their original **ASPECT RATIO**, and to get all the extra **OUT-TAKES** and film background. Everyone thinks it stands for digital video disc, but it really is digital versatile disc (that is a good one to memorize for quizzes).

ECU: extreme close-up, just a bit of the face, the hand – a detail (see **SHOT ABBREVIATIONS**).

EDITOR: the person who joins the chosen bits of different **TAKES** together to make the finished program. In film the person is also known as the **CUTTER**.

ELS: extreme long shot, everything at a great distance (see **SHOT ABBREVIATIONS**).

END BOARD (also **TAIL SLATE**): used when the **CLAPSTICK BOARD** is put on the end of a **TAKE** (maybe because it was forgotten, or because it was difficult to focus on it at the start). An **END BOARD** held upside down with the jaws open means the **SHOT** was done without any sound (see also **MOS**).

ESTABLISHING SHOT: the **SHOT** at the beginning of a scene that lets the audience know where they are. It can be a **SHOT** of the exterior of the house where everyone is talking inside; more interestingly it can be the first **SHOT** inside the house where the first speaker by an amazing coincidence just has to move all round the room, and so show the audience who else is there and what the room looks like.

EXTREME CLOSE-UP: (see **ECU**).

EXTREME LONG SHOT: (see **ELS**).

EYELINE: the direction your eyes take when looking at someone else. **DIRECTORS** (and actors) also like the camera to "get onto the **EYE-LINE**" – it means that both eyes of the actor will be seen. A matching **EYELINE** means that the eye directions of two actors in two **SHOTS** to be intercut must complement each other in having the same angle of looking, and so convince the audience that the actors are indeed looking at each other.

F-STOP (also **APERTURE**): the size of the opening of the iris that lets light into the lens on the camera. The higher the number, the less light gets in.

FG: foreground.

FILL LIGHT: the soft light that fills in the shadows caused by the **KEY LIGHT**.

FINE CUT: the final assembly of the material. This is usually how it will be when shown to an audience.

FIRST ASSISTANT: (see **ASSISTANT DIRECTOR**).

FISH EYE LENS (also **BUG EYE LENS** or **WIDE ANGLE LENS**): a very wide angle lens. If you get too close to it, it makes you look as if you have a huge nose and very small ears.

FISHPOLE: hand-held portable **BOOM**.

FLAG: anything used to stop stray light getting to the camera lens and so creating a flare. Also used to take sunshine off actors, or to put wanted shadows in place.

FLOOR MANAGER: the **DIRECTOR**'s link on a television studio floor, the equivalent to **ASSISTANT DIRECTOR** or **FIRST ASSISTANT** in the film world.

FLOOR PLAN: a bird's eye view of the scenery, with the positions of the cameras (and often the actors as well) marked in. This allows sound and lights to plan where to put their equipment to get the desired effects.

FLUFF: an actor tripping over a word, or saying the wrong one. (Sometimes called a **FLUB**.)

FOCUS PULL: (see **RACK FOCUS**).

FOLEY: the replacement and addition of footsteps, animal noises, and so on to make the effects in a scene sound correct. Because there is often a lot of noise around (the sound of the **DOLLY** moving, for example), there is the need for a lot of this. Now you know what that mysterious **FOLEY** credit means that you have seen at the end of all movies; it is named after the individual who invented the process.

FORMAT: (see **ASPECT RATIO**).

FREEZE FRAME: where the action is "frozen" by keeping one picture going; a good way of ending a scene if you can't think of a better one.

GAFFER: chief electrician.

GAFFER TAPE: heavy duty adhesive tape, used on a set for just about every fixing job.

GOLDEN HOUR: This is the twenty minutes or so of useful shooting time after the sun sets, when there is no direct sunshine but a wonderful glow to everything. **DIRECTORS** love to use this light, since it means that everyone has to hang around all day, and the **DIRECTOR** only has to work for those twenty minutes (all right, I am sure there are other things going on).

GREEN SCREEN (was **BLUE SCREEN** when I started – so I am showing how long I have been around): This means that the film you are booked to play in, with you looking forward to all those exotic locations, ends up with you standing in front of a **GREEN SCREEN** in a stuffy studio where the unnatural green color can be replaced by the inevitable computers with those locations you never got to visit.

GREENROOM: where the actors wait before coming onto the set to act. The place where they may run their lines with other actors, if they are not hiding in their trailers. Originally theater stages had green carpets, and going onto the stage was known as going onto the green – so the place to wait was of course the **GREENROOM**.

GREENSMEN: those on the set or **LOCATION** who take care of all the greenery, making winter look like spring by planting fake flowers and bushes.

GRIP: He transports and sets up the camera equipment, especially **TRACKS**, and pushes the **DOLLY**. The **KEY GRIP** is in charge.

HAIR IN THE GATE: now mostly confined to the history books. When shooting on film it was a minute bit of fluff or emulsion in the camera that will show up as one of those black worms you occasionally saw at the edges of the screen – and it meant you had to do the whole thing all over again. All **SHOTS** used to end therefore with the **CAMERA OPERATOR** ordering someone to "check the gate."

HAND-HELD: when the camera is hoisted onto the **CAMERA OPERATOR**'s shoulder, and goes chasing all over to follow exciting action. It is often used to make things seem more "realistic" (that is, more wobbly, and resembling the sort of **SHOTS** coming from news cameras).

HD: (see **HIGH DEFINITION**).

HEAD TO HEAD CONTINUITY: When we are shooting matching over-the-shoulder **SHOTS**, we will do the first one, and then we will do the **REVERSES**. Because both the actors' heads are in both **SHOTS**, they will have to move their heads at the same time in the same way both times, to get their head **CONTINUITY** just right and enable the **EDITOR** to **CUT** from one **SHOT** to the other.

HIGH DEFINITION (also **HD**): the **DIGITAL** system that gives a result almost indistinguishable from 35mm film, and the reason for its imminent demise.

HONEY WAGON: the American **LOCATION CATERING** van.

HOT SET: Everything is ready on the set for a **TAKE** – so do not touch a thing!

IDIOT CARDS (also **CUE CARDS**): large sheets onto which the performer's lines are written (so that all those moody glances away from their fellow actors are just looking for their next line). Also used for a talk show host to tell them where the next "joke" is lurking.

IN THE CAN: a satisfactory recording or **TAKE**, as in "we have got it **IN THE CAN!**"

INDIE: an independently produced film, the main effect on you being that you will be paid much less, or even asked to accept deferred payment, or "a share of the profits," which amazingly nearly always means a zero salary.

INKY DINKY: a small light placed near the camera that will put a sparkle into your eyes. It is well worth waiting for it to be installed (or even asking for it, if you have the nerve).

JIB ARM (also **DOLPHIN ARM**): an arm attached to the **DOLLY** that allows the camera to go up and down a reasonable amount.

JUICERS: (see **SPARKS**).

JUMP CUT: cutting from one picture to another with a huge difference in size, or in **LOCATION**, or in time continuity (much loved and used in music videos). The shock effect is the intention. It is also used as a term to describe two **SHOTS** that the **DIRECTOR** wants to **CUT** between, but the **EDITOR** refuses to, because it would be a **JUMP CUT**.

KEY LIGHT: the main light for an actor, coming in from the front of and to the side of you.

KILL: stop, or turn off; "**KILL** that light; **KILL** that lawn mower" (see also **STRIKE**).

LETTERBOX: When showing a **WIDE SCREEN** film on a less wide screen, in order to keep the original **ASPECT RATIO** black strips are put at the top and bottom of the picture, **LETTERBOXING** it. This makes it look like – you guessed it – a letterbox.

LEVEL: vocal level, as in the **MIXER** asking you, "Can you give us some more **LEVEL**?" Be very careful how much more you give (if at all).

LIGHTING CAMERAMAN: (see **DOP**).

LINE PRODUCER: the producer in charge of daily expenses, and so does on film what the **PRODUCTION MANAGER** does on smaller projects – signs expense forms, and announces that there is no money for any more time on this **LOCATION**.

LINE UP: getting everything in position for a **SHOT**. Also what all the cameras in a **MULTI-CAMERA** studio have to do together to get them balanced with each other.

LIP SYNC: the sound and movement of a speaker being correctly together. Occasionally when using the sound from one **TAKE** with the picture of another, we briefly go out of **LIP SYNC** and you wonder how that happened.

LOCATION: the place away from base or the studio where scenes are shot in real surroundings. Often it means **LOCATION CATERING** where actors can overeat, and sometimes get an overnight stay – there is a theory that overindulgence in food or whatever is allowed, since they all tell each other "on **LOCATION** doesn't count."

LOCK IT DOWN: Once the camera and actor rehearsals have come up with a sequence that the **DIRECTOR** likes, then this order is made to keep it and be ready to repeat it for the **TAKE**.

LOCKED-OFF CAMERA: a camera that is fixed in position and shot size for a static **SHOT**, often of an explosion or a car crash, where the **CAMERA OPERATOR** does not want to be present. Sometimes used to denote a camera that is only shooting one particular thing or person (a child or animal) and will follow it wherever it goes.

LONG SHOT: (see **LS**).

LOOSE SHOT: plenty of space around the subject, so you can happily wave your arms around (see also **TIGHT SHOT**).

LOSE THE LIGHT: when the natural daylight is about to become too dim, and everyone goes round shouting "We must get this shot **IN THE CAN** before we **LOSE THE LIGHT**."

LOW LOADER: a trailer onto which a car is put, and then pulled behind the truck with the camera, so that when filming the car and its occupants, it looks as if they are driving through the countryside. It also explains why actors driving and acting are able to take their eyes off the road for so long – someone else is steering.

LS: long shot, the complete figure, with a bit of space above and below (see **SHOT ABBREVIATIONS**).

MACGUFFIN: yet another innovation by Alfred Hitchcock, which is defined as something that is not really important, but is necessary to make the plot work, such as a ticking bomb, a wine bottle containing radioactive ore, or a murder that causes an exploration of family relationships and brings a community together.

MARK: tape or chalk (or indeed sandbag) to indicate where an actor should stand, or where you should come to after a move: "**MARK** those positions." "Make sure you **HIT THE MARK**." Also used to indicate that the **CLAPSTICK BOARD** should now be used at the top of the scene.

MASK: Something in front of something else is said to **MASK** it, whether it is one actor on another, a piece of furniture, or a cut out in front of the camera to prevent it seeing something it should not.

MASTER SHOT: a wide angle **SHOT** of the whole scene, done first so that everyone knows what lighting and positional moments have to be matched for all subsequent **SHOTS**. The whole scene will sometimes be done in this **SETUP**, so the **EDITOR** always has something to **CUT** to in an emergency (but quick-shooting **DIRECTORS** often have no time for this).

MATTE BOX: the thing in front of the camera lens that holds masks and filters. If you fling yourself about too energetically, you are apt to hit it with your head or hands.

MCU: medium close-up, chest to top of head (see **SHOT ABBREVIATIONS**).

MEDIUM CLOSE-UP: (see **MCU**).

MEDIUM SHOT (also **MID-SHOT**): (see **MS**).

METHOD ACTING: the system of acting that stresses emotional reality, so that the actor has to experience the real emotion at the moment they perform, or at least in their preparation. This would make all death scenes impossible to act of course, but that does not stop them. It is definitely not what this book is about, but is based on the theories of Stanislavski.

MID-SHOT: (see **MS**).

MISE-EN-SCÈNE: (see **DEVELOPING SHOT**).

MIXER: the person who mixes together the various inputs from the different microphones to get good sound.

MONTAGE: a series of **SHOTS** or short scenes to convey a whole period of time: as in telling the story of the rise of a star by having **SHOTS** of a train chugging across a map, intercut with **SHOTS** of ever larger auditoriums exploding with enthusiasm. It is also used to describe editing that is concerned not with narrative, but with contrasting images that together tell a story.

MORPHING: when the computer uses **DIGITAL** effects to change your face on the screen in a seamless way from lovable you to that of, say, a wolf.

MOS (also **MUTE**): made without sound. Romantics like to believe that it was early German directors in Hollywood saying "mitout sound," but it was more likely they were saying "mit-out sprache" (we all prefer the first version).

MOTION CAPTURE: When an exotic creature – such as a dragon, a giant, or a Gollum – is required to display human qualities of movement or even of expression, then an actor has sort of ping pong balls stuck all over him or her, with all movements and reactions recorded by an encircling array of cameras, so the eventual computer-created character can be invested with the very human qualities that were required by the script.

MS: medium shot, waist to head (see **SHOT ABBREVIATIONS**).

MULTI-CAMERA: a studio with anything from three to seven video cameras all available to record the program, with the **SWITCHER** cutting from one camera to another.

MUTE: (see **MOS**).

NAR: reputedly put on his script by Cary Grant for scenes where he just stood around, meaning "no acting required."

NG: no good (written on the script by the **PRODUCTION ASSISTANT** or **SCRIPT SUPERVISOR** after a technically imperfect **SHOT**, or when the acting is considered not up to scratch).

NODDY: the shot of an interviewer nodding, cut in with the interview to make it look as if they agree with all that is being said. It is, of course, shot after the interviewee has long gone.

NTSC: National Television System Committee, and *not* Standards Committee, as some would have. The color system for television used in the US, which was the first in the world. It is now also the least effective system (the penalty for being first). Rudely known in the trade as Never the Same Color twice (alternative systems are **PAL** and **SECAM**).

NUMBER ONES: the positions at the top of the scene – so the **ASSISTANT DIRECTOR** can shout "**NUMBER ONES** please!" and all the actors immediately rush to where they should be, or at least look as if they are, as they **TAKE IT FROM THE TOP**.

OB: outside broadcast.

OFF BOOK: knowing your lines, so you don't have to tuck the script into your waistband. If you can't get **OFF BOOK**, you can always pretend that you are the sort of actor who needs to keep everything semi-improvised and spontaneous.

OFF-CAMERA (OC): (see **OUT-OF-VISION**).

OFF-MIKE: lines given that have not been picked up clearly by the microphone. Often caused by the actors delivering the lines in a direction they did not do in rehearsal, or by the **BOOM** operator not getting the microphone into the correct position.

OFF-SCREEN (OS) (also **OFF-CAMERA**): (see **OUT-OF-VISION**).

ONE-SHOT: (see **SINGLE**).

OOV: (see **OUT-OF-VISION**).

OSS: over-the-shoulder **SHOT**.

OTT: Over the top; usually applied to an actor's performance (and usually only referring to the vocal level!).

OUT-OF-SYNC: the opposite of **LIP SYNC**, where the movement of the lips does not match the sounds heard.

OUT-OF-VISION (OOV): an action or voice that is not seen on the screen. The **DIRECTOR** may ask you, "Can you **OOV** your lines from the bedroom?"

OUT-TAKE: those bits of a show that were originally mistakes (but now seem to be done on purpose to feed those programs that feature them as we watch actors and anchor persons fall over, forget lines, walk into walls, etc.).

OVERLAP: when your dialogue is said at the same time as another character's. It is one of the most common reasons for "going again."

PAL: phased alternating line. The color system developed and used by Germany, and by most of Europe, except France (naturally – see **SECAM**).

PAN: rotating the camera through an arc: "**PAN** left; **PAN** right; **PAN** up." Technically, it should be "**TILT UP**," but that is the way it often goes.

PER DIEM: the expenses you get each day for food, and sometimes accommodation; from the Latin for "by the day, daily" (you knew that, didn't you?).

PICK UP: If a shot goes wrong in the middle – especially if an actor **FLUFFS** a line – the **DIRECTOR** sometimes shouts out for the actor to repeat the line straight away, without stopping the shoot. If just one bit of a **TAKE** is to be repeated and not the whole thing, this is also known and marked as a **PICK UP**. With **DIGITAL** recording meaning we are not wasting expensive film, this is becoming much more common.

PILOT: the trial program of what we all hope will turn into a long-running series. Many trek to Hollywood for the "**PILOT** season"; good luck! (You'll need it.)

PLAYBACK: If there is something to be checked, it can be done by playing back the **TAKE**.

POINT OF VIEW (POV): shows the scene the way the character would see it. Often the camera is put where it can get your **POV**, such as your view of the dead body on the floor, the letter you are reading, and so on.

POLECAT: telescopic pole that can be jammed between floors and ceilings, between cross beams and walls, allowing lights to be hung where no light ought to go.

POST-PRODUCTION: all that happens to a production after the shooting has finished, such as editing, **DUBBING**, and **SPECIAL EFFECTS**. With everything being **DIGITAL** these days, this process can now take longer than planning and shooting the film itself, and cost correspondingly more.

POV: (see **POINT OF VIEW**).

PRACTICAL: working, as in "can we have this bedside light **PRACTICAL**?" Also used to describe anything that actually works, like a stove, sink, or radio.

PRODUCER: the person who is really in charge, whatever the **DIRECTOR** says. They are responsible for all financial and administrative aspects of the production, and why anyone would want to do the job is beyond me – all aggravation, with little thanks or appreciation.

PRODUCTION ASSISTANT: the assistant to the **DIRECTOR**; the person also responsible for logging all **SHOTS**, and timing them. In television they also note down all **TIME CODES**, as well as doing the

CONTINUITY notes – oh, and they are sometimes asked to get the coffee as well. (No, I would never dare.)

PRODUCTION MANAGER: the coordinator of all business and technical matters; the person to whom **DIRECTORS** plead for just a few more minutes, as they are sure they will get the **SHOT** next time.

PULL FOCUS (also **FOCUS PULL**): (see **RACK FOCUS**).

PULL-BACK: to move the camera away.

PUSH-IN: move the camera in closer. Especially in a **MULTI-CAMERA** studio; for example, "Camera 3 **PUSH-IN** to the announcer." It is sometimes also used to get the camera to **ZOOM** in a bit.

Q: (see **CUE**).

RACK FOCUS (also **PULL FOCUS**): changing the focus from foreground to background, or vice versa – much loved by trendy **DIRECTORS** (me too!).

RADIO MIKE: small microphone hidden about you, which picks up your voice and transmits it by radio via a bulky lump hidden in your clothing. Picks up all thumps and noises, often goes wrong, and can cause problems if you keep wearing it and don't switch it off when going about your daily business not on the set. (Yes, we can still hear you, and if you are unwise enough to criticize us in your trailer...)

REACTION SHOT: the **SHOT** of one actor doing or "thinking," while the other is speaking.

REVERSES: shooting in the opposite direction to what we have just done. After shooting all the **SHOTS** of the person speaking to you, we will now **TURN ROUND** to do all your **REVERSES**.

RHUBARB (or **WALLA**): the noise that a crowd can be asked to make to prove they are alive and not **CGI** images. Actual words are not said, to prevent the extras and walk ons (called background artists to make them feel better) arguing that as they are speaking they should be paid as actors.

ROLL CAMERA (also **TURN OVER**): what you say to start the camera to shoot a **TAKE**. If using single camera **DIGITAL**, you flatter your **CAMERA OPERATOR** if you use the film term of **TURN OVER** instead, for then we can all pretend we are making major movies, rather than nice domestic dramas.

ROLLING SPIDER (also **WHEELED TREE**): a spreader that keeps the camera legs apart, with wheels attached. Should only be used to move the camera from place to place, but is often sneakily used as a simple **TRACK** (spider, tree – who said crews had no romance in their souls?).

ROSTRUM CAMERA: a fixed camera that shoots static **SHOTS** of books, pictures, and so on, which will usually be slotted into a documentary or news program.

ROUGH CUT: the first rough putting together of a sequence or complete show. It is often used as much to work out what to cut to get the program onto time as it is to see how effective it all is going to be.

RUNNING: what the **CAMERA OPERATOR** says when they have heard **TURN OVER (ROLL CAMERA)**, started the camera, and it is ready and stabilized to start shooting.

RUNNING ORDER: the actual order in which the scenes will be recorded.

RUNNING TIME: the length of a program.

RUSHES: (see **DAILIES**).

SCANNER: a purpose-built truck or van that serves as the mobile control room used for video cameras on **LOCATION**.

SCRIM: gauze or netting put over a lamp or window to diffuse the light. If the sun comes out or goes in during the day, you may have to wait while the **GAFFER** or **DOP** puts **SCRIM** on or off the windows.

SCRIPT GIRL, SCRIPT SUPERVISOR: (see **CONTINUITY**).

SCRUB: (see **STRIKE**).

SECAM: the color television system used by France (sequential couleur avec memoire), and sold by them to Russia, so they now have to use it as well (see also **PAL** and **NTSC**).

SECOND UNIT: subsidiary to the main shoot, filming bits that do not involve the main actors, or such things as a **LONG SHOT** of a car when you cannot really tell that it is not the star driving it. The **SECOND UNIT DIRECTOR** will be in charge.

SETUP: the camera's position; a certain number of **SETUPS** are expected each day, depending on the scale of the production.

SHOOTING RATIO: the amount of film shot compared with the amount that will be in the final production. Approximately, film dramas have a **SHOOTING RATIO** of 10:1, film documentaries of 30:1, and **DIGITAL** dramas of about 5:1 or less.

SHOOTING SCRIPT: the final approved script, often with cameras and cutting points marked in.

SHOT ABBREVIATIONS: (see **ECU, BCU, CU, MCU, MS, LS, ELS**). The actual sizes of the shots vary slightly between production companies, and from country to country, so check what everyone on the crew thinks they are.

SHOTS: the pictures taken by the camera.

SIGHT LINE: the line of vision someone takes; a **SIGHT LINE** from one actor to another, or from an audience member to the screen or a person on a stage.

SINGLE SHOT (also **ONE-SHOT**): of one person, usually in a **MEDIUM CLOSE-UP**.

SLATE: (see **CLAPSTICK BOARD**).

SOFT: out of focus. To prevent this, the camera crew will ask you to stand on the different **MARKS** you have to hit for a sequence, so they can note down the focus points for the camera, often using a measuring tape.

SPARKS (also **JUICERS**): electricians, often strangely absent when there is a good football game being televised.

SPECIAL EFFECTS: anything that is achieved by tricks, such as miniatures, **GREEN SCREEN**, split screens, and so on, but now mostly dominated by the **DIGITAL** effects that seem to rule the world of the screen.

SPEED: what the **MIXER** calls out when the sound recorder is stabilized, and so the **CAMERA OPERATOR** can **TURN OVER** for a **TAKE**. In the video world the **CAMERA OPERATOR** also calls this out when the camera is ready for the **TAKE**.

SPLIT DIALOGUE: When actors are so far apart that the **BOOM** cannot be close enough to get both of them, then two microphones will be used, and the **MIXER** will record the two parts of the dialogue on two different or split **TRACKS**. The **MIXER** is always keen to know in advance if there will be any **SPLIT DIALOGUE** in a scene, so they can arrange for a second **BOOM** operator, or install a second microphone.

STAND-IN (also **DOUBLE**): a near likeness of a main performer who literally stands in for him as a **SHOT** is lined up. This prevents the tedium of lighting a scene and **MARKING** up where the performer should stand from exhausting the main talent. This allows the star to spend more time in his trailer, concentrating on his performance, or whatever.

STEADICAM: trade name for the device of harness and springs that allows the **CAMERA OPERATOR** wearing it to run after the performers and have the camera steady, more or less. (Well, it is sometimes also referred to as Wobblycam by those who prefer the macho of **HAND-HELD**.)

STORY LINE: the brief synopsis of a film or production; the ongoing stories (as opposed to scripts) as planned for a soap drama.

STORYBOARD: a cartoon-like layout of all the **SHOTS** planned and how they relate to each other, so everyone concerned (**DIRECTOR**, **PRODUCER**, **DOP**, **MIXER**, designer) can anticipate problems and plan for them. Some major movies like *Gone with the Wind* had all the **STORYBOARDS** drawn and colored before the **DIRECTOR** was even contracted.

STRIKE (also **SCRUB**): remove or take away; "**STRIKE** the furniture"; "**STRIKE** that idea" (see also **KILL**).

SWISH PAN (also **ZIP PAN, WHIP PAN**): a very quick swing of the camera, leaving the background as a blur. Often used to join two similar sequences together, one **SWISH PAN** melding into the next one.

SWITCHER (also **VISION MIXER**): the person in the studio who switches between the video cameras, choosing which one's output is to be broadcast (live shows) or recorded.

TAIL SLATE: (see **END BOARD**).

TAKE: the individual **SHOT**, which is often repeated (as a **RETAKE**). Do not despair if they do a great number of these – there are many reasons for going again other than wanting better performances (see also **TAKE IT FROM THE TOP**).

TAKE IT FROM THE TOP: start the scene from the very beginning, from the first moment of the scene – and so from the top of the page.

TELECINE: the machine from the old days that allowed any program made on film to be easily transmitted on any television system (**NTSC**, **PAL**, or **SECAM**).

TELEPHOTO: a very long lens that makes distant people look as if they are near. It also makes them look as if they are walking fast but getting nowhere.

TELEPROMPTER (also **AUTOCUE**): trade name for the device in the studio that has the script rolling across the camera lens as far as the reader is concerned, so you at home are amazed they can speak so well without referring to their notes or script.

THREE-SHOT: three people in frame (**3-S**).

TIC: ironic – as in "tongue in cheek."

TIGHT SHOT: close; the opposite of a **LOOSE SHOT**, so do not wave your arms about (see also **LOOSE SHOT**).

TILT UP/DOWN: the camera **TILTING UP** to look up, **TILTING DOWN** to look down; newcomers say **PAN** up/down, which gets very scornful looks from the crew.

TIME CODE: the way **DIGITAL** recordings can be found, with each **TAKE** having its unique **TIME CODE**, which allows the editor to find any particular **SHOT**, as long as someone remembered to write down the times for the individual **SHOTS** and **TAKES**.

TRACKING: (see **DOLLYING**).

TRACKS: the actual rails or planks put down for the **DOLLY** to travel along. Also the different places the **MIXER** will put the different sounds on, the dialogue on one, this voice on another, background on yet another, and so on. These days, many **TRACKS** are used to feed the many loudspeakers used in surround sound.

TREATMENT: halfway between a **STORY LINE** and a **SHOOTING SCRIPT**. An indication of how the production will be, without all the dialogue.

TROMBONE: (see **VERTIGO EFFECT**).

TRUCKING: (see **DOLLYING**).

TURN OVER: always used to start off a film camera.

TURN ROUND: to move the camera and lights (usually by 180 degrees) so that we can do all the **REVERSES**.

TURNAROUND: when a project is in search of another backer; when one set is changed for another; or the agreed gap between finishing work one day and starting work on the next.

TWO-SHOT (also **DOUBLE**): two people in the frame (**2-S**).

UNIT: all the people involved in the filming, especially when away from base on a **LOCATION**. The place where everyone arrives and centers around is the **UNIT BASE**, equipped with **UNIT BATHROOMS**, **UNIT PARKING**, and – naturally – **UNIT LOCATION CATERING** (see also **SECOND UNIT**).

UPSTAGE: farther away from camera. This is a term taken from the theater, where in the old days the stages slanted up to back, so being **UPSTAGE** meant also being farther from the audience. (An actor **UPSTAGING** you is one farther away, and so not seen by you, who is doing stuff that the audience will watch rather than you.)

VERTIGO EFFECT (also **DOLLY ZOOM**): was called a **TROMBONE**, but renamed in honor of the genius who first used it in the film *Vertigo* – Alfred Hitchcock. The camera goes **TRACKING** in and the lens **ZOOMS** out, so the subject remains the same but the background perspective changes, seeming to get further away – Steven Spielberg memorably did this in *Jaws*. You can get the opposite effect by **TRACKING** out and **ZOOMING** in, as Martin Scorsese does in *GoodFellas*.

VISION MIXER: (see **SWITCHER**).

VOICE-OVER (VO): the disembodied voice that speaks while pictures are shown; the voice exhorting you to buy the product, or narrating the documentary. It is adored by actors who like to be paid without having to memorize lines.

WALK ON: what extras used to be called. Now they have elevated titles, such as background artists, supporting artists, and anything else that keeps them happy, and their fees down.

WALTER PLINGE: (see **ALAN SMITHEE**).

WHEELED TREE: (see **ROLLING SPIDER**).

WHIP PAN: (see **SWISH PAN**).

WIDE ANGLE LENS: (see **FISH EYE LENS**).

WIDE SCREEN: any **FORMAT** wider than the old standard 4:3 (or 1.33:1). All films are now made **WIDE SCREEN**, and most television programs have changed to the wider **FORMAT**.

WILD TRACK: the sounds and effects recorded after the actors have said their lines, as well as the **BUZZ TRACK** or **ATMOS**. Sometimes this will be the business that the actors have just done: "Can we just **WILD TRACK** you walking upstairs without the dialogue?" Sometimes they may **WILD TRACK** a line of yours that you **FLUFFED** during the **TAKE**.

WIPE: a person or object going across the screen, often used to motivate a **CUT**. Also a **WIPE** is a transition between two scenes, when the incoming **SHOT** pushes the previous one off the screen.

WRANGLER: the person responsible for animals on the set, with the thankless task of getting them to **HIT THE MARKS**.

WRAP: the end, either of a day's shooting or of the whole project. "It's a **WRAP**" is encouraging if you have worked hard all day, discouraging if you are still trying to get one last **SHOT** into the camera.

WS: wide shot.

ZIP PAN: (see **SWISH PAN**).

ZOOM: changing the field of view by using a varifocal lens. Since it is something we cannot do with our own eyes, it tends to bring attention to the mechanics of the shot unless it is hidden or motivated by actor movement.

ZOOM LENS: the actual adjustable lens that allows the camera to **ZOOM** in and out, or when used very fast to **CRASH ZOOM**. Modern **DIRECTORS** often use the **ZOOM LENS** instead of moving the camera, or even commit the unpardonable sin of shooting an unmotivated **ZOOM** (and purists like me suck their teeth in horror).

BIBLIOGRAPHY

Books relating to screen acting

Here is a list of the books I have consulted – books which are on my shelves – about screen acting. The ones I have found particularly useful and think you might like a lot I have marked with a *, but this is purely a personal opinion. You may well find great insights in any of the following books (some of whose opinions I do not agree with). I have updated the list since the second edition, adding new ones, and leaving off those that (alas) have gone out of print.

Books on film and television acting

Barr, Tony. *Acting for the Camera*. William Morrow Paperbacks, 1997.
Bernard, Ian. *Film and Television Acting*. Focal Press, 1997.
Caine, Michael. *Acting in Film*. Applause Theatre Books, 2000.
Cardullo, Bert. *Playing to the Camera*. Yale University Press, 1999.
Carlson, Steve. *Hitting Your Mark*. Michael Wiese Productions, 2006.
Churcher, Mel. *Acting for Film: Truth 24 Times a Second*. Virgin Books, 2003.
Comey, Jeremiah. *The Art of Film Acting*. Focal Press, 2002.
Fridell, Squire. *Acting in Television Commercials for Fun and Profit*. Three Rivers Press, 2009.
Haase, Cathy. *Acting for Film*. Allworth Press, 2003.
Hirsch, Foster. *Acting Hollywood Style*. Kobal Collection. Harry N. Abrams, 1996.
Kramer, Lovell. *Screen Acting*. Routledge, 1999.
Pudovkin, V.I. *Film Technique & Film Acting*. Sims Press, 2007.
White, Daniel L. *Acting for Film and Television*. CreateSpace Independent Publishing Platform, 2013.

Books by or about actors and acting training

Barkworth, Peter. *About Acting*. Bloomsbury Methuen Drama, 1992.
Blum, Richard A. *Working Actors: The Craft of Television, Film and Stage Performance*. Focal Press, 1989.

231

Boleslavsky, Richard. *Acting – The First Six Lessons*. Martino Fine Books, 2013.
Brown, D.W. *★You Can Act*. Michael Weise Productions, 2009.
Hurtes, Hettie Lynne. *Agents on Actors*. Back Stage Books, 2000.
Mamet, David. *★True and False*. Faber and Faber, 1998.
Stevens, Jon. *★Actors Turned Directors*. Silman-James Press, 1998.

Books about the film/television medium (with references to acting)

Badham, John. *★John Badham on Directing*. Michael Weiss Productions, 2013.
Badham, John, and Craig Modderno. *I'll Be in My Trailer*. Michael Weiss Productions, 2006.
Bordwell, David, and Kristin Thompson. *Film Art*. McGraw-Hill Higher Education, 2012.
Breskin, David. *★Inner Views: Filmmakers in Conversation*. Da Capo Press, 1997.
Goldman, William. *Adventures in the Screen Trade*. Abacus, 1996.
Lumet, Sidney. *★Making Movies*. Bloomsbury Publishing, 1996.
Mamet, David. *★On Directing Film*. Penguin Books, 1992.
Owens, Jim, and Gerald Millerson. *★Television Production*. Focal Press, 2012.
Searle, Judith. *★Getting the Part*. Limelight Editions, 2004.
Sherman, Eric. *★Directing the Film*. Acrobat Books, 1976.

Books by Patrick Tucker and Christine Ozanne

Tucker, Patrick. *Secrets of Acting Shakespeare*. Routledge, 2002.
Tucker, Patrick. *First Folio Speeches for Men*. Oberon Books, 2004.
Tucker, Patrick. *First Folio Speeches for Women*. Oberon Books, 2004.
Tucker, Patrick, and Christine Ozanne. *★The Actor's Survival Handbook*. Routledge, 2005.
Tucker, Patrick, and Christine Ozanne. *Award Monologues for Men*. Routledge, 2007.
Tucker, Patrick, and Christine Ozanne. *Award Monologues for Women*. Routledge, 2007.
Ozanne, Christine. *Closet Star* (in preparation).

Audio by Patrick Tucker and David H. Lawrence XVII

★Secrets of Screen Acting. The Podcast. 2008. www.secretsofscreenacting.com

INDEX OF FILM AND
TELEVISION DRAMAS

The director of the film, and the year it was first released, are also noted

INDEX OF ACTORS

GENERAL INDEX

007 15, 76, 110
180 degree rule 189, 191, 211, 215

About Acting 115, 231
Academy Ratio vii, 23
Acting 101 109–10
Acting for the Edit 190
action props 169, 211
Actor Prepares, An 110
Actors Studio 109
AD (assistant director) 2, 212
America (American) 15, 29, 34, 65, 85, 94, 96, 109–10, 189, 211–12, 220
angle 2, 41, 48, 78, 97, 163, 187–8, 213–15; camera 144, 212–13; reverse 2, 47, 105, 180, 197, 220, 225, 228
Antony and Cleopatra 109
Ashley 135
assistant director 46, 82, 174, 180, 202–3, 212, 218, 223
Attias, Dan 2
Audience of One 45, 50–1, 97, 162, 168, 179, 198
Australia 105
Austrian 92
autocue 163, 212, 228
avatar 113
Avid 216

back light 155, 212
bat-and-ball 151
BBC i, 26, 81, 92, 174
Besson, Luc 118
Bête, La 171

big close-up (BCU) (tight close-up) 10, 13–14, 55, 74, 126, 128, 143–4, 156, 192, 196, 204, 213
block 113, 139–40, 143, 145–6, 213
Blum, Richard A. 16, 231
boom 46, 73–4, 76–7, 140, 144–5, 173, 176, 201–3, 213, 223, 227; shadow 140, 144,
Boyle, Danny 165
British 15, 18, 97, 129, 199
Broadway 10, 12, 19, 30, 134

camera A, camera B 29, 211
camera angle 144, 212–13; cards 144–5, 213; left/right 45–6, 176, 213
camera operator, person 2, 33–4, 45, 50, 74, 76, 140–1, 144, 155, 169, 176, 187, 195, 201, 203, 213, 217, 221, 225–7
Cameron, James 30, 43, 121, 165, 183
Canada 105
casting director, person 92, 93, 100, 123, 124, 127–8, 131–4, 139
CGI 28, 113, 119, 213, 225
Chabrol, Claude 77
cheat, cheating 13, 15, 37, 40, 42–3, 47–9, 51–4, 146, 156, 172, 176, 180, 195–6, 204, 214
Christina's World 34
Churchill, Winston 83
clapper board 203, 214
Cleopatra 109
close-up (CU) 8, 18–19, 25, 28, 30, 34, 40–1, 48, 51, 55, 63, 73–80, 84, 92, 115, 126–7, 131, 142, 145, 153, 155, 158, 173–4, 181, 186–8, 190, 196–7, 203–4, 206–9, 214–15

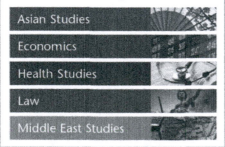
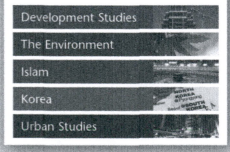